Dwelling on Grief
Narratives of Mourning Across Time and Forms

LEGENDA

LEGENDA is the Modern Humanities Research Association's book imprint for new research in the Humanities. Founded in 1995 by Malcolm Bowie and others within the University of Oxford, Legenda has always been a collaborative publishing enterprise, directly governed by scholars. The Modern Humanities Research Association (MHRA) joined this collaboration in 1998, became half-owner in 2004, in partnership with Maney Publishing and then Routledge, and has since 2016 been sole owner. Titles range from medieval texts to contemporary cinema and form a widely comparative view of the modern humanities, including works on Arabic, Catalan, English, French, German, Greek, Italian, Portuguese, Russian, Spanish, and Yiddish literature. Editorial boards and committees of more than 60 leading academic specialists work in collaboration with bodies such as the Society for French Studies, the British Comparative Literature Association and the Association of Hispanists of Great Britain & Ireland.

The MHRA encourages and promotes advanced study and research in the field of the modern humanities, especially modern European languages and literature, including English, and also cinema. It aims to break down the barriers between scholars working in different disciplines and to maintain the unity of humanistic scholarship. The Association fulfils this purpose through the publication of journals, bibliographies, monographs, critical editions, and the MHRA Style Guide, and by making grants in support of research. Membership is open to all who work in the Humanities, whether independent or in a University post, and the participation of younger colleagues entering the field is especially welcomed.

ALSO PUBLISHED BY THE ASSOCIATION

Critical Texts
Tudor and Stuart Translations • *New Translations* • *European Translations*
MHRA Library of Medieval Welsh Literature

MHRA Bibliographies
Publications of the Modern Humanities Research Association

The Annual Bibliography of English Language & Literature
Austrian Studies
Modern Language Review
Portuguese Studies
The Slavonic and East European Review
Working Papers in the Humanities
The Yearbook of English Studies

www.mhra.org.uk
www.legendabooks.com

TRANSCRIPT

Transcript publishes books about all kinds of imagining across languages, media and cultures: translations and versions, inter-cultural and multi-lingual writing, illustrations and musical settings, adaptation for theatre, film, TV and new media, creative and critical responses. We are open to studies of any combination of languages and media, in any historical moments, and are keen to reach beyond Legenda's traditional focus on modern European languages to embrace anglophone and world cultures and the classics. We are interested in innovative critical approaches: we welcome not only the most rigorous scholarship and sharpest theory, but also modes of writing that stretch or cross the boundaries of those discourses.

TRANSCRIPT

1. *Adapting the Canon: Mediation, Visualization, Interpretation*, edited by Ann Lewis and Silke Arnold-de Simine
2. *Adapted Voices: Transpositions of Céline's Voyage au bout de la nuit and Queneau's Zazie dans le métro*, by Armelle Blin-Rolland
3. *Zola and the Art of Television: Adaptation, Recreation, Translation*, by Kate Griffiths
4. *Comparative Encounters between Artaud, Michaux and the Zhuangzi: Rationality, Cosmology and Ethics*, by Xiaofan Amy Li
5. *Minding Borders: Resilient Divisions in Literature, the Body and the Academy*, edited by Nicola Gardini, Adriana Jacobs, Ben Morgan, Mohamed-Salah Omri and Matthew Reynolds
6. *Memory Across Borders: Nabokov, Perec, Chamoiseau*, by Sara-Louise Cooper
7. *Erotic Literature in Adaptation and Translation*, edited by Johannes D. Kaminski
8. *Translating Petrarch's Poetry: L'Aura del Petrarca from the Quattrocento to the 21st Century*, edited by Carole Birkan-Berz, Guillaume Coatalen and Thomas Vuong
9. *Making Masud Khan: Psychoanalysis, Empire and Modernist Culture*, by Benjamin Poore
10. *Prismatic Translation*, edited by Matthew Reynolds
11. *The Patient, the Impostor and the Seducer: Medieval European Literature in Hebrew*, by Tovi Bibring
12. *Reading Dante and Proust by Analogy*, by Julia Caterina Hartley
13. *The First English Translations of Molière: Drama in Flux 1663-1732*, by Suzanne Jones
14. *After Clarice: Reading Lispector's Legacy in the Twenty-First Century*, edited by Adriana X. Jacobs and Claire Williams
15. *Uruguayan Theatre in Translation: Theory and Practice*, by Sophie Stevens
16. *Hamlet Translations: Prisms of Cultural Encounters across the Globe*, edited by Márta Minier and Lily Kahn
17. *The Foreign Connection: Writings on Poetry, Art and Translation*, by Jamie McKendrick
18. *Poetics, Performance and Politics in French and Italian Renaissance Comedy*, by Lucy Rayfield

Dwelling on Grief

Narratives of Mourning Across Time and Forms

❖

Edited by Simona Corso,
Florian Mussgnug, and Jennifer Rushworth

LEGENDA

Transcript 22
Modern Humanities Research Association
2022

Published by Legenda
an imprint of the Modern Humanities Research Association
Salisbury House, Station Road, Cambridge CB1 2LA

ISBN 978-1-83954-034-9 (HB)
ISBN 978-1-83954-035-6 (PB)

First published 2022

Copy-Editor: Charlotte Brown

CONTENTS

ACKNOWLEDGEMENTS

Some of the essays in this volume stem from a conference on 'Mourning: Different Times, Different Forms' held at Roma Tre University in May 2019. Looking back at the conference at the point of putting this book together in spring 2021, the idea of international travel and of conferences in person now seems remarkable and remarkably distant. We would like to express our thanks to University College London's Cities Partnership Programme for their support of the original conference and the cost of image rights for this publication, as well as to our hosts at the Department of Modern Languages, Literatures and Cultures at Roma Tre. We also thank the Society for Italian Studies for their contribution. We are grateful to Matthew Reynolds for accepting this edited volume in his fine book series, *Transcript*, and to Graham Nelson, the Managing Editor at Legenda, for his invaluable support at every stage. We also wish to thank the anonymous reader who provided us with constructive feedback on the volume, Matthew Salisbury who lent us his attentive ear to English style, and Alexandra Lee and Charlotte Wathey for helping us through the production process.

NOTES ON THE CONTRIBUTORS

Luca Aversano obtained a PhD in Musicology at the University of Cologne, with a thesis on the diffusion of Austro-German instrumental music in Italy in the early 1800s. He has been Lecturer in the History and Philology of Musical Text at the University of Parma. From 2001 to 2004 he worked at the University of Florence. Since 2005 he has taught Musicology and History of Music at Roma Tre University. In 2012 he was awarded the Mittner Preis for Musicology, in the field of Italian-German studies. In 2018 he was awarded the Italian Music Critics' Prize 'Franco Abbiati'.

David Bowe is an Irish Research Council Postdoctoral Fellow and co-director of the Centre for Dante Studies in Ireland at University College Cork. He works on lyric and other literature from the thirteenth to the fifteenth centuries, including the works of Dante and their reception. His publications include *Poetry in Dialogue in the 'Duecento' and Dante* (Oxford University Press, 2020) and essays on gender, subjectivity, and temporality in medieval lyric. He has edited the first publication of Rachel Owen's *Inferno Illustrations* for Bodleian Library Publishing (2021) and his poems have been performed at the Victoria and Albert Museum (V&A) and appeared in the Shakespeare centenary volume *Project 154* and in Live Canon and *Aesthetica* prize anthologies.

Elena Buia Rutt is a poet, translator, and literary critic who holds degrees in Philosophy and Literature, and an MA in Journalism. As a journalist, she contributes to the cultural pages of the *Osservatore romano*. Her main translation works include poems by Rowan Williams, poems by Mary Oliver, and Flannery O'Connor's *Prayer Journal*. Elena's first book of poems, *Ti stringo la mano mentre dormi* (Fuorilinea) was published in 2012, and her second (*Il mio cuore è un asino*, Nottetempo) in 2015. Her most recent book of poems, *La sete* (Aragno), was published in December 2019.

Simona Corso is Associate Professor of English Literature at the Roma Tre University. Her research interests cover the tradition of the European novel and the novel in English, from the eighteenth century to the present. Her publications include *Narrating the Passions: New Perspectives from Modern and Contemporary Literature* (with Beth Guilding, 2017); *Postcolonial Shakespeare* (with Masolino d'Amico, 2009); *Automi, termometri, fucili* (2004); and articles on Shakespeare, Ben Jonson, James Joyce, Martin Amis, Derek Walcott, V. S. Naipaul, J. M. Coetzee, and the myth of Robinson Crusoe. Her novel *Capodanno al Tennis Club* (2002) was awarded the Premio Mondello Opera Prima in 2003.

Susan Irvine is Quain Professor of English Language and Literature at University College London (UCL). She is the author of *Old English Homilies from MS Bodley 343* (1993) and *The Anglo-Saxon Chronicle MS E* (2004), and co-author (with Malcolm Godden) of *The Old English Boethius* (2009) (winner of the International Society of Anglo-Saxonists 'Best Edition' Prize), and *The Old English Boethius with Verse Prologues and Epilogues* (2012). She is President of the Society of Teachers of Old English in Britain and Ireland, and serves on various international advisory boards and councils. She was awarded the Anneliese Maier Research Award by the Alexander von Humboldt Foundation in 2015.

Catherine Keen is Professor of Dante Studies in the Italian Department at UCL. She is currently Senior Co-Editor of the journal *Italian Studies*. Her research interests cover Dante's *Commedia* and his minor works, especially relating to his thought on politics and exile, themes addressed in her monograph *Dante and the City* (2003). She has also published on the early Italian lyric tradition, with a special interest in the poetry of Cino da Pistoia, and on the translation and reception of classical literature in Duecento and Trecento Italy, particularly the works of Cicero and of Ovid.

Luca Marcozzi is Associate Professor of Italian Literature at Roma Tre University. His books and essays include *Petrarca lettore di Ovidio* (2001), *La biblioteca di Febo* (2002), *Petrarca platonico* (2011), the edition of the *Fabulae centum* (1564) by Gabriele Faerno (2006), and the chapter 'The Making of the *Canzoniere*' in *The Cambridge Companion to Petrarch* (2015). He edited a *Lessico critico petrarchesco* (2015) and authored with Francisco Rico the entry 'Petrarca, Francesco' for the *Dizionario Biografico degli Italiani* (2015) (then in *I venerdì del Petrarca*, with the same Rico, 2016, awarded the De Sanctis prize). He has published several essays on Dante; he edited the volume *Dante e la retorica* (2017) and a commentary on the late fifteenth-century Antonio Grifo's illustrations to the *Divine Comedy* (2015); his *Dante e il mondo animale* (edited with Giuseppe Crimi, 2013) won the Lombroso Prize. More recently, he has focused on Renaissance literature (*Bembo*, 2017). He is the co-director of the journal *Petrarchesca* and of the series *Dulces musae*. In 2013 he taught on the PhD courses at the University of Notre Dame as a Fulbright Distinguished Chair.

Timothy Mathews is Emeritus Professor of French and Comparative Criticism at UCL. In his writing and translating he explores what relating to art can tell us about relating to people. His interests include relations of literary and visual art, translation, and creative critical writing. He has written on, amongst others, Guillaume Apollinaire, Aimé Césaire, Roland Barthes, Michel Houellebecq, W. G. Sebald, Cees Noteboom, Max Ernst, Jean Fautrier, Alberto Giacometti, Agnès Thurnauer, Antoni Tàpies, and William Kentridge. His most recent monograph is *Alberto Giacometti: The Art of Relation* (2013). He is co-translator with Delphine Grass of Michel Houellebecq, *The Art of Struggle*, and with Luce Irigaray of her *Everyday Prayers*. He is currently completing a book of creative critical 'chronicles', and preparing translations of Guillaume Apollinaire and Roland Barthes. He is a member of the Academy of Europe and Officier dans l'Ordre des Palmes Académiques.

Florian Mussgnug is Professor in Italian and Comparative Literature at UCL. He has published widely on twentieth- and twenty-first-century literature, with a particular focus on literary theory, experimental literature, and narrative prose fiction. His *The Eloquence of Ghosts: Giorgio Manganelli and the Afterlife of the Avant-Garde* (2010) was awarded the Edinburgh Gadda Prize in 2012. He is co-investigator for the five-year AHRC-funded research project 'Interdisciplinary Italy 1900–2020: Interart/Intermedia'.

Zoe Papadopoulou is an artist who doubles as a tour guide at Highgate Cemetery. Her practice aims to engage a wide range of audiences in ethically challenging issues around illness, end of life, death, and scientific research through workshops and direct participation. Her work takes many forms from writing to installation and performance and has been shown at the V&A, the Wellcome Trust, the ICA, the National Museum of China, the Science Gallery Dublin, and the Van Boijmans Museum, amongst others.

Helena Phillips-Robins is a Research Fellow at Selwyn College, Cambridge. Previously she was a Research Fellow at the British School at Rome and the Centre for Research in the Arts, Social Sciences and Humanities (CRASSH), Cambridge. She specialises in medieval Italian literature and culture with a particular interest in Dante, theology and religious practices, and visual cultures. She has published on Dante, liturgy, and theology in *Italian Studies* and *Bibliotheca Dantesca*, and her monograph *Liturgical Song and Practice in Dante's 'Commedia'* was published by Notre Dame Press in 2021. She is also a contributor to the *Tesoro della Lingua Italiana delle Origini* project (a historical dictionary of the Italian language before 1375, directed by the Accademia della Crusca).

Jürgen Pieters is Professor of Literature at Universiteit Gent (Belgium), where he teaches courses on literary theory and the history of poetics. He has published books on Stephen Greenblatt's New Historicism (Amsterdam University Press, 2001), the topos of the conversation with the dead (Edinburgh University Press, 2005) and the Dutch seventeenth-century poet Constantijn Huygens (Poëziecentrum, 2014). He has edited scholarly volumes on the work of Roland Barthes, Catherine Belsey, and Vladimir Nabokov's *Lectures on Literature*. His most recent book is *Literature and Consolation: Fictions of Comfort* (Edinburgh University Press, 2021).

Aarathi Prasad has a PhD in molecular genetics and works on interdisciplinary research in development and health at the UCL Institute of Global Health. In her spare time she studies bio-archaeology and writes books about the history and future of science, technology, and medicine.

Jennifer Rushworth is Associate Professor in French and Comparative Literature at UCL. She has published two books, *Discourses of Mourning in Dante, Petrarch, and Proust* (Oxford University Press, 2016) and *Petrarch and the Literary Culture of Nineteenth-century France* (Boydell Press, 2017). She was the recipient of the Society for French Studies's Malcolm Bowie Prize 2015, for an article on 'Proust, Derrida, and the Promise of Writing'. Her article on 'Mourning and Intermittence between

Proust and Barthes' won the *Paragraph* Essay Prize 2016, awarded that year for the best essay on the topic of 'Mourning'.

Uta Staiger directs the European Institute at UCL. Her research sits at the intersection of modern European thought, culture, and politics, with a particular interest in twentieth-century German philosophy. She is also UCL's Pro-Vice-Provost (Europe), a member of the Russell Group EU Advisory Group and the Scottish Council on European Relations, and a Senior Fellow of the Centre for European Studies at Canterbury Christ Church University. She holds a PhD from the University of Cambridge, gained with a scholarship from the Gates Cambridge Trust, and was a post-doctoral fellow at CRASSH. She was previously educated at the Universities of Edinburgh, Konstanz, and Girona.

Adina Stroia is Lecturer in French and Francophone Studies at Newcastle University. Her research interests lie in the areas of life-writing, trauma studies, psychoanalysis, hauntology, and thanatography, as well as visual studies. She has most recently published an interview with Camille Laurens, 'L'Écriture depuis soi', in *Dalhousie French Studies* and the article 'The Traumatic Structure of the *récit de mort*: Camille Laurens's *Philippe*' in *Contemporary French and Francophone Studies*. Her present research project engages with representations of ageing in Agnès Varda's late documentary work.

INTRODUCTION

❖

Simona Corso, Florian Mussgnug, Jennifer Rushworth

As this book goes to press, more than 300 million people worldwide have contracted COVID-19, and the number of global deaths has exceeded 5.5 million. Communities and countries are struggling to find an adequate political response to the pandemic, to limit contagion, and to protect those who are most exposed. For political philosopher Michael J. Sandel, 'the pandemic reminded us of our vulnerability, of our mutual dependence'.[1] It has given shape to new practices of care, fresh modes of wakefulness, and a heightened attention to the quotidian. It has also revealed troubling hierarchies of power and exposed stark social inequalities. Most tragically, it has normalized mass death, to a degree that was unfamiliar to most, in the prosperous global North. As the pandemic spreads, the need for a moral and cultural response is increasingly felt by many. Beyond the strictures of self-isolation and 'social distancing', people long for experiences of community and for mutual bonds of solidarity and compassion. Just as importantly, the global emergency has increased the need for collective mourning and for ways to commemorate the victims of the pandemic. At the time of this writing, it is too early to tell how societies and individuals will emerge from the experience of COVID-19, and whether it will inspire new forms of community and care. We write this introduction in the hope that our book, and our collective examination of the long and diverse history of cultural practices and poetic forms of mourning, will inspire meaningful responses to such unprecedented and challenging times. In this way, we wish to make a small contribution to the enormous tasks that lie ahead.

Mourning, as the experience of the pandemic reminds us, crosses the dividing lines between life and literature, and blurs any attempted opposition of the private and the familial versus the professional and the academic. This insight about the imbrication of life and writing is framed in the essays that follow. We suggest, with Jacques Derrida, that 'On ne peut pas tenir un discours *sur* le "travail du deuil" sans y prendre part [...]. Il n'y a donc pas de métalangage quant au langage où s'engage un travail du deuil' [One cannot hold a discourse *on* the 'work of mourning' without taking part in it [...]. There is thus no metalanguage for the language in which a work of mourning is at work].[2] One of the connecting threads of our volume is this tension between consideration of discourses *on* mourning across different disciplines and fields — in particular, Comparative Literature, Modern Languages, English, Medieval Studies, Political Thought, Music, Biology, and the Environmental Humanities — and an acknowledgement of the ways in which metalanguage breaks down and is punctuated by experience.[3]

Readers are likely to recognize in the quotation from Derrida engagement with Freudian terminology, that of mourning understood as a 'travail du deuil' or 'work of mourning' (in the original German, *Trauerarbeit*).[4] Two interconnected aspects of the Freudian heritage are vital within mourning studies: questions of terminology, and the fact that the cementation of Freud as a touchstone has involved too reductive an approach to his work. Put simply, Freud's thoughts on mourning have been reduced to one short essay, 'Trauer und Melancholie' [Mourning and Melancholia] (1917).[5] As is well known, this essay presents a binary opposition between, on the one hand, the work of mourning as a slow but sure process taking place over time and leading teleologically to a desirable end of mourning and, on the other hand, melancholia as a blocked, halted experience of endless grief, which is therefore considered pathological and unnatural. However, subsequent texts by Freud undermine this binary, with, for instance, a famous letter to Ludwig Binswanger from April 1929 stating instead that 'although we know that after such a loss the acute state of mourning will subside, we also know we shall remain inconsolable and will never find a substitute. [...] And actually this is how it should be'.[6] From this perspective, an end to mourning is no longer viewed as possible and the foundational distinction between mourning and melancholia collapses. With this theoretical collapse (which, following Leo Bersani, we consider to be a vital part of what makes Freud's writings so intriguing), terminological distinctions are once more thrown into disarray.[7] Some of our contributors do return to Freud's notion of mourning as work (see especially Simona Corso's Chapter 10 and Zoe Papadopoulou's Epilogue), but this work is no longer understood as finite, as in Freud's original conception of the work of mourning, but rather as ongoing and inconclusive — in the words of Papadopoulou, as a 'work in progress'.

Alongside this revision to the Freudian model (itself, as we have noted, reductive in comparison to later texts by Freud), our contributors have also sought other theoretical frameworks. The diversity and heterogeneity of our perspectives, we suggest, is characteristic of the highly plural field of mourning studies, which has developed from the active dialogue between different disciplines and experiences.[8] Looking beyond Freud, the writings of Roland Barthes have been particularly important to our project, since he writes about grief both as a reader of other mournful texts and from the point of view of personal experience, in a return to Derrida's point that to write about mourning is to take part in mourning. Barthes's *Journal de deuil* [*Mourning Diary*], a collection of dated index cards written in the two years following his mother's death and published only posthumously in 2009, offers us rich and moving reflections on the experience of grief. One of these reflections relates to issues of terminology, and once again suggests a challenge to the Freudian tradition:

> Deuil/Chagrin
> (Mort de la Mère)
>
> Proust parle de *chagrin*, non de *deuil* (mot nouveau, psychanalytique, qui défigure).

> [Mourning/Suffering
> (Death of the Mother)
> Proust speaks of *suffering*, not *mourning* (a new, psychoanalytic word, one that distorts).][9]

There are multiple questions of translation here, from the absent original German term to the English where 'mourning' cannot be said to be 'a new psychoanalytic word' and where 'chagrin' seems poorly rendered by 'suffering'. In our book title, by already including both grief and mourning, we have tried to avoid the technical language 'that distorts' (according to Barthes), while also acknowledging that clusters of terms congregate around mourning and cannot be clearly separated from one another (not even, as we have seen, the original binary of mourning and melancholia).[10] Setting aside matters of vocabulary, however, what is also important about this quotation from Barthes is that literature is presented as a 'body of knowledge' on an equal footing to psychoanalysis and not only as an 'object' to which psychoanalysis might be applied.[11] We have sought to reflect this intuition by foregrounding the concept of *narratives* of mourning: a term which, we suggest, is more plural and less fraught than that of 'literature'. Chapters in this volume trace these narratives across different moments in time, from the earliest evidence of human burial to the contemporary period, and across different forms. These forms include different literary genres (theatre, poetry, memoir, essay) but also different disciplines. In this attention to form, we also share a conviction that each particular narrative is bound up with the form of grief experienced and narrated.[12]

Up until this point, we have been considering terminological and theoretical questions regarding the experience of what is variously described as mourning or grief. Let us note here that our volume does not rely on the related concept of trauma, and, more specifically, does not consider what E. Ann Kaplan and others have called 'collective trauma'.[13] The decision to differentiate between trauma and grief was taken for two reasons. First, we observe that research in trauma studies has foregrounded the 'unimaginable', especially in its profound engagement with the Holocaust. As Jenny Edkins explains:

> Events of the sort we call traumatic [...] strip away the diverse commonly accepted meanings by which we lead our lives in various communities. They reveal the contingency of the social order and in some cases how it conceals its own impossibility.[14]

Traumatic experiences, according to this approach, cannot be expressed in the symbolic structures of language: they 'can only be *shown*, in a negative gesture, as the inherent failure of symbolisation'.[15] Our understanding of grief, by contrast, focuses on the ethical and aesthetic possibilities of literary expression as a necessary form of cultural mediation. Secondly, our interest in this volume centres on narratives that articulate unique experiences of loss, as exemplified by the death of a loved person. We do not explore the relation, across different scales, between personal and collective loss, or the complex interconnections between individual, national, and cultural trauma. In certain chapters, nonetheless, personal grief is necessarily set against a backdrop of collective grief, whether historical — the Second World

War, in chapters on the engraver Laurence Whistler and on the composer Dmitri Shostakovich — or more contemporary, with in particular Chapter 12 by Florian Mussgnug reflecting on the present challenges of COVID-19 and the climate crisis.

Before turning to the structure and contents of our volume in greater detail, we would like to consider our other key titular term: dwelling. The *OED* defines the verb 'to dwell on, upon' as follows:

> To spend time upon or linger over (a thing) in action or thought; to remain with the attention fixed on; now, *esp.* to treat at length or with insistence, in speech or writing; also, to sustain (a note) in music.

We have been drawn to the term 'dwelling' in these particular senses, and understand writing about mourning as a relational activity: a form of lingering over a loss both in action (the action of artistic production) and in thought, as a form of fixed attention, and as an insistence upon loss. In many cases, we also see artistic practice as a way to sustain — extend, prolong — mourning, in the musical sense given above. Mussgnug's chapter associates this relational quality of grief with affirmative ethics and the practice of care, which he explores through environmental philosophy and the work of Emmanuel Levinas. It is evident that our project is motivated by attentiveness to mourning as an ongoing, unfinished and unfinishable, yet ever-changing experience.

The connection between mourning and dwelling is beautifully put in the following extract from a talk by Thom van Dooren and Deborah Bird Rose, which we come to through Donna Haraway's citation of this passage in *Staying with the Trouble* (2016):

> Mourning is about dwelling with a loss and so coming to appreciate what it means, how the world has changed, and how we must *ourselves* change and renew our relationships if we are to move forward from here. In this context, genuine mourning should open us into an awareness of our dependence on and relationships with those countless others being driven over the edge of extinction [...]. The reality, however, is that there *is* no avoiding the necessity of the difficult cultural work of reflection and mourning. This work is not opposed to practical action, rather it is the foundation of any sustainable and informed response.[16]

Van Dooren and Rose draw our attention to contexts of mourning that go beyond human relationships. This attention to the more-than-human world is explored in the chapters by Aarathi Prasad and Mussgnug. It also shapes our wider understanding of the temporality and scope of mourning, across the different sections of this volume: what we consider significant about the quotation is both Van Dooren's and Rose's definition of mourning as 'about dwelling with a loss' and the argument that this dwelling 'is not opposed to practical action'. In other words, dwelling is not isolation or self-isolation, self-indulgence, or inactivity; rather, it is difficult and necessary 'cultural work'. Dwelling is the 'foundation' for awareness and self-awareness of mortality, with the understanding that such an awareness will make change and moving forward possible.

In a more literary-philosophical fashion, our understanding of dwelling has also been shaped by the writings of Martin Heidegger, particularly his essays

'Building Dwelling Thinking' and '"...Poetically Man Dwells..."'.[17] 'Building Dwelling Thinking' deals more broadly with the question of the relationship between building and dwelling, and particularly points to the (in Heidegger's view) lamentable fact that the German *bauen* has come to mean merely 'to build' and has lost its earlier, etymological sense of 'to dwell'. Heidegger initially defines 'to dwell', quite predictably, as 'to remain, to stay in a place', but then develops it into the defining feature of humanity, with an associated meaning of '*sparing and preserving*'.[18] He writes that 'to be a human being means to be on the earth as a mortal. It means to dwell' and that, similarly, 'dwelling is [...] the basic character of human being'.[19] For him, dwelling is time-bound as well as space-bound, and establishes an essential 'oneness' between 'earth and sky, divinities and mortals'.[20] In this sense, dwelling is inherently material, 'always a staying with things'.[21]

In the second essay, Heidegger takes a phrase from a late poem by Friedrich Hölderlin as his inspiration for a reflection on the relationship between dwelling and poetry. He writes: 'Poetry is what really lets us dwell. But through what do we attain to a dwelling place? Through building. Poetic creation, which lets us dwell, is a kind of building'.[22] Reading Hölderlin's poem, Heidegger further defines poetry as follows: 'To write poetry is measure-taking, understood in the strict sense of the word, by which man first receives the measure for the breadth of his being. Man exists as a mortal. He is called mortal because he can die'.[23] Poetry takes the measure of our human mortality, not in a reductive, mathematical sense but rather in the sense of greater understanding, awareness, and appreciation.

The same connection between poetry and dwelling is the catalyst for Giorgio Agamben's *Stanze: la parola e il fantasma nella cultura occidentale* [*Stanzas: Word and Phantasm in Western Culture*], appropriately so since Agamben's book is explicitly dedicated 'In memoriam Martin Heidegger'.[24] In *Stanzas*, Agamben takes as his epigraph Dante's definition of *stanza* from the *De vulgari eloquentia*, 'hoc est mansio capax, sive receptaculum' [that is, a capacious dwelling or receptacle], thereby suggesting, like Heidegger but also pre-Heidegger (through Dante), an intimate connection between poetry and dwelling.[25] In his introduction, Agamben elaborates on this connection, writing 'of the *stanza* through which the human spirit responds to the impossible task of appropriating what must in every case remain unappropriable'.[26] Agamben has in mind here first and foremost *gaudium* [joy], but his later definition of melancholy as 'the imaginative capacity to make an unobtainable object appear as if lost' means that it is also a question of mourning, too. Here Agamben makes a bold and unsettling claim about the relationship between poetry and melancholy: that 'melancholy succeeds in appropriating its own object only to the extent that it affirms its loss'.[27] As is true of the examples in the chapters that follow, to write about mourning is not only to affirm a loss, but also to establish a relationship — even a relationship of attempted appropriation — with the love object as lost, through this very loss.

The claims of Heidegger and Agamben are focused on poetry, and poetry is present in our volume particularly in the Old English and medieval Italian traditions.[28] We would like to extend their insights to other forms of writing and art too. As noted, mourning means 'dwelling with a loss' (in van Dooren and Rose's words), but it is art (in our examples, particularly the art of both poetry and narrative) which creates a space for this dwelling. While writing may allow particular mourners to dwell with and give form to their own grief (as is the case, especially, in the grief memoirs explored by Corso in the present volume), a final related term to dwelling makes space for the reader, too. In her chapter on Dante, Helena Phillips-Robins uses the term 'indwell' to describe the multiple relationships of different people to the same text. As she writes, with reference to the work of David Ford, indwelling is 'a defining feature of liturgical prayers, namely that their words can be spoken, indwelt, by diverse people in a great variety of ways'.[29] We would like to propose that this kind of 'indwelling' is a feature not only of liturgical prayers, but also of other texts and forms, including literary expressions of grief. As Rushworth and Corso explore in particular, reading about another's grief can involve both recognition (one 'use of literature', according to Rita Felski) and identification (Barthes's own term for his reading of Proust).[30] Mournful texts and other works of art give us ways in which to describe, understand, or confront our own experiences of grief. To borrow Ford's terms, summarized by Phillips-Robins: these works can be 'indwelt, by diverse people in a great variety of ways'.

* * * * *

The volume is organized in four parts. The first part, 'The Poetry of Lament', takes as its focus canonical expressions of mourning from the Middle Ages, with a particular focus on the Italian lyric tradition. The second part, 'Lineages of Grief', considers how later readers have responded to and reimagined medieval discourses of mourning, not only in text but also in the art of glass engraving. The third part, 'The Politics of Mourning', focuses on interdisciplinary examples from a broad expanse of time, from the earliest human remains and classical theatre to the music of Shostakovich. The fourth part, 'Breaking the Silence', looks at three recent trends in writing about grief: on the one hand, the florescence of intimate literary texts responding to real-life experiences of loss, understood both as grief memoirs (in the anglophone tradition) and, in French, as *récits de mort*; on the other hand, the more collective experience of grief as characterized in contemporary writings about the climate crisis.

The opening chapter of the volume sets out very clearly the imbrication of medieval literature and modern theory that is one of the throughlines of our project in its mixing of different times and forms. In 'The Poetry of Mourning in the *Vita nova*: An Agambenian Reading' (Chapter 1), Catherine Keen takes as her primary focus the youthful prosimetrum of the medieval Italian poet Dante Alighieri, his *Vita nova* [New Life].[31] This work narrates Dante's amorous and poetic apprenticeship, as he learns how to love and how to write guided by his beloved Beatrice. Part of the originality of Dante's work is that he seeks to write poetry after the death of the beloved, whereas in earlier traditions such as troubadour poetry the death of the beloved would ordinarily mean the end of poetry. Keen considers the end of poetry in a rather different sense, turning to comments on Dante made by Giorgio Agamben in his essay collection *La fine del poema* [*The End of the Poem*]. As Keen cites, Agamben notes that 'the rubric *Vita nova* delimits an undecideability between what is lived and what is poeticized'.[32] Taking this comment as her starting point, Keen analyses the presence and language of mourning in Dante's *Vita nova*, a text she summarizes as a tale of four funerals and a wedding. From this perspective, what emerges is that the death of Beatrice is but one loss that the text recounts; as such, Keen is interested in showing the importance of mourning in this fictional society beyond that of Dante's individual experience. Keen traces moments of hesitation, fragmentation, and silence in Dante's use of the vernacular and, especially, in his formal alternation of prose and poetry, but also shows how mourning is a collective experience, with poetry at the boundary of the private and the public. Keen draws upon different aspects of Agamben's thought, including melancholia and the phantasmatic, but returns in the end to this question of an 'undecideability between what is lived and what is poeticized'. Keen finds this undecidability embodied in the open, unresolved ending of Dante's *Vita nova*, which resists closure by putting forward a promise of future writing. Textually, then, the end of the text with its potential end to mourning is always provisional and liable to be resumed.

Dante's resumption of the tale of his love for Beatrice even after her death leads, most famously, to his *Commedia* (known in English as his *Divine Comedy*, although the adjective is a later, posthumous addition to the title). This is not to say that the end of the *Vita nova* was intended as a prophecy of the *Commedia*, nor should this textual leap be allowed to detract from Dante's intervening works (including the *Convivio*, most prominently). Still, Helena Phillips-Robins's 'Voicing Lament: Poet and Reader as Mourners in Dante's *Commedia*' (Chapter 2), does turn to the *Commedia*, and in particular to the very intertextually rich moment of mourning for Virgil that we find in *Purgatorio*, XXX. In this scene, it is as if mourning is inevitable and constant, even if the mourned object may change; at the very moment that Dante is reunited with Beatrice, he loses his guide Virgil, addressed here very poignantly as 'dolcissimo patre' (literally, 'sweetest father') (*Purgatorio*, XXX. 50). Critics have written extensively about how Dante's shock and grief at Virgil's sudden disappearance are mediated by quotations from Virgil's own works, in particular the mourning of Orpheus for Eurydice as recounted in the *Georgics*.[33] Phillips-Robins shows how this scene is framed by a broader discourse about the ethics of mourning, with a particular focus on medieval sermons which tend to proscribe excessive grief for the death of loved ones where this is likely to obstruct or take the place of mourning for oneself, for one's own sins and distance from God. In the words of Beatrice to Dante, 'pianger [...] conven' (literally, 'weeping is appropriate, worthwhile, fitting': *Purgatorio*, XXX. 57), but the question is: weeping for what or for whom? Phillips-Robins also suggests that the reader becomes emotionally involved in this scene, perhaps mournfully so but certainly in terms of compassion (which, etymologically, means 'suffering with'). From this perspective, the specific example of Dante's mourning for Virgil and the reader's response to these lines is read by Phillips-Robins in the broader context of Dante's overall aim for his *Commedia*: that is, in her words, the possibility for the *Commedia* to assist us 'to live out relationships of loving compassion over the course of our whole lives'.

In his work *In Praise of Love*, Maurice Valency rather dramatically claims that 'after Dante, the rate of mortality among angelic ladies' rose 'abruptly and alarmingly', in recognition of the paradigm shift that Dante's work provokes (as noted above, the setting of the new example that poetry should continue after rather than cease on the death of the beloved).[34] Certainly, what Valency claims is supported by the subject of Luca Marcozzi's 'Mourning in and around Petrarch' (Chapter 3). Petrarch's debt to Dante has been much discussed, with many claiming that Petrarch's *Canzoniere* is a sort of *Vita nova* without the prose.[35] Marcozzi also discusses the resonances between these two works, with particular attention to the way in which mourning is anticipated in both works, prior to the death of the beloved. Yet Marcozzi is also keen to show how Petrarch wishes to distance himself from the previous poetic tradition of lament. This desire is particularly evident in the case of the first *canzone* on the death of Laura, *Rvf* 268, which, as Marcozzi shows, has a complex editorial history of repeated rewritings, and includes the marginal annotation in one version 'non videtur satis triste principium' [the beginning is not seen to be sufficiently sad]. Here we see Petrarch grappling directly with the challenges of how to express sadness adequately and in poetry. Marcozzi suggests that Petrarch's distancing of himself from the lyric tradition is one way of allowing the expression of grief not to be dulled by poetic convention.

At the same time, however, Marcozzi also reminds us that Petrarch is not merely the author of vernacular poetry and that his sources of inspiration are classical as well as vernacular. In terms of the former, the injunction against excessive grief is traced by Marcozzi in both pagan and Christian writers, with, for instance, Augustine reportedly weeping for only one day on the occasion of his mother's death. If the medieval sermons cited by Phillips-Robins tend to allow weeping for the death of a loved one, so long as it is not at the expense of weeping for one's own sins, the classical attitude — especially that of Stoical forbearance — is much starker and less forgiving. Marcozzi cites from Petrarch's Latin letters in support of a similar interdiction against excessive displays of grief, although he also sees a turn away from weeping even in the *Canzoniere*. Strikingly, Marcozzi suggests a precise date, the year 1350, after which Petrarch turns from mourning to consolation and, by extension, in his own writing from lyric poet to moral philosopher. Marcozzi concludes his chapter by explaining that Petrarch offers us two models of mourning: the tradition of consolation continued from the Classics and (more distinctive to the later Petrarch especially) a rational acceptance of death as natural and inevitable. The latter, for Marcozzi, is Petrarch's humanist legacy for the twenty-first century.

The second part of the volume turns to post-medieval expressions of grief which are predicated upon intimate familiarity with medieval literature, not only the late thirteenth- and fourteenth-century Italian poetic tradition but also earlier Old English poetry. In his grief memoir *Levels of Life* (a text discussed subsequently in Corso's chapter), Julian Barnes writes that 'griefs do not explain one another, but they may overlap. And so there is a complicity among the griefstruck'.[36] It is this same kind of 'overlap' or 'complicity' that is argued for in this section, with particular attention to the way in which the medieval poetry of lament is revived in new contexts.

In 'Roland Barthes's Mournful Dante' (Chapter 4), Jennifer Rushworth considers the way in which Barthes's experience of grief at his mother's death is mediated by his reading of the medieval Italian poet. A symbiotic relationship is thus established between the two; Dante helps Barthes to express his own grief, but Barthes also changes the way in which we read Dante. We have noted above that Dante critics tend to frown upon the reading, possible only in hindsight, of the end of the *Vita nova* as a prophecy of the *Commedia*. Yet the example of Barthes is a case in point as to how tempting this reading remains, with Barthes accordingly identifying the *Commedia*'s opening 'selva oscura' [dark wood] as a site of mourning for Beatrice. Rushworth reviews the commentary tradition's typical interpretations of the 'selva oscura' and finds that Barthes's reading of the 'selva oscura' as grief is an exciting, affective revision to previously established readings of the 'selva oscura' as ignorance, vice, sin, error, exile, Florence, Italy, or civil war. Barthes offers us a version of Dante that is personal and griefstruck. His version is also markedly partial, in that Barthes never finds a way out of the 'selva oscura' of grief, but rather dwells in and on this space. Rushworth therefore contrasts Barthes's reading of Dante with that of another mournful reader, Joseph Luzzi, who turns to Dante in the wake of the sudden loss of his wife in a car accident.[37] Unlike Barthes, Luzzi ultimately follows Dante out of the 'selva oscura'. Both Luzzi and Barthes identify with Dante through a shared experience of grief; the different outcomes in their writing, however, show how this identification remains remarkably fluid and open-ended. In other words, if, as Rushworth argues, Dante offers us a model for grief, this model is far from singular or one-sided.

In Chapter 5, 'From Medieval Text to Modern Glass: Expressions of Mourning in *The Dream of the Rood* and Laurence Whistler', Susan Irvine examines how an early medieval poem is reimagined by a twentieth-century glass engraver in the window of a church in Dorset (St Nicholas's, Moreton). Irvine grounds her comparative analysis in a rich variety of source material, including Whistler's study of Old English at Oxford, where he likely first encountered the poem. She also reads Whistler's window for its visual intertexts, both explicit (the Alfred Jewel, now held in the Ashmolean Museum in Oxford, which takes the place of the head of Christ on the cross) and potential (Salvador Dalí's painting of Christ of St John of the Cross). In Irvine's reading, Whistler's window depicts a variety of forms of grief: not only, most obviously, mourning for Christ's death as in its explicit textual inspiration, *The Dream of the Rood*, but also more implicit and personal grief, that of Whistler for his brother Rex. Rex, himself a noted painter, was killed in action in the Second World War at the age of thirty-nine. The window's medieval intertext is therefore overlaid with a personal loss shared by many in Whistler's generation (not to mention a further dedicatee in the presence of the inscription of the window as commemorating one Noel Findlay). Early medieval and twentieth-century griefs thus intertwine, but what is specific to the medieval example, as Irvine shows, is that it suggests that mourning and rejoicing are inextricable and, moreover, that mourning is a means of transcendence and access to the divine. The foundation of this interpretation is, of course, the very paradox of the Crucifixion as celebrated in *The Dream of the Rood* (both text and eponymous window), where the cross is at the same time joyfully bedecked with jewels and mournfully covered in tears and blood. This coexistence of mourning and rejoicing is, as Irvine highlights, peculiarly appropriate to Whistler's medium, since (in his own words discussing the art of engraving) 'the light needs the dark to be intelligible'.[38]

The final chapter of the second section, Jürgen Pieters on 'The Poet's Mourning and the Philosopher's Consolation: René Descartes's Letter of Condolence to Constantijn Huygens' (Chapter 6), explores a lineage of grief that goes back to Petrarch and, like Marcozzi's earlier chapter on Petrarch, also explores ways out of mourning — consolation and self-consolation, in particular. Pieters does not necessarily recommend consolation as a solution to mourning, since he remarks that modern readers are likely to find such injunctions rather cold and unfeeling. Nonetheless, he does find consolation to be a pre-eminent philosophical response to mourning in the early modern period, with a Christian inflection that makes it distinct from its classical forerunner. The focus of Pieters's chapter is the Dutch poet and diplomat Constantijn Huygens. The death of his wife on 10 May 1637 is the catalyst for Huygens's famous sonnet 'Op de dood van Sterre' [On the occasion of Stella's death], written some eight months afterwards and also known under the Pauline Latin phrase 'Cupio dissolvi' [longing to be dissolved]. In this sonnet, Huygens imagines his dead wife in highly Petrarchan terms as a 'Sterre', that is, as a star waiting for him in heaven. Around three centuries after it was written, Petrarch's vernacular poetry remains a current model for the expression of love and grief. Pieters emphasizes, nonetheless, how Huygens's desire for death as reunion with his wife is tempered by his awareness of his earthly commitments and obligations, both familial (his children) and professional. The importance of survival and continuation is also raised by a letter from Descartes to Huygens, on the occasion of the same loss. As Pieters shows, Descartes warns Huygens against despair and opposes reason and mourning, in particular by arguing for a rational acceptance of death. While Huygens's sonnet is Petrarchan in its expression of acute mourning, Descartes's letter is Petrarchan in a different sense in reminding us of the role granted by Petrarch to reason as a restraint upon grief (see Chapter 3 in the present volume). Huygens annotates Descartes's letter with the following line from Petrarch's *Canzoniere*: ''l desir vive, et la speranza è morta' [desire still lives, but hope is dead] (*Rvf* 277, 4), as if rebutting Descartes's message.[39] In this refusal of consolation, and a concomitant refusal to remarry, Pieters finds Huygens's grief ultimately to be as inconsolable as the definition of mourning offered by Freud in the letter to Ludwig Binswanger cited earlier in this Introduction.

The third part of this volume is devoted to 'The Politics of Mourning'. Doubtless, mourning is always political, since, after all, the personal is political and mourning takes place within and is inflected by broader societal structures and norms. Still, the chapters in this section present a particular connection between mourning and politics, focused on questions of burial, conflict, and tradition. Uta Staiger's '"I did it. I do not deny it": Mourning, Tragedy, and the Law in Contemporary Philosophy' (Chapter 7) explores the social and political ramifications of mourning, with particular attention to the relationships between individuals, community, and the law. Her corpus comprises classical Greek theatre, in particular Sophocles's *Antigone*, a play which presents a very striking example of a conflict between individual and familial grief, on the one hand, and socio-political norms and expectations, on the other. Following Bonnie Honig's reading of *Antigone*, Staiger highlights the dual meaning of 'to grieve': 'both to express grief and to litigate or seek redress for a wrong'.[40] Staiger's essay partly traces the way in which *Antigone* has been reread by philosophers from Hegel onwards, thus proving paradigmatic for modern reflections upon grief. Staiger's essay also explores other models of mourning beyond the Freudian, in particular drawing upon theories of mournful introjection versus melancholic incorporation developed by Jacques Derrida and by Nicolas Abraham and Maria Torok. As Staiger shows, mourning practices help us both to define and question the limits of the polis, who pertains to it, and what is permissible in it. By extension, as she concludes, mourning also tells us something about the practices and ethical aspirations of political and legal philosophy itself.

Musicologist Luca Aversano takes as his focus a particular string quartet: no. 8 in C minor, op. 110, by the twentieth-century Russian composer Dmitri Shostakovich (Chapter 8). He is particularly interested in how individual and collective mourning is expressed in this work, and offers an analysis of the musical language of the quartet, in relation to both traditional musical expressions of mourning (in particular, the model of the funeral march and the choice of the key of C minor) and more specific models, which include a revolutionary song, works by Wagner and Tchaikovsky, and several of Shostakovich's own compositions. Aversano also shows how the quartet is bound up in broader political reflection. Shostakovich wrote it while staying near Dresden for the filming of *Five Days, Five Nights*, a film whose score he was commissioned to compose. Shostakovich's grieving reaction at the sight of this devastated city, for Aversano, seems to be expressed in the eventual dedication of the quartet 'To the victims of fascism and war', although the authorship of this dedication remains uncertain. Ultimately, Aversano suggests that the apparent contradiction between the personal and the collective, in Shostakovich's work, is reconciled through its blending together of self-citation and quotations from the broader musical tradition. This insight concerning the embeddedness of the individual within the historical is framed by Aversano in specifically musical terms. The implications for other disciplines, and specifically for the study of literature, however, are striking.

In 'The Ontology of Mourning' (Chapter 9), Aarathi Prasad provides a highly interdisciplinary approach to the politics of mourning involving archaeology, anthropology, and biology, and which is also situated within the new field of 'evolutionary thanatology', as defined by primatologist James Anderson, archaeologist Paul Pettitt, and zoologist Dora Biro.[41] Prasad considers evidence of burial practices amongst our earliest human relations, understanding funeral rites as evidence of symbolic thought around death, loss, and grief. As Prasad explains, the forms and organization of burial sites reflect broader societal understanding that we can attempt to reconstruct. At the same time, she also shows how much of this evidence is subject to ongoing debate and uncertainty: for example, whether particular Neanderthal graves contain traces of pollen because flowers were deliberately placed there with the dead, or whether the pollen got there through other less intentional or non-human means. In the final part of her essay, Prasad turns to the animal kingdom in order further to challenge any assumption of an intrinsic connection between mourning and *Homo sapiens*. Prasad focuses on evidence of forms of grief among our closest genetic relatives, non-human apes, as well as similar tales involving elephants and insects. From this perspective, Prasad suggests a chemical basis for mourning that is cross-species, although typical of those particular species that are defined as 'eusocial', that is, sharing certain characteristics such as living in groups with overlapping generations and shared care for offspring.[42] Prasad's chapter provides a very important scientific challenge to many literary-philosophical assumptions about mourning, in particular the view of Giambattista Vico (summarized by Robert Pogue Harrison) that 'to be human means above all to bury', because of the etymological connection between *human* and *humus* (earth).[43] At the same time, Prasad does conclude by suggesting that there may indeed be a difference between human and non-human experiences of loss, with the latter a shorter-term, more passive process of grief and the former, instead, a much longer-term and more active experience of mourning.[44]

The final part of the volume is entitled 'Breaking the Silence'. In this section, contributors consider new expressions of grief which have broken through the silence of the taboo surrounding death characteristic of much of the twentieth century, at least according to Philippe Ariès.[45] This taboo is introduced in Simona Corso's 'A Grief Narrated: The Contemporary Grief Memoir' (Chapter 10), which begins by considering the embarrassment and silence that has surrounded mourners from C. S. Lewis in *A Grief Observed* (1961) onwards. As Corso shows, the emergence of the grief memoir as a significant literary genre in recent years calls into question this taboo surrounding death and suggests that literature may provide, in contrast, a space in which to dwell upon grief. Corso focuses on three examples: Julian Barnes's *Levels of Life* (2013), a story in three parts whose final part narrates the author's grief at his wife's sudden death from cancer; Max Porter's *Grief is the Thing with Feathers* (2016), a strange, poetic text which brings to life Ted Hughes's Crow as a figure for and guide through grief, and which responds to the author's earlier experience of the death of his father; and Philip Roth's *Patrimony: A True Story* (1991), which narrates the last illness and death of the author's father. Beyond an analysis of each text, Corso's essay considers, more broadly, the authors' purposes and motivations in writing these texts, as expressed in their work, as well as the reasons for the popularity of such texts among readers. Corso concludes that writing about mourning is most successful where it achieves a particular literary form. For Corso, some degree of consolation (returning to a theme explored in Chapters 3 and 6) is possible through a linguistic dwelling on grief that is a form of survival for the author and potential comfort, through recognition, for the reader.[46] Thus, while literature does not put an end to mourning, it may — in the words of Don Paterson, cited by Corso — 'help us feel less alone in our experience of [grief]'.[47]

Adina Stroia's 'Visualizing Mourning: The Legacy of Roland Barthes's *La Chambre claire*' (Chapter 11) explores the relationship between mourning and photography as established in Barthes's final book *La Chambre claire* (translated into English as *Camera Lucida*) and as developed by subsequent French writers. As Stroia shows, Barthes views photography as intimately connected to death not only because it records and represents a moment in the past that has been lost but also because, for Barthes, it is connected to the death of his own mother and the photographs of her that survive. After introducing Barthes's very personal theory of photography, Stroia turns to a reader of Barthes who engages explicitly with Barthes's text in a short book on the death of her son shortly after birth: Camille Laurens's *Philippe* (1995). Stroia understands Laurens's text as part of a literary genre that has become increasingly popular in French culture in recent years: the *récit de mort*, which she defines — with some overlap with the genre of the grief memoir discussed by Corso — as 'an account in which the events recounted are of a non-fictional nature, written by an author who entertained a close relationship with the deceased'. According to Stroia, this genre has what she terms 'a photographic logic': while some texts may include photographs, others invoke photographs through ekphrasis as well as through their very form in the frequent fragmentation of their structure and *mise-en-page*. Famously, the most moving photograph of *La Chambre claire* is the so-called 'Winter Garden Photograph' of the mother which Barthes describes but does not include, since it would not have the same affective, wounding quality for the reader as it does for the author. Even in texts without photographs, therefore, absent photographs take on a kind of textual presence and significance. To conclude, Stroia considers a final, more recent *récit de mort*: *Deuil* (2018), by the writer and poet Dominique Fourcade. Fourcade and Laurens share a publisher, P.O.L. (the initials of Paul Otchakovsky Laurens), and Fourcade's text is in fact dedicated to mourning this publisher, who died in a car accident at the start of 2018. For Stroia, Fourcade's text represents the case of a *récit de mort* that has become too clichéd and whose self-awareness and by now predictable formal features of fragmentation and so forth bespeak affectation more than affect. Stroia's chapter thus asks vital questions about the future of the *récit de mort* as a genre, with particular concern about how the authenticity that is so important to this genre can survive the ossification of increasingly entrenched formal conventions.

Finally, Florian Mussgnug turns to the more-than-human world to suggest that mourning is always communal and that all expressions of grief are bound up with the wider, shared needs of the living (Chapter 12). Mussgnug observes that encounters with grief place an excessive demand on the mourner. They mark a burden that exceeds what is socially acceptable and test the limits of reasonable accommodation. According to Mussgnug, this makes mourning structurally similar to care, which is likewise shaped by its relation to what he describes, following philosophers Emmanuel Levinas and Simon Critchley, as an *infinite demand*. Responsibility towards the other, according to this tradition of thought, is non-reciprocal, asymmetrical, and non-chosen.[48] It does not arise out of a social contract, but exists *before* individual freedom. Mussgnug specifically focuses his attention on two contexts, where the shared vulnerability of humans and non-humans calls for expanded grief. First, he discusses the recent experience of the coronavirus pandemic, which he describes as a powerful reminder of the omnipresence of death, but also of the inexhaustible, generative force of human and more-than-human communities, and of the strength of social ties. Secondly, he pays attention to the unfolding environmental emergency, and specifically to the mass extinction of non-human species, as a result of habitat destruction, pollution, invasive species, human population growth, and overharvesting. Mussgnug engages the work of human geographer Andreas Malm to argue that these seemingly different scenarios of existential risk are, on closer inspection, inextricably entangled.[49] He also proposes that they call, in similar ways, for new expressions of expanded grief, beyond the individualizing focus of the traditional poetic elegy. In the second half of his chapter, Mussgnug develops this idea with a specific focus on the plight of the honeybee, its long history as a companion species, and its recent exposure to environmental stress and threats.

While the above accounts for the twelve chapters which make up this volume, these four parts are interspersed by creative contributions which we have numbered as *intermezzi*. As in its musical sense, these *intermezzi* are short pieces that we intend as 'connecting links between the main divisions' (*OED*). They respond, as anticipated at the outset of this Introduction, to Derrida's observation that there can be no metalanguage of grief. They demonstrate that mourning is always personal and never purely academic, always part of life and never only a literary theme. The first intermezzo is by the medievalist and poet David Bowe, who responds to poems from Petrarch's *Canzoniere* discussed in Chapters 3 and 6 and gives life, once more, to Petrarch's language of mourning. The second intermezzo is by the academic and translator Timothy Mathews, and takes the form of a book review of Kristina Carlson's short novel *Mr Darwin's Gardener* (2013), in the translation of Emily Jeremiah and Fleur Jeremiah.[50] The third intermezzo is a selection of poems by the contemporary Italian poet Elena Buia Rutt, translated into English by Andrew Rutt. The volume's Epilogue is the text of 'Grief — a Work in Progress' by Zoe Papadopoulou, which was first performed at the Southbank Centre in London on 5 March 2017 as part of their 'Belief and Beyond Belief' festival. These four creative interventions reflect, in a practical, intimate way, on the enduring relationship between mourning and writing. In other words, they dwell with loss and offer a space for dwelling on grief.

Notes to the Introduction

1. Michael Sandel, *The Tyranny of Merit: What's Become of the Common Good?* (London: Allen Lane, 2020), p. 4.
2. Jacques Derrida, 'Louis Marin (1931–1992): à force de deuil', in *Chaque fois unique, la fin du monde* (Paris: Galilée, 2003), pp. 175–204 (pp. 177–78); 'By Force of Mourning: Louis Marin', in *The Work of Mourning*, ed. and trans. by Pascale-Anne Brault and Michael Naas (Chicago: University of Chicago Press, 2001), pp. 142–64 (pp. 142–43).
3. Let us also highlight from the outset that this interdisciplinarity, along with our consideration of a very broad expanse of human time, is one of the distinctive aspects of our volume in relation to other studies of mourning that either focus on one author, one particular period of time, or one language.

4. For a discussion of the term and its translation into other languages, including the Italian 'lavoro del lutto (*or* del cordoglio)', see Jean Laplanche and J.-B. Pontalis, *The Language of Psycho-analysis*, trans. by Donald Nicholson-Smith (London: Hogarth Press, 1973), pp. 484–85.
5. Sigmund Freud, 'Mourning and Melancholia' [1917], in *The Standard Edition to the Complete Psychological Works of Sigmund Freud*, ed. and trans. by James Strachey, 24 vols (London: Hogarth Press, 1953–74), XIV (1957), 243–58.
6. *Letters of Sigmund Freud 1873–1939*, ed. by Ernst L. Freud and trans. by Tania Stern and James Stern (London: Hogarth Press, 1961), p. 386. Key critics who have called attention to Freud's abandonment of his position in his essay 'Mourning and Melancholia' include especially: Richard Goodkin, *Around Proust* (Princeton, NJ: Princeton University Press, 1991), pp. 127–45; Anna Magdalena Elsner, *Mourning and Creativity in Proust* (New York: Palgrave Macmillan, 2017), pp. 12–13. Most recently, see Madelon Sprengnether, *Mourning Freud* (London: Bloomsbury Academic, 2018).
7. See Leo Bersani, *The Freudian Body: Psychoanalysis and Art* (New York: Columbia University Press, 1986). An excellent cross-period anthology of texts on the related topic of melancholy is the following: *The Nature of Melancholy: From Aristotle to Kristeva,* ed. by Jennifer Radden (Oxford: Oxford University Press, 2000).
8. Recent contributions include *The Power of Death: Contemporary Reflections on Death in Western Society*, ed. by Maria-Jose Blanco and Ricarda Vidal (New York: Berghahn, 2014); Thomas W. Laqueur, *The Work of the Dead: A Cultural History of Mortal Remains* (Princeton, NJ: Princeton University Press, 2015); Simon Stow, *American Mourning* (Cambridge: Cambridge University Press, 2017); Elsner, *Mourning and Creativity in Proust*, and Sprengnether, *Mourning Freud*, as previously mentioned; *The Materiality of Mourning: Cross-disciplinary Perspectives*, ed. by Zahra Newby and Ruth E. Toulson (Abingdon: Routledge, 2019); *Variations on the Ethics of Mourning in Modern Literature in French*, ed. by Carole Bourne-Taylor and Sara-Louise Cooper (Oxford: Peter Lang, 2021).
9. Roland Barthes, *Journal de deuil: 26 octobre 1977–15 septembre 1979*, ed. by Nathalie Léger (Paris: Seuil/Imec, 2009), p. 168; *Mourning Diary*, ed. by Nathalie Léger and trans. by Richard Howard (London: Notting Hill Editions, 2011), p. 156. For further discussion of this point as it relates to Proust's novel, see Elsner, *Mourning and Creativity in Proust*, pp. 8–9 and 33–34.
10. At the end of her chapter, Aarathi Prasad suggests a distinction between grief as 'a short-term active process' versus mourning as 'an active, long-term process', with reference to Robert Marrone, 'Grieving and Mourning: Distinctions in Process', *Illness, Crisis & Loss*, 6 (1998), 320–32. This distinction is not one that other contributors follow, however.
11. We take up here terms from Shoshana Felman's discussion of the relationship between psychoanalysis and literature in 'To Open the Question', in *Literature and Psychoanalysis: The Question of Reading: Otherwise* (= *Yale French Studies*, 55/56 (1977)), 5–10 (repr. as *Literature and Psychoanalysis: The Question of Reading: Otherwise* (Baltimore, MD: Johns Hopkins University Press, 1982)).
12. For a similar view of the inextricability of form and desire, see Manuele Gragnolati, *Amor che move: linguaggio del corpo e forma del desiderio in Dante, Pasolini e Morante* (Milan: Il Saggiatore, 2013).
13. E. Ann Kaplan, *Trauma Culture: The Politics of Terror and Loss in Media and Literature* (New Brunswick, NJ: Rutgers University Press, 2005). For a recent overview of the field of literary trauma studies, see *The Routledge Companion to Literature and Trauma*, ed. by Colin Davis and Hanna Meretoja (Abingdon: Routledge, 2020).
14. Jenny Edkins, *Trauma and the Memory of Politics* (Cambridge: Cambridge University Press, 2003), p. 5.
15. Slavoj Žižek, *The Plague of Fantasies* (London: Verso, 1997), p. 217.
16. Thom van Dooren and Deborah Bird Rose, 'Keeping Faith with the Dead: Mourning and De-extinction' (10 November 2013) <https://thomvandooren.org/2013/11/02/keeping-faith-with-death-mourning-and-de-extinction/> [accessed 3 November 2020]. Cited in Donna J. Haraway, *Staying with the Trouble: Making Kin in the Chthulucene* (Durham, NC: Duke University Press, 2016), pp. 38–39.

17. Both essays are cited from the collection of Martin Heidegger's essays, *Poetry, Language, Thought*, trans. by Albert Hofstadter (New York: Harper Colophon Books, 1971), pp. 143–61 and pp. 211–29 respectively. 'Bauen Wohnen Denken' [Building Dwelling Thinking] was given as a lecture on 5 August 1951 and first published in 1952; '"...dichterisch wohnet der Mensch..."' was given as lecture on 6 October 1951 and first published in 1954. Both can be found in Heidegger, *Vorträge und Aufsätze* (Pfullingen: Neske, 1954).
18. Martin Heidegger, 'Building Dwelling Thinking', in *Poetry, Language, Thought*, pp. 143–61 (pp. 146 and 149).
19. Ibid., pp. 147, 148.
20. Ibid., p. 149.
21. Ibid., p. 151.
22. Martin Heidegger, '"...Poetically Man Dwells..."', in *Poetry, Language, Thought*, pp. 211–29 (p. 215).
23. Ibid., pp. 221–22.
24. Giorgio Agamben, *Stanze: la parola e il fantasma nella cultura occidentale* (Turin: Einaudi, 1977); *Stanzas: Word and Phantasm in Western Culture*, trans. by Ronald L. Martinez (Minneapolis: University of Minnesota Press, 1993). Agamben has repeatedly placed his theory of aesthetic singularity in the tradition of Heidegger and Hölderlin. See, most recently, Giorgio Agamben, *La follia di Hölderlin: cronaca di una vita abitante (1806–1843)* (Turin: Einaudi, 2021). While the Italian philosopher's ambitious deployment of transhistorical analogy is suggestive, his disavowal of historical context appears problematic, especially at the level of political orientation. We take this opportunity to refer to the recent debate provoked by the publication of Heidegger's notebooks. See *Reading Heidegger's 'Black Notebooks' 1931–1941*, ed. by Ingo Farin and Jeff Malpas (Cambridge, MA: MIT Press, 2016) and *Heidegger's 'Black Notebooks': Responses to Anti-semitism*, ed. by Andrew J. Mitchell and Peter Trawny (New York: Columbia University Press, 2017).
25. Quotation from Dante, *De vulgari eloquentia*, II. ix. 2, in the English translation cited in Agamben, *Stanzas*. Agamben reiterates this quotation from Dante in his 'Introduction', p. xvi. Chapter 1 in our volume, by Catherine Keen, returns to Agamben, although to his essays on *The End of the Poem* rather than to *Stanzas*.
26. Agamben, *Stanzas*, p. xviii.
27. Ibid., p. 20.
28. For further recent exploration of mourning in poetry, see *A Gaping Wound: Mourning in Italian Poetry*, ed. by Adele Bardazzi, Francesco Giusti, and Emanuela Tandello (Oxford: Legenda, forthcoming).
29. David Ford, *Self and Salvation: Being Transformed* (Cambridge: Cambridge University Press, 1999), pp. 127–29.
30. See Rita Felski, 'Recognition', in *Uses of Literature* (Oxford: Blackwell, 2008), pp. 23–50; Roland Barthes, '*Longtemps, je me suis couché de bonne heure*', in *The Rustle of Language*, trans. by Richard Howard (Berkeley & Los Angeles: University of California Press, 1989), pp. 277–90.
31. The debate about the title of Dante's work, whether in Latin (*Vita nova*) or Italian (*Vita nuova*), need not concern us overly here, although contributors have tended to opt for the former, in the wake of Dante, *Vita nova*, ed. by Guglielmo Gorni (Turin: Einaudi, 1996).
32. Giorgio Agamben, 'The Dictation of Poetry', in *The End of the Poem: Studies in Poetics*, trans. by Daniel Heller-Roazen (Stanford, CA: Stanford University Press, 1999), pp. 76–86 (p. 84).
33. See, for instance, Rachel Jacoff, 'Intertextualities in Arcadia: *Purgatorio* 30.49–51', in *The Poetry of Allusion: Virgil and Ovid in Dante's 'Commedia'*, ed. by Rachel Jacoff and Jeffrey T. Schnapp (Stanford, CA: Stanford University Press, 1991), pp. 131–44.
34. Maurice Valency, *In Praise of Love: An Introduction to the Love-poetry of the Renaissance* (New York: Schocken Books, 1982), p. 271.
35. On the two poets, see at least *Petrarch and Dante: Anti-Dantism, Metaphysics, Tradition*, ed. by Zygmunt G. Barański and Theodore J. Cachey Jr (Notre Dame, IN: University of Notre Dame Press, 2009). On the *Canzoniere* as a prose-less *Vita nova*, see Germaine Warkentin, 'The Form of Dante's "libello" and its Challenge to Petrarch', *Quaderni d'italianistica*, 11.2 (1981), 160–70. Petrarch named his poetic collection in Latin *Rerum vulgarium fragmenta* [Fragments of Things

in the Vernacular], hence the abbreviation *Rvf* for the individual poems, although posterity has tended to prefer the vernacular title *Canzoniere*.

36. Julian Barnes, *Levels of Life* (London: Jonathan Cape, 2013), p. 72.
37. Joseph Luzzi, *In a Dark Wood: A Memoir of Grief, Healing and the Mysteries of Love* (London: William Collins, 2015).
38. Laurence Whistler, *The Image on the Glass* (London: John Murray, in association with the Cupid Press, 1975), p. 43.
39. Francesco Petrarca, *Canzoniere*, ed. by Marco Santagata, rev. edn (Milan: Mondadori, 2010); *The Complete Canzoniere*, trans. by A. S. Kline <https://www.poetryintranslation.com/PITBR/Italian/Petrarchhome.php> [accessed 6 November 2020].
40. Bonnie Honig, *Antigone, Interrupted* (Cambridge: Cambridge University Press, 2013), p. 119.
41. James R. Anderson, Dora Biro, and Paul Pettitt, 'Evolutionary Thanatology', *Phil. Trans. R. Soc. B*, 373 (2018) <https://royalsocietypublishing.org/doi/full/10.1098/rstb.2017.0262> [accessed 5 August 2021].
42. Edward O. Wilson and Bert Hölldobler, 'Eusociality: Origin and Consequences', *Proceedings of the National Academy of Sciences USA*, 120 (2005), 13367–71 <https://www.pnas.org/content/pnas/102/38/13367.full.pdf> [accessed 7 September 2021].
43. Robert Pogue Harrison, *The Dominion of the Dead* (Chicago: University of Chicago Press, 2003), p. xi. That said, Harrison does not limit humanity to a particular species, but rather explains that for him (if not for Vico) 'humanity [...] is a way of being mortal and relating to the dead' (p. xi).
44. As noted above, Prasad's distinction here between grief and mourning draws upon Marrone, 'Grieving and Mourning'.
45. Such is the thesis, at least, of Philippe Ariès, *The Hour of Our Death*, trans. by Helen Weaver, 2nd edn (New York: Knopf, 2004).
46. The term 'recognition' being understood in the way proposed by Felski, *Uses of Literature*, pp. 23–50.
47. Don Paterson, 'Introduction', in *The Picador Book of Funeral Poems*, ed. by Don Paterson (London: Picador, 2012), p. xiii.
48. See Emmanuel Levinas, *Autrement qu'être ou au-delà de l'essence* (Dordrecht: Kluwer Academic, 1996); Simon Critchley, *Infinitely Demanding: Ethics of Commitment, Politics of Resistance* (London: Verso, 2007).
49. Andreas Malm, *Corona, Climate, Chronic Emergency: War Communism in the Twenty-first Century* (London & New York: Verso, 2020).
50. Kristina Carlson, *Mr Darwin's Gardener*, trans. by Emily Jeremiah and Fleur Jeremiah (London: Peirene, 2013).

PART I

The Poetry of Lament

CHAPTER 1

The Poetry of Mourning in the *Vita nova*: An Agambenian Reading

Catherine Keen

In a brief comment on Dante Alighieri's *Vita nova* (*c.* 1293/95), the philosopher and critic Giorgio Agamben notes how 'the rubric *Vita nova* delimits an undecideability between what is lived and what is poeticized'. He comments that:

> Dante consciously plays with the title of the work, so that it is impossible to decide once and for all if in the title one is to find a reference to what is lived or to what is poeticized, to the 'book' (*libro*) of memory (in which one finds the title *Incipit vita nova*) or to the 'booklet' (*libello*) in which the poet transcribes what the reader will read.[1]

In the large body of critical writings on Dante's first substantial authored work, there is abundant discussion of its chosen title and of the metaphors of book and booklet introduced in its opening words.[2] Agamben's readings of Dante, and of medieval theories and practice of poetry form part, rather, of his exploration of how creative and literary language divides between poetry and prose and of how language confronts the limitations and finitude of human experience.[3] The *Vita nova*, which presents Dante's own authorially selected series of lyric poems framed by expository prose and extended between multiple imagined time-frames of experience and composition, lends itself well to such enquiry. In Dante, Agamben suggests, the commitment to following 'use' rather than 'art' by writing in vernacular rather than formalized, grammatically regulated Latin (*gramatica*), is to embrace the instability but also the affective primordiality of lived experience; whilst the tension that surrounds the openings and still more the closures of lyric utterance underscore the vernacular's transience via form as well as medium.[4] 'To speak in the vernacular is to precisely experience this incessant death and rebirth of words, which no grammar [*gramatica*] can fully treat', Agamben argues.[5]

In this essay I explore how, in both its formal and linguistic structures, Dante's *Vita nova* exploits the tension between 'what is lived and what is poeticized' in relation to the theme of mourning. Especially, I examine how the work leaves space to the eloquence of hesitations, fragmentations, and silences that inhere in the literary choices to use vernacular and to alternate between prose and lyric contents, both for Dante and for the book's inscribed poetic communities, including Beatrice, the central female protagonist whom the narrator loves, and whose death marks a pivotal moment within the text. The discussion begins with reflections on the *Vita nova*'s prose elements, reviewing how Dante positions them in relation to the 'widow' metaphor used to describe the disruption of the textual succession of prose and poetry units following his account of Beatrice's death. Next, focusing primarily on lyric contents, I consider the introduction of mourners and mourning into the text, as both Dante and Beatrice participate in rituals of funeral, lament, and commemoration, finally leaving Dante as survivor mourning Beatrice herself. I review the text's strategies of inclusion and omission with regard to public and social versus private and interior expressions of grief via Agamben's 'phantasms', the imagined beings of lyric discourse. Finally, in a review of the motif of selection and copying, I reflect on the alternative afterlives that Dante obliquely imagines for his poetry, especially in the increasingly uneven copying situations ascribed to the post-mortem, 'widowed' lyrics.

A Book of Memory and of Mourning: Prose

The theme of loss and mourning is present within the *Vita nova* from its opening phrases. The presentation of the entire text as a selection drawn from the narrator's book of memory confronts the reader immediately with the idea of retrospection across what is distant, disrupted, or absent:

> In quella parte del libro de la mia memoria dinanzi a la quale poco si potrebbe leggere, si trova una rubrica la qual dice: *Incipit vita nova.* Sotto la qual rubrica io trovo scritte le parole le quali è mio intendimento d'assemprare in questo libello; e se non tutte, almeno la loro sentenzia. (*VN* I. 1)
>
> [In my Book of Memory, in the early part where there is little to be read, there comes a chapter with the rubric: *Incipit vita nova.* It is my intention to copy into this little book the words I find written under that heading — if not all of them, at least the essence of their meaning.][6]

These opening lines prompted Agamben's declaration on the 'undecideability between what is lived and what is poeticized'. As readers, they tell us that the physical pages that we follow in the *libello*'s interpretive transcription will always be incomplete and fall into a silence that remains provisional, since the living writer's memory-book is *in fieri*, forever moving ahead of the poetic or scribal record. The book's ending anticipates this, too. Not only does it offer a tantalizing promise of more to come, from an author in continually evolving literary apprenticeship, but it anticipates a permanent falling into silence at the moment of his own death and transition into paradise, beyond the limits of earthly discourse:[7]

> Appresso questo sonetto apparve a me una mirabile visione, ne la quale io vidi cose che mi fecero proporre di non dire piú di questa benedetta, infino a tanto che io potessi piú degnamente trattare di lei. [...] Sí che, se [....] la mia vita duri per alquanti anni, io spero di dire di lei quello che mai non fue detto d'alcuna;

> e poi piaccia a colui che è Sire de la cortesia, che la mia anima sen possa gire a vedere la gloria de la sua donna, cioè di quella benedetta Beatrice, la quale gloriosamente mira ne la faccia di colui *qui est per omnia secula benedictus.* (*VN* XLII. 1–3)
>
> [After I wrote this sonnet there came to me a miraculous vision in which I saw things that made me resolve to say no more about this blessèd one until I would be capable of writing about her in a nobler way. [...] Accordingly, if [...] my life continue for a few more years, I hope to write of her that which has never been written of any other woman. And then may it please the One who is the Lord of graciousness that my soul ascend to behold the glory of its lady, that is, of that blessèd Beatrice, who in glory contemplates the countenance of the One *qui est per omnia secula benedictus* [who is forever blessèd].]

Structural incompletions, omissions, and alternatives are crafted into the *Vita nova* from beginning to end and, besides being declared overtly in these opening and closing prose statements, achieve prominence at different internal moments.[8]

Memory and mourning are intrinsic to the work from the start. The phraseology first introducing Beatrice as 'la gloriosa donna de la mia mente' (*VN* II. 1) would immediately tell medieval audiences that her enjoyment of paradisal glory means she is already dead, as Mark Musa's translation stresses, calling her 'the *now* glorious lady of my mind' (my emphasis).[9] Structurally, the ordering of the prose strongly marks the disruptive consequences of Beatrice's death for protagonist, book, and writer. Its earlier sections frame almost every lyric between two prose presentations of its thematic and rhetorical content: first, an account of the supposed biographical circumstances of its composition (the *ragione*); at the end, an analytical 'division' (*divisione*) of its formal structure follows the poem.[10] From the moment of Beatrice's death announcement, the *divisione* is moved to join the *ragione* ahead of the poem, leaving it 'widowed': 'E acciò che questa canzone paia rimanere piú vedova dopo lo suo fine, la dividerò prima che io la scriva; e cotale modo terrò da qui innanzi' [And in order that this *canzone* may seem to remain all the more widowed after it has come to an end, I shall divide it before I copy it. And from now on I shall follow this method] (*VN* XXXI. 2). The phrasing emphatically echoes the biblical quotation from Lamentations that precedes the announcement of Beatrice's death: '*Quomodo sedet sola civitas plena populo! facta est quasi vidua domina gentium*' [How doth the city sit solitary that was full of people! how is the mistress of the Gentiles become as a widow] (*VN* XXVIII. 1, Lam. I. 1).[11] Thus the shock of Beatrice's death is matched by a deep re-structuring of the book's narrative pattern, rooted in biblical paradigms of grief. The change means there is no longer any in-page textual separation between the emotional biography of Dante-the-lover and the controlled rhetorical commentary of Dante-the-poet, which become a single textual unit.

After Beatrice's death, the lyric thus always stands as the end-stop — or at least, the point of falling into silence — to a unit of thought. To extend one of Agamben's notes on 'The End of the Poem', this restructuring exposes the 'decisive crisis' that accumulates at a poem's ending, where metrical and semantic structures seek to be reconciled. Previously, the closing *divisione* analysing each lyric's rhetorical components has contained the poem's energies and bridged lyric and narrative realities. Agamben posits that a lyric *tornada* or *envoi* marks a kind of 'institutional necessity', 'as if for poetry the end implied a catastrophe and loss of identity so irreparable as to demand the deployment of very special metrical and semantic means'. In the *Vita nova*, the prose *divisione* has performed a function of retrospection across the completed lyric similar to a metrical *tornada*, and its changed position after Beatrice's death is presented as marking crisis and deprivation: structural widowhood. Now, more intensely than before, 'the poem [will] leave behind it only an empty space in which [...] truly *rien n'aura eu lieu que le lieu*'.[12]

The Mourner's Lament: Phantasm and Poeticization

We can thus extend Agamben's explorations of how the organized discourse of poetry confronts the problems of ending and of empty space, in the case of the *Vita nova*, to include the discursive units of *ragione*-lyric-*divisione* and, even more, the 'widowed' units of *ragione*-*divisione*-lyric. Looking elsewhere in Agamben's work, his discussions of melancholia, loss, and memory in relation to medieval love poetry also cast light on mourning rituals within the *Vita nova*, as another element that 'delimits an undecideability between what is lived and what is poeticized'.[13] For Agamben, the love discourse of the *Vita nova* and its commitment to the vernacular's transience coalesce in Beatrice, 'the name of the amorous experience of the event of language at play in the poetic text itself'.[14] This 'event of language' expresses the 'threshold' aesthetic Agamben sees in thirteenth-century love literature, where lyrics are dominated by images of the beloved generated from sense observation, but interiorized as 'phantasms' within the discursive subject, such that possession and desire can be subjugated via a kind of mediated co-presence satisfied by the act of poetic articulation itself.[15] 'Medieval psychology [...] conceived of love as an essentially phantasmatic process involving both imagination and memory, in an assiduous tormented circling around an image painted or reflected in the deepest self,' he notes.[16]

A trajectory of this dispossessed, phantasmic love discourse within the *Vita nova* can, I suggest, be traced over the arc of its four funerals (and a wedding — though one that takes on dangerously funereal traits). Beyond my pun on the film title *Four Weddings and a Funeral*, Agamben's emphasis on the priority of poeticization over (auto)biography makes Beatrice's imagined death and funeral, in the lyric 'Donna pietosa e di novella etate' [A lady, tender in heart and young] (*VN* XXIII. 17), just as 'real' as the three deaths claimed as external events.[17] In the latter, the protagonist and/or his beloved Beatrice participate in social observances that mark, externally, real-world deaths and losses but also provoke the articulation of mournful poetry directed inwards towards and between the image-persons populating the spaces of lyric rather than external cityscapes.[18] Proleptic and imagined as well as real deaths, and losses of both a distant and an intimate nature increasingly saturate the narrative, as Dante's book works towards, around, and beyond the central death of Beatrice, and reconfigures its conceptualization of loss and mourning.[19]

The *Vita nova*'s prose conveys from the outset that Beatrice is already dead and in glory, and more specific encounters with death and mourning are introduced from early on. Even the first two poems intertwine images of love with those of deathly loss. In the first sonnet, presenting in double phantasm the imagined beings of its lyric subject's dream-vision, the beloved is wrapped in a shroud-like sheet. Its troubadoric image of eating the lover's burning heart recalls love's traditional fatality;[20] while the prose shows the authenticity of its deathly premonition by citing the response sonnet embracing this interpretation, Guido Cavalcanti's 'Vedesti, al mio parere, onne valore' [I think that you beheld all worth] (*VN* III. 14).[21] The second poem provides the *Vita nova*'s first quotation from the Book of Lamentations that is later directly linked to Beatrice's death. A vernacular translation calls to 'O voi che per la via d'Amor passate' [O you who pass by on Love's way] (*VN* VII. 3, l. 1), making the *via d'Amor* a locale for Jerusalemic mourning; the *divisione* directly quotes the Latin source text, 'O vos omnes qui transitis per viam, attendite et videte si est dolor sicut dolor meus' [O all ye that pass by the way, attend, and see if there be any sorrow like to my sorrow] (*VN* VII. 7, Lam. 1.12).[22] Yet the melancholy is directed again into a domain of lyric phantasms: according to the prose, 'O voi che per la via' appropriated Jeremiah's mourning discourse for an indirect and metaphorical loss, lamenting the departure on a voyage (not the death) of a woman (not Beatrice) who has 'screened' Dante's true love (though love for Beatrice is itself a source of suffering and sorrow).

The sonnet's lament matches what Agamben identifies as a Freudian sense of melancholia, 'the paradox of an intention to mourn that precedes and anticipates the loss of the object'.[23] The early preoccupation with absence expands thanks to overtly indirect social and poetic projections of loss onto and into simulacra of the beloved and of the poetry that utters her into being, whilst also managing to speak truthfully about Beatrice (and about the melancholy surrounding her approaching loss). Thus, the third and fourth poems swiftly move us from citational to historical mourning, at the first funeral: the lament of 'O voi che per la via' did indeed, it proves, anticipate a death.[24] For the only time in the *Vita nova*, Dante-narrator claims to have witnessed the real-world mourning rituals in person. The victim is a young woman companion of Beatrice, 'lo cui corpo io vidi giacere sanza l'anima in mezzo di molte donne, le quali piangeano assai pietosamente' [I saw her body without the soul, lying in the midst of many ladies who were weeping most pitifully] (*VN* VIII. 1). Like the preceding lyric's anticipatory quotation from Lamentations, this funeral stands in proleptically for those following, and it produces the first experiments in explicitly funereal poetry. The resulting two sonnets both publicize painful confrontation with bodily death, yet internalize mourning, like love, into the space of lyric with its projected image-persons, as the allegorical phantasms of Love and Death mingle with the equally projected lyric figures of the poet and the mourning women.

The intertextual inferences of the eaten heart sonnet come close to realization at a wedding banquet, where the lover undergoes a near-death experience when overwhelmed by his beloved's proximity. In the related two sonnets, fictive personae dramatize the fatality of intense desire. The first portrays the lover's transformation into a ghostly 'figura nova' [strange figure] or 'figura d'altrui' [figure of another] (*VN* XIV. 11–12, ll. 3, 12), empty of any personal substance. In the second, death warnings are shouted not only by Love but by the inanimate fabric of the wedding-hall, as the phantasms of lyric space become themselves spatial beings. If the first sonnet's human form is transformed into an empty shell, here stones acquire voice. Their menacing '"Moia, moia"' ['Die, Die'] (*VN* XV. 4, l. 8) anticipates the '"morra'ti, morra'ti"' ['You will die, you will die'] (*VN* XXIII. 22, l. 42) called by lamenting women in the *canzone* 'Donna pietosa', a little later in the narrative, where Dante hallucinates his own and Beatrice's inevitable deaths.[25] Even in the laudatory *canzone*, 'Donne ch'avete intelletto d'amore' [Ladies who have understanding of love] (*VN* XIX. 5), praise of Beatrice involves recognition that 'Madonna è disïata in sommo cielo' [My lady is desired in highest heaven] (*VN* XIX. 9, l. 29), anticipating a heavenwards journey that inevitably implies bodily death.[26]

The remaining three funerals are not witnessed materially by the protagonist. On the death of Beatrice's father, the lover is screened from direct knowledge of Beatrice's grief, and even from talking to her female companions, by gender-segregated mourning conventions (*VN* XXII. 3). Replaying some of the dynamics of the opening lines of 'O voi che per la via', the weeping lover becomes a spectacle for women leaving the house of mourning and passing him by; Beatrice remains enclosed within. Poet and women maintain decorous silence in the prose; but by eavesdropping on their conversations the poet imagines lyric dialogues where he and they attempt to represent the absent Beatrice's grief. The dialogue thus projected out of the streetscape and into the confines of two sonnets permits an Agambenian prioritization of poeticized over lived experience, as words never spoken even within the prose fiction are uttered by the lyric's image-persons of lover and women.

After her father's funeral come death and mourning rituals for Beatrice herself, along with further layerings of ineffability, interiority, and distance between poet and beloved. In 'Donna pietosa', the sick protagonist realizes his own and his beloved's mortality, and imagines in detail both the ascent of Beatrice's soul to heaven, and funeral rites performed for her on earth. The *canzone* borrows from the scenarios of the previous two deaths (of the young woman, and Beatrice's father), which adds contextually to its ambiguity as a 'vano imaginar' [delusive vision] or 'imaginar fallace' [false vision] (*VN* XXIII. 23, 26, ll. 44, 65), a product of melancholic substitutions and anticipations of loss.[27] As well as creating echoes from elsewhere in the narrative, the mourning scenes of 'Donna pietosa' are enriched by borrowings from the Gospel accounts of the Crucifixion, with eclipse and earthquake marking Beatrice's death as a Christological event.[28] These biblical allusions both underline the mediated nature of the poem's mourning imagery, but also stress that it offers a fundamentally truthful way of thinking about Beatrice, literally central to the *libello*: not only to its exploration of her salvific role in the narrator's life experience, but also numerically central to the prosimetrum's formal construction, being the sixteenth of its thirty-one collected poems.[29]

Fragments of Mourning Discourse: Falling into Silence

The announcement of Beatrice's historical death that 'Donna pietosa' anticipates is accompanied by escalating statements about the impossibility of authentically capturing the poet's mourning in verse. The *libello*'s third *canzone* is, or should have been, the lyric 'Sí lungiamente m'ha tenuto Amore' [Love has possessed me so long] (*VN* xxvii. 3). But the poem is left hanging as a single stanza, and, uniquely in the *Vita nova*, the narrator presents a poem claimed to be incomplete.[30] Returning to Agamben's commentary on the perils of poetic endings, we truly take the measure of the impending crisis when, for the only time in the narrative, 'the poem leaves behind it only an empty space', not only lacking analytical *divisione* but interrupted in a way that marks the 'catastrophe' of ending that here implies a sense of the radical loss of poetic subjecthood as well as of textual sound and sense.

The inclusion of the unfinished lyric precedes a new structural and conceptual confrontation with the crisis of absolute loss; and the struggle to convey absence and incompletion is hereafter actualized in increasing fragmentation of the narrative record.[31] Transcription of the uncompleted lyric is disrupted by the return of the opening words of Lamentations: '*Quomodo sedet sola civitas plena populo! facta est quasi vidua domina gentium*'. The narrative stutters across the sudden incursion of this Latin phrase: only after copying Jeremiah's text does the narrator mark his *canzone*'s disruption: 'Io era nel proponimento ancora di questa canzone, e compiuta n'avea questa soprascritta stanzia, quando lo Signore de la giustizia chiamòe questa gentilissima a gloriare' [I was still engaged in composing this *canzone*, in fact I had completed only the stanza written above, when the God of Justice called this most gracious one to glory] (*VN* xxviii. 1). Temporality and articulation are thus both fragmented, already 'widowed', although the extent of the loss and its structural implications are not yet evident.[32] Famously, no direct account of Beatrice's death appears: it is literally unspeakable.

Only after a long passage on the event's numerological significance is the biblical citation picked up and glossed as expressing the condition of the poet and his whole community after Beatrice's death. When we finally reach the third complete *canzone*, 'Li occhi dolenti per pietà del core' [My eyes that grieve because of my heart's anguish] (*VN* xxxi. 8), with the fourth of the book's phantasmically staged lyric mourning scenes, the lover confronts its unspeakability — the woman's name is linked to definitive loss ('Ita n'è Beatrice in l'alto cielo' [Beatrice has departed to heaven on high], *VN* xxxi. 10, l. 15), while the speaker's voice dwindles and is displaced into his own lyric projections. His role as mourner is embodied finally within the personified poem itself, which melds into the imagined crowd of mourning women as a 'figliuola di trestizia' [daughter of sorrow] (*VN* xxxi. 17, l. 75) whose genealogy derives from the primacy of the poetic over the biographical order of existence.[33]

As for '*Quomodo sedet sola civitas*', the code-switching between the discursive Latin *gramatica* of power and institutions, into the vernacular of poetry, love, and loss, is a vital element in the *libello*'s mourning poetics. Dante reshapes the Jerusalemic lament to fit the unnamed city where the love-fiction is located, describing it as 'la sopradetta cittade quasi vedova' [the aforementioned city [...] left as if a widow] (*VN* xxx. 1), shifting into the vernacular that, for Agamben, intrinsically articulates the transience of the human condition.[34] The scriptural Latin provides a half-opening for social and civic modes of discourse: 'onde io, ancora lagrimando in questa desolata cittade, scrissi a li principi de la terra alquanto de la sua condizione, pigliando quello cominciamento di Geremia profeta: *Quomodo sedet sola civitas*' [and I, still weeping in this barren city, wrote to the princes of the land describing its condition, taking my opening words from the prophet Jeremiah [...]: *Quomodo sedet sola civitas*] (*VN* xxx. 1). Latin epistolography, however, is declaredly out of place for the interiorized poetic environment of the *libello*, and unlike the *canzone* 'Sí lungiamente', transcribed in its unfinished entirety, the finished Latin epistle is absent from the narrative. The allusion to it stands in tension with the suppression of detail concerning the crisis-moment of Beatrice's death and omission of any funeral visualization. If Beatrice, as Agamben suggests, 'is the name of the amorous experience of the event of language at play in the poetic text itself', Dante's refusal to narrate her death and burial locates the book's new life (*vita nova*) in poetry, with its vivifying phantasms, rather than in biography, history, and Latin's institutional power.[35] The event is thus appropriately accompanied within the narrative by linguistic and formal hesitations: by oscillation between Latin and vernacular, complete and incomplete texts, transcription and omission; and by increasing recourse, in the remaining narration, to a poetics of fragment, fantasy, and unrealized or not-yet-realized alternative utterance.

From here onwards, Dante's statements about his chosen audiences and about his *libello*'s selection and transcription of materials become ever more susceptible to fragmentation or silencing. The major signal of disruption is the prose *divisioni*'s repositioning to their 'widowed' place before the lyrics, noted above. This draws attention to Dante's authority as the shaping author and editor of a work drawn from his own intriguingly absent-yet-present book of memory; but also renounces some of that control, by stressing the 'collapse into silence' that Agamben finds in the crisis of poetic endings.[36] The book marks this crisis clearly, hinting at the multiple, fragmented afterlives of the *Vita nova*'s component poems via allusions to elements that are not present in the *libello*, to poems whose meanings elude contemporary audiences, or to rewritings and exchanges glimpsed only in part.

After the unfinished 'Sí lungiamente' and the missing *Quomodo sedet* epistle, the formal *planctus* of 'Li occhi dolenti' is followed by two more funeral lyrics, 'Venite a 'ntender li sospiri miei' [Come and hear my sighs] (*VN* xxxii. 5) and 'Quantunque volte, lasso!, mi rimembra' [Alas, whenever I remember] (*VN* xxxiii. 5). The poems' laments are elaborately ventriloquized performances. They are commissioned by a friend of the narrator, Beatrice's brother, who conceals his objective ('simulava sue parole', *VN* xxxii. 2) by claiming he wants to commemorate a different woman's death, inviting his accomplished friend to voice words on his behalf. To complicate this already elaborate screening, the first-person voice in 'Venite a 'ntender' incorporates and conceals the lover's own mourning for Beatrice beneath the voice of its commissioning patron. Similarly, the prose unfolds a hidden distinction between the patron's and poet's subject-positions in the two grieving stanzas of 'Quantunque volte'. We may return to Agamben's 'threshold' or 'labyrinth' arguments about how medieval poetry employs phantasm and simulacra to interiorize the tension between desire and its inevitable absence and loss. To let the poet go 'into the heart of what [is kept] at a distance', the identities of the dead woman, of the voices saying 'I', and of the poet producing them all become increasingly elusive and indirect.[37]

Like the moment of Beatrice's actual death, its anniversary is recorded in another disrupted poem, 'Era venuta ne la mente mia' [There had come into my heart] (*VN* xxxiv. 7).[38] Contrary to the incomplete 'Sí lungiamente', disruption here produces poetic excess. Two alternative opening quatrains to the sonnet record two perspectives on the speaker's acts of grieving, with his mournful introspection represented either as a solitary tableau, in the first incipit, or as a moment witnessed by others, in the second. In this episode, we glimpse Dante as visual artist as well as poet, sketching angels on his writing-tablet, although of course his drawings are absent from our reading experience.[39] The second incipit, addressing the bystanders who watch him sketching, makes this a historical moment that pins the poem to social spaces inhabited by the author and his audience; yet the external encounter is subordinated, in both prose and lyric, to the interior realm where the persons of poetry or painting constitute the speaker's central experiential focus.[40] As readers, we have the choice to begin with either or both of the quatrains as the poem's stuttering starting point, offering us at least three alternative versions of the poem; but always depriving us of its author's angelic decorations. We can never recuperate the writing-tablets where the *Vita nova*'s mournfully yearning protagonist sketched words and/or images, and neither we nor he can fix the sonnet into regular, unified diction contained within a stable frame. It is 'widowed' both of prose *divisione* (that is, the *divisione* stands in the post-mortem widowed position, ahead of the poem) and of accompanying 'figure d'angeli' (figures of angels: *VN* xxxiv. 3), as it falls precariously into silence.

The struggles and screenings incorporated into the first year's poetry of mourning anticipate more serious complications that arise when the demonstrative empathy of a 'donna gentile' [gracious lady] with the lover's sorrow nearly leads to recovery from grieving and a new love story with a woman who closely replicates Beatrice's external traits. But with another phantasmic moment that doubles back to the dalliances with 'screen women' near the start of the book, a dream vision of Beatrice re-immerses the lover in his devotion to her, and to the problem of articulating her love and loss effectively in mourning verse.[41] The timing of the 'donna gentile' interlude falls significantly after the end of a year's mourning, during which the lover has been immersed in recalling the past ('ne la quale mi ricordava del passato tempo': *VN* xxxv. 1). Its distractions are punctured only by a deeper memorial retrospection that follows the dream of Beatrice: a recursion that perpetuates mourning but also promises to impose order on it (as expressed also by the *libello*'s open ending): 'ricordandomi di lei secondo l'ordine del tempo passato' [remembering her in the sequence of past times] (*VN* xxxix. 2). As Donato

Pirovano notes, the *libello* achieves its open-ended resolution by embracing the melancholy of perpetual absence, turning to poetry to create a verbal 'reliquary' in and through which the lover's devotion can be maintained.[42]

The last two lyrics, with their prose frames, constitute phantasmic reliquaries in recalling how medieval pilgrimage engaged with the liminality of relics as material emblems of the transcendent realm. In the penultimate sonnet, the poet imagines telling a group of pilgrims passing through his city how this apparent waystop is a Jerusalemic 'città dolente' [sorrowing city] (*VN* XL. 9, l. 6). In the final poem, in turn, the poet's own 'peregrino spirito' [pilgrim spirit] (*VN* XLI. 10, l. 8), in the form of a wordless sigh, travels to behold Beatrice in paradise, a vision too ineffable for coherent speech. The book's closing words, as we saw above, end the book without definitively resolving its narrative and instead anticipate speech-acts and silences yet to come, to fill still-unwritten pages in the book of the poet's future memory.[43]

The final poem's phantasmic pilgrimage crystallizes the preoccupation with absence and displacement running through the *libello*'s closing sections. It is introduced however with an explicitly social and patronal opening scenario that envisages a possible re-ordering or alternative genesis of the *Vita nova*, which is often overlooked. Another kind of silence or absence arises in the prose notes explaining its genesis as prompted by a request from 'due donne gentili [...] pregando che io mandassi loro di queste mie parole rimate' [two gentlewomen [...] requesting that I send them some of my poetry] (*VN* XLI. 1). The request looks back over the narrator's lyric past, since the women's invitation shows knowledge of existing poetic production; but it looks forward too, since it prompts him to write 'una cosa nuova' [something new] (*VN* XLI. 1). This new poem, 'Oltre la spera che piú larga gira' [Beyond the sphere that circles widest] (*VN* XLI. 10), becomes the last lyric transcribed within the pages of the *Vita nova*. Yet Dante also notes that the poem was one of three sent to the women, in a micro-series of mourning poems drawn from the post-mortem lyrics for Beatrice.[44] The resulting sequence is one that readers can put together from within the text, but which we must manufacture for ourselves: Dante does not transcribe it. We cannot be sure about its precise shape, either. Its constituent poems are listed in reverse chronological sequence: so would the putative page sent to the women begin with the brand-new 'Oltre la spera' (*VN* XLI), followed by 'Deh peregrini' (*VN* XL), and finally 'Venite a 'ntender' (*VN* XXXII), the funeral poem commissioned by Beatrice's kinsman, in the order listed in the prose *ragione* (*VN* XLI. 1)? Or would the poet have sent his lyrics in what the *Vita nova* suggests is the correct narrative order, with 'Venite a 'ntender' first, then 'Deh peregrini', and finally 'Oltre la spera'? Each choice would significantly affect the emotive charge of a sequence in which the balance between mourning and consolation varies depending on whether it begins or ends with 'Oltre la spera'.

Compressing, disrupting, and fragmenting the *Vita Nova's* lyric sequence, the authorized but absent micro-collection sent to the women remains focused on mourning. Its new poem, 'Oltre la spera', introduces the consolatory note that continues into the final prose ending of Dante's prosimetrum. Yet famously, even those final sentences dissolve into narrative absence and ineffability. They project the *Vita nova*'s opening premise of incomplete transcription away from the past and into the future, from the book of memory to the book of the not-yet-known, contingent and unpredictable. Agamben comments on 'the undecideability between what is lived and what is poeticized' in Dante's *libello*.[45] Up to its closing pages, new starting points and uncompleted utterances proliferate around the words we read, taking us from the newness of the incipit through to the closing poetic 'cosa nuova'. As readers, we continually confront the gap between what is said and unsaid, what is biography and what is literature. At the end of the *Vita nova*, we are assured there is more of both to come. For the moment, both the final poem and the final prose have to fall into a silence that accepts its own incompletion, and acknowledges the loss of Beatrice as something for which the mourning, earth-bound writer cannot find words.

Notes to Chapter 1

1. Giorgio Agamben, 'The Dictation of Poetry', in *The End of the Poem*, pp. 76–86 (p. 84).
2. The *Vita nova* is henceforth in this chapter referenced as *VN*. For recent bibliography on the book/booklet image, see at least Albert Russell Ascoli, *Dante and the Making of a Modern Author* (Cambridge: Cambridge University Press, 2008), esp. pp. 175–201; Michelangelo Picone, 'La teoria dell'*auctoritas* nella *Vita Nova*', *Tenzone*, 6 (2005), 173–91; H. Wayne Storey, 'Following Instructions: Remaking Dante's *Vita Nova* in the Fourteenth Century', in *Medieval Constructions in Gender and Identity: Essays in Honor of Joan M. Ferrante*, ed. by Teodolinda Barolini (Tempe: Arizona Center for Medieval and Renaissance Studies, 2005), pp. 117–32; Jelena Todorović, *Dante and the Dynamics of Textual Exchange* (New York: Fordham University Press, 2016). Fundamental for some of the mourning themes discussed here is the connection with elegy traced in Stefano Carrai, *Dante elegiaco: una chiave di lettura per la 'Vita nova'* (Florence: Olschki, 2006). In this essay I adopt the Latin title *Vita nova* based on Dante's inscribed incipit, *VN* I. 1; all references to the *Vita nova* follow Donato Pirovano's edition in Dante Alighieri, *Vita nuova; Rime*, ed. by Donato Pirovano and Marco Grimaldi (Rome: Salerno, 2015), pp. 77–289.
3. This essay draws especially on two of Agamben's collections. First, *Categorie italiane: studi di poetica* (Venice: Marsilio, 1996), whose title underlines how engagement with Italian literature in particular informs its reflections, a prominence lost in the English translation's title (n. 1 above), though this rightly avoids confining the essays to a 'national literature' focus (see Anthony Adler, 'Deconfabulation: Agamben's Italian Categories and the Impossibility of Experience', *Diacritics*, 43.3 (2015), 68–94 (pp. 82–89)). Secondly, *Stanze*; in English, *Stanzas*. On Agamben's literary thought, as distinct from the *Homo Sacer* series, I found especially helpful Adler, 'Deconfabulation'; Paolo Bartoloni, 'Dante Alighieri', in *Agamben's Philosophical Lineage*, ed. by Adam Kotsko and Carlo Salzani (Edinburgh: Edinburgh University Press, 2017), pp. 125–30; William Watkin, *The Literary Agamben: Adventures in Logopoiesis* (London: Continuum, 2010).
4. Agamben explores Dante's vernacular/*gramatica* distinction in 'The Dream of Language', in *The End of the Poem*, pp. 43–61; the titular essay 'The End of the Poem' focuses on problems of ending, in *The End of the Poem*, pp. 109–15.
5. Agamben, 'The Dream of Language', p. 54; and on vernacular and *gramatica* more widely in Dante's thought, pp. 53–61. See also Gary P. Cestaro, *Dante and the Grammar of the Nursing Body* (Notre Dame, IN: University of Notre Dame Press, 2003).
6. Prose translations throughout are from *Dante's 'Vita Nuova'*, ed. and trans. by Mark L. Musa (Bloomington: Indiana University Press, 1973); lyrics from *Dante's Lyric Poetry*, ed. and trans. by Kenelm Foster and Patrick Boyde, 2 vols (Oxford: Clarendon, 1967).
7. On the open ending's promise of future writing, see Jennifer Rushworth, *Discourses of Mourning in Dante, Petrarch, and Proust* (Oxford: Oxford University Press, 2016), pp. 119–20, 135, 139–41.
8. Agamben's 'End of the Poem' highlights the 'crisis' associated with poetic closure (pp. 112–13,

and see below): in Dante's experimental book form, his opening and closure chiastically articulate a similar 'crisis of identity' for the booklet recounting a poeticized life-experience.

9. See Charles Singleton, 'The Death of Beatrice', in *An Essay on the 'Vita nuova'* (Cambridge, MA: Harvard University Press, 1949), pp. 6–24 (p. 7). Teodolinda Barolini stresses Dante's insistent narratological prolepsis from incipit onwards, in '*Cominciando dal principio infino alla fine*: Forging Anti-narrative in the *Vita nuova*', in *Dante and the Origins of Italian Literary Culture* (New York: Fordham University Press, 2006), pp. 175–92 (esp. pp. 183–90).
10. The apparently biographical material uses verbs such as *narrare, trattare, ragionare* [narrate, treat, tell], or the noun *ragione*, a partial calque of the Occitan *razo* which Agamben also discusses in *The End of the Poem*: see Watkin, *The Literary Agamben*, pp. 35–38. On *Vita nova*'s *ragioni* and *divisioni*, see Ascoli, *Dante and the Making of a Modern Author*, pp. 179–81; Todorović, *Dante and the Dynamics of Textual Exchange*, pp. 115–21 (esp. p. 119); Federica Pich, 'On the Threshold of Poems: A Paratextual Approach to the Narrative/Lyric Opposition in Italian Renaissance Poetry', in *Self-Commentary in Early Modern European Literature, 1400–1700*, ed. by Francesco Venturi (Leiden: Brill, 2019), pp. 99–134 (pp. 101–05).
11. See Ronald Martinez, 'Mourning Beatrice: The Rhetoric of Threnody in the *Vita nuova*', *MLN*, 113.1 (1998), 1–29 (esp. pp. 17, 20); repr. in *Dante: The Critical Complex*, ed. by Richard Lansing, 8 vols (New York: Routledge, 2003), I, 127–55. See also Carrai, *Dante elegiaco*, pp. 86–89.
12. All from Agamben, 'The End of the Poem', pp. 112–14. The French quotation is from Stéphane Mallarmé: 'nothing will have taken place but the place'.
13. Agamben, 'The Dictation of Poetry', p. 84.
14. Agamben, 'Dream of Language', p. 58.
15. Bartoloni, 'Dante Alighieri', pp. 125–27. For the *VN* in Agamben, *Stanzas*, see esp. '*Spiritus phantasticus*', pp. 90–101; 'Spirits of Love', pp. 102–10.
16. Agamben, 'Eros at the Mirror', in *Stanzas*, pp. 73–89 (p. 81); see also *Stanzas*, Part I, 'The Phantasms of Eros'.
17. *Four Weddings and a Funeral*, dir. by Mike Newell (Rank, 1994). I classify the *Vita nova*'s four funerals as those of Beatrice's friend (*VN* VIII) and father (XXII), and the imagined (XXIII) then genuine death of Beatrice (XXVIII); each is however dramatized multiple times in the text, in both prose and lyric iterations.
18. On the *Vita nova*'s lyric phantasms and the influence of Guido Cavalcanti (another of Agamben's key medieval poets), see Gianfranco Contini, 'Cavalcanti in Dante', in *Un'idea di Dante* (Turin: Einaudi, 1970), pp. 143–58. See also Giuseppe Mazzotta, 'The Language of Poetry in the *Vita nuova*', *Rivista di studi italiani*, 1.1 (1983), 3–14.
19. Martinez reads 'the unfolding of the plot of the *Vita nuova* as a series of separations and losses', 'Mourning Beatrice', pp. 15–16; while Fabio Camilletti reads the book as 'a progressive refinement of love and poetry through loss': *The Portrait of Beatrice: Dante, D. G. Rossetti, and the Imaginary Lady* (Notre Dame, IN: University of Notre Dame Press, 2019), p. 17. See also Jeremy Tambling, 'Thinking Melancholy: Allegory and the *Vita nuova*', *Romanic Review*, 96.1 (2005), 85–105 (p. 99), on the link between death and memory. Singleton's 'Death of Beatrice' argues for the reality of the *libello*'s visions, especially the imagined death in 'Donna pietosa'.
20. On the eaten heart, see Simon Gaunt, *Love and Death in Medieval French and Occitan Courtly Literature: Martyrs to Love* (Oxford: Oxford University Press, 2006), pp. 77–81 (drawing extensively on Agamben's *Homo Sacer* studies); Heather Webb, *The Medieval Heart* (New Haven, CT: Yale University Press, 2010), pp. 156–63.
21. See Carrai, *Dante elegiaco*, pp. 23–24; Manuele Gragnolati, '(In-)Corporeality, Language, Performance in Dante's *Vita Nuova* and *Commedia*', in *Dante's Plurilingualism: Authority, Knowledge, Subjectivity*, ed. by Sara Fortuna, Manuele Gragnolati, and Jürgen Trabant (Oxford: Legenda, 2010), pp. 213–22 (p. 217); Michelangelo Picone, 'Dante e Cino: una lunga amicizia. Prima parte: i tempi della *Vita nova*', *Dante*, 1 (2004), 39–53 (pp. 42–46).
22. See Tambling, 'Thinking Melancholy', pp. 89–90.
23. Agamben, 'The Lost Object', in *Stanzas*, pp. 19–21 (p. 20). On the Freudian melancholia of the episode's 'screen memories', see Tambling, 'Thinking Melancholy', pp. 102–03.
24. Nancy Vickers terms this 'proleptic citation': 'Widowed Words: Dante, Petrarch, and the

Metaphors of Mourning', in *Discourses of Authority in Medieval and Renaissance Literature*, ed. by Kevin Brownlee and Walter Stephens (Hanover: University Press of New England, 1989), pp. 97–108 (p. 100).

25. Martinez, 'Mourning Beatrice', pp. 21–22; Mazzotta, 'The Language of Poetry in the *Vita nuova*', pp. 7–8.
26. Martinez links the image to *planctus* traditions ('Mourning Beatrice', p. 14).
27. Agamben, 'Introduction', in *Stanzas*, pp. xv–xix (pp. xvii–xviii).
28. Singleton, *An Essay on the 'Vita nuova'*, pp. 18–20; Tambling, 'Thinking Melancholy', pp. 21–25. On the *Vita nova*'s elision of corporeal death and salvific emphasis on the glory of changed, celestial life, see Camilletti, *The Portrait of Beatrice*, pp. 15–17.
29. Singleton, *An Essay on the 'Vita nuova'*, pp. 6–7, 18; Barolini explores how the abundant detail in the poem and its frame, contrasting with the 'black hole' surrounding the death event itself, interact to support or to undermine Dante's self-projection as an 'exemplary narrator' (*Dante and the Origins of Italian Literary Culture*, pp. 185–87).
30. Barolini, *Dante and the Origins of Italian Literary Culture*, pp. 188–89; David Bowe, 'Rubrics and Red Dresses: Ordering the *Vita nova*', *LaRivista*, 8.1 (2020), 5–29 (p. 19); Rushworth, *Discourses of Mourning in Dante, Petrarch, and Proust*, pp. 117–19; Tambling, 'Thinking Melancholy', pp. 91–92. Monostrophic *canzoni* were produced by contemporary lyricists, so the poem is potentially complete; the prose commentary claims otherwise.
31. See Francesca Southerden, 'Lost for Words: Recuperating Melancholy Subjectivity in Dante's Eden', in *Dante's Plurilingualism*, ed. by Fortuna, Gragnolati, and Trabant, pp. 193–210 (pp. 193–95).
32. Barolini, *Dante and the Origins of Italian Literary Culture*, pp. 187–89.
33. Martinez, 'Mourning Beatrice', pp. 16–18; Southerden, 'Lost for Words', p. 201; Vickers, 'Widowed Words', pp. 105–08; see Agamben, 'The Dictation of Poetry', p. 84.
34. Agamben, 'Dream of Language'; Bartoloni, 'Dante Alighieri', p. 126.
35. Agamben, 'Dream of Language', p. 58.
36. Agamben, 'End of the Poem', p. 115.
37. Agamben, 'Introduction', in *Stanzas*, p. xviii.
38. Southerden, 'Lost for Words', p. 197.
39. See Federica Pich, 'L'immagine "donna de la mente" dalle *Rime* alla *Vita Nova*', in *Le Rime di Dante*, ed. by Claudia Berra and Paolo Borsa (Milan: Cisalpino, 2010), pp. 345–76. Gorni speculates on the possible Y-shaped or 'winged' transcription of the dual incipits as a *carmen figuratum*: 'Nota al testo', in Dante Alighieri, *Vita Nova*, ed. by Gorni, pp. 338–40; Camilletti provides a rewarding, extended discussion of the episode's word-image relationships (*The Portrait of Beatrice*, pp. 19–34).
40. See Agamben on the 'image in the heart' motif: 'Eros at the Mirror', p. 81.
41. Rushworth, *Discourses of Mourning in Dante, Petrarch, and Proust*, pp. 127–32, with a Freudian reading that chimes with Agamben's 'Lost Object' discussion; Bowe, 'Rubrics and Red Dresses', pp. 21–22.
42. Donato Pirovano, 'Nota introduttiva', in *Vita nuova; Rime*, ed. by Pirovano and Grimaldi, pp. 3–36 (p. 24). See Seeta Chaganti's studies of the 'poetics of enshrinement' that creates textual and performative reliquaries in verse: *The Medieval Poetics of the Reliquary: Enshrinement, Inscription, Performance* (New York: Palgrave Macmillan, 2008).
43. See Rushworth, *Discourses of Mourning in Dante, Petrarch, and Proust*, pp. 135–41; Camilletti, *The Portrait of Beatrice*, pp. 32–33.
44. Martinez calls it a 'germinal mini-anthology of the *libello* itself [...] that emphasizes the domination of mourning' ('Mourning Beatrice', p. 13).
45. Agamben, 'The Dictation of Poetry', p. 84.

CHAPTER 2

Voicing Lament: Poet and Reader as Mourners in Dante's *Commedia*

Helena Phillips-Robins

This essay asks whether, how, and why a literary text might invite readers to mourn. I focus on one episode from Dante's *Commedia*, an episode that is among the most intense of Dante's reflections on grief. The scene forms the climax of the Dante character's journey through purgatory, and stages a simultaneous loss and encounter: Virgil, who has become as father and mother to Dante, disappears, without warning, in the moment that Beatrice, Dante's beloved who had died ten years before, arrives. The experience of loss and grief is mediated through an extended dialogue with other texts, both classical and Christian. I focus on one of these dialogues — Dante's rewriting of Orpheus's lament from Virgil's *Georgics* — and specifically on the type of engagement that I suggest this passage invites from the reader of the *Commedia*. I suggest that Dante not only invites readers to interpret this depiction of grief, but also gives readers a script for their own voicing of compassionate grief.

Dante explicitly declares that one of his aims in writing the *Commedia* was to help effect the moral and spiritual transformation of his readers.[1] One way in which Dante proclaims the salvific mission of his text is by claiming that this is a poem that is true. As Christian Moevs has shown, this is not a claim that the *Commedia* is an objective report of events and things, a report of how things really are in the afterlife. Rather, it is a claim that the *Commedia* mediates, if only partially, the ultimately reality, which Dante calls God or love. It is a claim that the *Commedia* has the potential to lead its readers into deeper relationships of love, with God and with fellow humans. The truthfulness of the *Commedia*, for Dante, lies in the reader's response to the poem, in whether the reader, over the course of their life, enters more fully into such relationships, or not.[2] All this has a bearing on my opening question — whether, how, and why the *Commedia* might invite readers to mourn — and I will return to Dante's understanding of the truthfulness of his poem towards the end of this essay. In that it is grounded in conceptions of truth and fiction in many respects different from modern ones, the *Commedia* offers perspectives on the relation between reader, writer, and text, that form a fruitful point of contrast with others of the works and time periods explored in this volume.

In this essay I draw on a number of medieval sermons. Preaching, much of which was directed at the laity, was the primary form of mass communication in the later Middle Ages, and so sermons, which survive in vast quantities, can be a rich resource for investigating concepts and practices that would have been available in the type of contexts in which Dante lived. I draw on sermons not as direct sources for Dante's thought, but as resources that can help us reconstruct the cultural frameworks in which Dante and his contemporaries made sense of their world. These findings can in turn further our understanding of the *Commedia*.[3]

Let us turn, then, to our scene from *Purgatorio*. The passage is worth citing at length for its dramatization of the utter shock of Beatrice's arrival and Virgil's disappearance. The passage begins with a host of angels who greet Beatrice:

Tutti dicean: '*Benedictus qui venis!*'
e fior gittando e di sopra e dintorno,
'*Manibus,* oh, *date lilïa plenis!*'
[...]
così dentro una nuvola di fiori
che da le mani angeliche saliva
e ricadeva in giù dentro e di fori,
sovra candido vel cinta d'uliva
donna m'apparve, sotto verde manto
vestita di color di fiamma viva.
E lo spirito mio, che già cotanto
tempo era stato ch'a la sua presenza
non era di stupor, tremando, affranto,
sanza de li occhi aver più conoscenza,
per occulta virtù che da lei mosse,
d'antico amor sentì la gran potenza.
Tosto che ne la vista mi percosse
l'alta virtù che già m'avea trafitto
prima ch'io fuor di püerizia fosse,
volsimi a la sinistra col respitto
col quale il fantolin corre a la mamma
quando ha paura o quando elli è afflitto,
per dicere a Virgilio: 'Men che dramma
di sangue m'è rimaso che non tremi:
conosco i segni de l'antica fiamma.'
Ma Virgilio n'avea lasciati scemi
di sé, Virgilio dolcissimo patre,
Virgilio a cui per mia salute die'mi;
né quantunque perdeo l'antica matre,
valse a le guance nette di rugiada
che, lagrimando, non tornasser atre.
'Dante, perché Virgilio se ne vada,
non pianger anco, non piangere ancora;
ché pianger ti conven per altra spada'.

[They spoke thus: '*Benedictus qui venis!*'
and, strewing petals upward and around:
'*Manibus,* oh, *date lilia plenis!*'

[...]
So now, beyond a drifting cloud of flowers
(which rose up, arching, from the angels' hands,
then fell within and round the chariot),
seen through a veil, pure white, and olive-crowned,
a lady now appeared to me. Her robe was green,
her dress the colour of a living flame.
And I, in spirit, who so long had not
been, trembling in her presence, wracked by awe,
began again to tremble at her glance
(without more evidence that eyes could bring,
but darkly, through the good that flowed from her),
sensing the ancient power of what love was.
But on the instant that it struck my sight —
this power, this virtue that had pierced me through
before I'd even left my boyhood state —
I turned aside (and leftwards) meaning now,
with all the hope and deference of some child
that runs when hurt or frightened to its mum,
to say to Virgil: 'There is not one gram
of blood in me that does not tremble now.
I recognize the signs of ancient flame.'
But Virgil was not there. Our lack alone
was left where once he'd been. Virgil, dear sire,
Virgil — to him I'd run to save my soul.
Nor could the All our primal mother lost,
ensure my cheeks — which he once washed with dew —
should not again be sullied with dark tears.
'Dante, that Virgil is no longer here,
do not yet weep, do not yet weep for that.
A different sword cut, first, must make you weep'.]
(*Purgatorio*, xxx. 19–57)

The angels greet Beatrice with a Christological *Benedictus* and a Virgilian funeral lament. The words 'manibus date lilia plenis', which in the *Aeneid* are used to mourn the death of Marcellus, Augustus's heir, as a tragedy of wasted potential, are used to greet Beatrice, as one who also died young, but who now lives in Christian eternity. The citation functions, as critics have discussed, through contrast. The flowers that were funerary lilies for Marcellus — a hollow, comfortless offering ('inane munus', *Aeneid*, vi. 885–86) — have become Christological flowers of celebration for Beatrice.[4] Dante asks readers to call to mind the terrible grief of the Marcellus story, and to reflect on the upending of reality brought about by the Crucifixion, which means that, in Dante's worldview, the pain of early death need no longer be the final word.

Within the narrative, Beatrice then appears and Dante, like a child running to its mother, turns, about to speak Virgil's own words to Virgil, to speak, in Italian, the words that in *Aeneid*, iv Dido speaks when she realizes she has fallen in love with Aeneas: 'conosco i segni de l'antica fiamma' [I recognize the signs of ancient flame], 'agnosco veteris vestigia flammae'. But as he fashions himself as a new, redeemed

Dido, Dante realizes that Virgil has gone.[5] Precisely when we might expect Dante's mourning to reach its end — he has been reunited with Beatrice — he starts to mourn a different loss.

In the tears Dante sheds for Virgil, mourning and compassion flow into one another, with no clear-cut boundary between the two. These are tears of bereavement; Virgil has left Dante and his companion 'scemi | di sé', deprived of himself. They are also tears of compassion because in the narrative of the *Commedia* Virgil, who is instrumental in helping Dante gain salvation, is himself consigned to limbo, the region of hell where the inhabitants experience no physical pain, but endlessly unfulfilled desire. There is, Beatrice emphatically declares, something problematic in Dante's tears. Yet although Beatrice lays great stress on her injunction, the injunction itself is ambiguous. Lines 55–57 can be read in the sense, 'do not weep yet for the fact that Virgil has gone; weep first for another grief' (as Robin Kirkpatrick's translation suggests), or in the sense, 'do not weep yet; weep later for another grief and not at all for Virgil'.[6] For reasons that will become clear over the course of this essay, I am taking Beatrice's words in the first sense. Reading along these lines, the issue is not that weeping for Virgil is per se wrong, but that Dante has to perform another type of weeping first. In the scene that follows Beatrice's injunction, Dante experiences the pain of recognizing how his sins have damaged his relationships with others and with God, and weeps in repentance (*Purgatorio*, XXX. 58–XXXI. 90). This recognition is the 'other sword cut' of Beatrice's speech.[7]

The dialogue that Dante sets up between weeping with grief for the death or loss of a friend and weeping in sorrow and penance for one's sins, is a question discussed by at least some medieval preachers. Some preachers present these types of weeping as concerning grief for the bodily death of a loved one and grief for the spiritual death of one's soul. An anonymous thirteenth- or fourteenth-century sermon on penance preserved as the opening text in a collection of Lenten sermons is one example. The sermon is not assigned to a particular day of the liturgical year, but contains material that, perhaps even more than is the case with other sermons, could be reused on multiple occasions requiring preaching on penance. The preacher quotes Ecclesiasticus 38:16, 'My son, shed tears over the dead', and then admonishes his listeners:

> But alas, there are many people who weep more for the bodily death of another person, than for the death of their own soul. Augustine says, 'Let a man know himself to be guiltily obstinate if he weeps for temporal ills or for the death of a friend, yet does not show, with tears, grief for his sins'.[8]

Another sermon in the same collection also quotes the Augustinian saying and similarly declares: 'A foolish man weeps for the bodily death of another person and yet does not weep for the death of his own soul'.[9] Both sermons seek to guide and prompt listeners to self-examination and penitence. The point seems to be not that one should not weep for one's loved ones, but that this is not the only type of weeping one should practise. The 'foolishness' consists in not also weeping at one's distance from God. Indeed, elsewhere preachers instruct listeners to weep for their sins as though bereaved, bereavement indicating the severity of the pain that one's distance from God — itself a type of bereavement — should provoke. The Dominican preacher Giovanni da San Gimignano, for example, in a sermon for Ash Wednesday (written 1304–14, surviving in numerous manuscripts), exhorts: a penitent 'should weep like one bereaved because he is no longer the son of our Father, God, or our Mother, the Church'.[10] The saying attributed to Augustine (though in fact from the Pseudo-Augustinian treatise *De vera et falsa poenitentia*) is quoted by Peter Lombard in the *Sentences*.[11] Aquinas reflects on the saying in his Commentary on the *Sentences* and, though in a different way, makes the point I suggest is implicit in the sermons in the manuscript cited above. Aquinas discusses reasons why one might be unable to weep: sometimes one is in too much pain, or one weeps in private with only God as witness. Sometimes, 'on account of the hardness of one's bodily constitution one cannot weep physical tears for one's sins; yet one weeps for the death of a friend, for this type of pain is more easily felt, and so more easily leads one to pour out tears'.[12] Again, the point seems to be not that weeping for loved ones is wrong, but that one should practise both types of weeping: weeping for loved ones and for one's sins.

These discussions resonate with Beatrice's command. The sermons are concerned with guiding and exhorting listeners to penance, as is Beatrice with Dante in *Purgatorio*, XXX. In the sermons, the need to weep at one's distance from God does not mean there is no place for weeping for loved ones. The sermons may make us more attentive to the fact that, even if the forcefulness of Beatrice's words might initially seem to indicate otherwise, *Purgatorio*, XXX does give space to lament for Virgil. Dante character's lament is cut off, but, as we shall see, Dante-poet performs a lament in the act of writing the canto. Various questions arise concerning Beatrice's injunction, the relation between penitential grief and grief for Virgil, and the relation between the laments of Dante character and Dante-poet, but the rest of this essay focuses on the poet's lament and its implications for the reader.

At line 49 Dante makes a notable shift, switching from transcribing the direct speech his character would have made to Virgil back to a narrative reporting mode, speaking as the poet in the here and now of writing the *Commedia*:

> Ma Virgilio n'avea lasciati scemi
> di sé, Virgilio dolcissimo patre,
> Virgilio a cui per mia salute die'mi.
>
> [But Virgil was not there. Our lack alone
> was left where once he'd been. Virgil, dear sire,
> Virgil — to him I'd run to save my soul.]
> (*Purgatorio*, XXX. 49–51)

Line 51 sends us back to the very beginning of the *Commedia*, when Dante, completely lost, entrusted himself to Virgil. The line encompasses the whole of Dante's journey so far, from the moment he turned to Virgil, 'die'mi', to the current moment in which his salvation, his 'salute', is certain. Dante's turning to Virgil is cast as an act of complete trust, a giving of self into another's power: 'die'mi', quite literally, 'I gave myself'. It is this witnessing to a human bond of affection and trust that gives this tercet much of its force. The affection continues from the previous line; Dante frequently uses the term *dolce* — meaning 'beloved' or 'dear', though carrying many further connotations — to describe Virgil, but nowhere else does he use the superlative *dolcissimo*. This is, indeed, the only time Dante uses *dolcissimo* to describe any person. The affection for Virgil to which Dante witnesses is also potentially an affection he has built up over the course of the poem in the reader. The efficacy with which Dante instils affection for Virgil in his readers is clear from the implicit, and sometimes explicit, observations of critics.[13] Virgil is a father, 'patre', to Dante, and, as in the image in the previous lines, a mother, within the narrative, and also on a metatextual level, in that Dante's poetry is, often in contradictory ways, indebted to that of Virgil.[14] The three-line lament — powerful because of its extreme economy of expression — encompasses Dante's whole journey thus far, the affection that binds him to Virgil, the reader's affection for Virgil, and Dante's debt to Virgil the poet.

The most striking feature of the lament, however, is the insistent repetition of Virgil's name. The importance of the act of naming Virgil is borne out by the surrounding lines, in which there is an intense focus on names: Dante is named for the only time in the poem (*Purgatorio*, XXX. 55) and he glosses the 'necessità' which justifies that naming (ll. 62–63), Beatrice emphatically names herself (l. 73), and Virgil is named twice more, making a total of five times in ten lines (ll. 46–55). These various acts of naming carry many implications, which I shall not rehearse here.[15] I note, rather, that the repetition of Virgil's name acts as a particularly heightened expression of grief. As Jennifer Rushworth observes, 'the proper name occupies a special place in narratives of mourning'.[16] The threefold 'Virgilio' points towards the absence of the one whose name is called and, as Kirkpatrick puts it, towards 'the wholly singular and irreplaceable existence' of the one named.[17] The act of repeating 'Virgilio' is an expression and a living out of grief at the loss of a particular irreplaceable human being.

In the text that Dante here rewrites, the expression of grief also culminates in the calling of the beloved's name. As is well known, Dante's threefold crying out for Virgil echoes Virgil's telling of the Orpheus and Eurydice myth at the conclusion of his *Georgics*.[18] Virgil's telling of the story ends:

> tum quoque marmorea caput a ceruice reuulsum
> gurgite cum medio portans Oeagrius Hebrus
> uolueret, Eurydicen uox ipsa et frigida lingua,
> a miseram Eurydicen! anima fugiente uocabat:
> Eurydicen toto referebant flumine ripae.

> [And even when Oeagrian Hebrus rolled in mid-current that head, severed from its marble neck, the disembodied voice and the tongue, now cold for ever, called with departing breath on Eurydice — ah, poor Eurydice! 'Eurydice' the banks re-echoed, all along the stream.][19]

The act of calling is made vividly present to the reader through the triple insistence on Orpheus's voice — 'uox ipsa', 'frigida lingua', 'anima fugiente' — and by the way in which Virgil, by moving 'Eurydice' between different feet and between different positions in the clauses, imitates the echo of the riverbanks.

In the *Georgics* the callings of Eurydice's name are all, in effect, direct speech; the first two 'Eurydice's are spoken by Orpheus's head, and the third 'Eurydice' is the echo created by the riverbank. The lament, constituted by the uttering of her name, is performed within the story, by the character, and then by the landscape. In the *Commedia*, however, the three 'Virgilio's are spoken not by the Dante character within the narrative, but by Dante-poet. These lines are immediately preceded by the direct speech, or rather the planned speech, of the Dante character: 'conosco i segni de l'antica fiamma'. But the threefold 'Virgilio' belongs to the poet's voice. Beatrice tells the Dante character that he must not yet weep for Virgil, but Dante-poet writes a lament for Virgil into the text of the *Commedia* itself. The weeping that Beatrice classed as so premature is given another, more lasting form. Lament for Virgil becomes an act that Dante not only describes, but actually performs in the process of writing the *Commedia*.

Peter Hawkins, writing on lines 49–51, observes, 'what follows immediately upon verse 48 [...] is undeniably valedictory, as pilgrim and reader alike acknowledge the present loss of one who has been our guide from the beginning'.[20] Hawkins does not elaborate further, the focus of his essay being Dante's rewriting and transcending of Dido's words from *Aeneid*, IV at *Purgatorio*, XXX. 48. But the suggestion that the reader, as well as the Dante character, will acknowledge the loss of 'our guide' reminds us of a crucial aspect of the *Commedia*, though one whose implications are rarely discussed: Dante invites, both explicitly and implicitly, the emotional engagement of his readers.[21] What modes of engagement, then, does Dante invite from the reader of lines 49–51?

To consider the possibilities offered to the reader here, we can turn to a passage from Dante's *Vita nuova*. After Beatrice's death her brother asks Dante to write a poem for him, prompting Dante to reflect on the modes in which grief might be expressed through such a poem:

> Onde poi, pensando a ciò, propuosi di fare uno sonetto, nel quale mi lamentasse alquanto, e di darlo a questo mio amico, acciò che paresse che per lui l'avessi fatto; e dissi allora questo sonetto, che comincia: *Venite a intender li sospiri miei.*
>
> [Then, thinking it over, I decided to compose a sonnet, to be sent to this friend of mine, in which I would express my sorrow in such a way that it would seem to be his. And so I wrote this sonnet which begins: *Now come to me.*][22]

The words of the sonnet are ones through which Dante expresses his own grief, but they are presented to Beatrice's brother as an expression of his, the brother's, sorrow. In the next chapter Dante continues reflecting on the sonnet and its recipient. He is concerned that the sonnet is an insufficient offering for a grieving relative and so writes a *canzone* for the brother too. For our purposes, however, the salient point is the further description of the sonnet: 'Poi che detto ei questo sonetto, pensandomi chi questi era a cui lo intendea dare quasi come per lui fatto, vidi che povero mi parea lo servigio e nudo a così distretta persona di questa gloriosa' [After I had composed this sonnet, I realized, thinking more about the person to whom I intended to give it as an expression of his own feelings, that the poem might seem a poor and empty favor for anyone so closely related to my lady now in glory]

(*Vita nuova*, XXXIII. 1). The sonnet is described again as 'quasi come per lui fatto'. The poem's words are offered to the brother as words through which he can give voice to his own grief. Dante composes the poem in such a way that both he and Beatrice's brother can indwell its words.[23] That is, both Dante and the brother can use its words to express their own particular sorrow, even if the brother is unaware of this double possibility. There are, of course, several differences between the ways in which poetry of lament is conceived in *Vita nuova*, XXXII and in *Purgatorio*, XXX; notably, in the *Vita nuova* Dante also plays on lyric tropes of secrecy and concealment that are less relevant to the purgatorial episode. But *Vita nuova*, XXXII does raise the possibility that poetry of mourning can offer words that are available to be spoken or indwelt by different people in different ways.[24] It is this possibility, I suggest, that is offered in the lament in *Purgatorio*, XXX.

Lines 49–51 are a lament performed not within, but outside the narrative, not by the character but by the poet. In making these lines a lament that is performed in the here and now of writing the *Commedia*, Dante makes these lines available as a lament to be performed in the here and now of reading the *Commedia*. As in the *Georgics*, it is in the calling of the beloved's name — 'Eurydicen [...] Eurydicen [...] Eurydicen' or 'Virgilio [...] Virgilio [...] Virgilio' — that the speaker or writer both expresses and lives out his grief. The act of sounding Virgil's name is performed every time that a reader speaks these words aloud, or, reading them silently, hears them in their head. One can, of course, read these lines with emotional detachment, one can read them without indwelling or taking up the emotional state of the speaking voice of the poet. But these lines also create the opportunity for a more involved engagement from the reader. Dante has constructed them such that the reader has the opportunity to speak Virgil's name, and, if they choose, to speak it as a lament. This is not to say that the reader can speak these lines in exactly the same way that Dante does. The narrative descriptions 'n'avea lasciati scemi | di sé' and 'a cui per mia salute die'mi' are not ones that in a strict sense the reader can speak as their own. But the reader is offered the opportunity to take up as their own the emotions that the lament expresses. The reader has the opportunity to articulate grief at Virgil's absence and compassion at his return to limbo, and, by expressing these intersecting griefs alongside Dante, to engage in a further act of compassion — that of mourning together with another human being.

Why might the reader be invited to lament for Virgil, who is, after all, only a character in a narrative? The *Commedia* is, in part, an extended meditation on how one relates, or fails to relate, to others in and through compassion.[25] Dante's whole journey is set in motion by the compassionate intercession of three people: the Virgin Mary, the 'donna [...] che si compiange' [a lady [...] who grieves] (*Inferno*, II. 94), Lucia, and Beatrice, who descends, weeping, to ask Virgil to be Dante's guide (*Inferno*, II. 116). The poem also invites us to reflect on compassion given to those for whom it might seem there is little point in having compassion, as in the story of Gregory the Great, whose prayers brought the emperor Trajan back from hell and secured his salvation (*Purgatorio*, X. 73–75; *Paradiso*, XX. 106–17). Compassion can be misdirected, as for example, when Dante, overcome with sympathy for Paolo and Francesca, faints as though dead (*Inferno*, v. 139–42). As he journeys through *Purgatorio*, Dante learns how to be, as he puts it, 'pierced through by compassion'. In the same lines he implicitly invites readers to share in that compassion, tacitly encouraging them not to behave like the 'omo duro':

> Non credo che per terra vada ancoi
> omo sì duro che non fosse punto
> per compassion di quel ch'i' vidi poi.
>
> [I can't believe that anyone on earth
> could be so hard that pity, at the sight
> that I saw now, would not have pierced him through.]
> (*Purgatorio*, XIII. 52–54)

When Beatrice descends to hell to commission Virgil to be Dante's guide, she promises to praise Virgil to God (*Inferno*, II. 70–74). From one perspective Beatrice's promise is, as Anna Maria Chiavacci Leonardi notes, theologically absurd. Virgil is in hell, so it would seem his status in the afterlife could in no way be changed by praising him.[26] Yet salvation, as Dante repeatedly dramatizes, *is* absurd. One factor that suggests we should take Beatrice's words seriously, and not as mere flattery or Beatrice forgetting the rules of the afterlife, is the central place of praise in Dante's thought; in *Paradiso* praise is a constitutive part of the souls' mode of being.[27] As Vittorio Montemaggi argues, taking Beatrice's words seriously does not mean claiming 'that Dante would like us to think Virgil is unequivocally saved'.[28] Rather, it means reflecting on the unresolved tension concerning Virgil, and acknowledging that for Dante, praise of another human — including one whom Dante's own worldview has seemingly placed beyond the possibility of salvation — has value. Dante envisages Beatrice celebrating Virgil. In having compassion for Virgil, the reader participates in those same dynamics in which care for another person draws those separated by time, space, and unknown futures into relation.

Yet, inviting our grief for Virgil could be seen as doing no more than drawing us into the narrative world. On the other hand, this is a narrative that declares itself to be true, not in that it 'objectively report[s] prior spatiotemporal events', but in that it claims the potential to effect the spiritual transformation of its readers.[29] For Dante, the truth of the *Commedia* lies in the reader's response, in whether, because of reading the *Commedia*, the reader enters more deeply into relationships of love with God and with fellow humans, or not. I would suggest we understand Dante's invitation to the reader to grieve for Virgil not as an invitation to believe that, outside the space of the poem, the historical Virgil really is in hell, but as an invitation to put into practice a truth that Dante dramatizes repeatedly in the *Commedia*: the need for humans to have (rightly directed) compassion for each other.

Of course, ultimately what for Dante is most important is not whether we have compassion for Virgil, but whether the *Commedia* assists us to live out relationships of loving compassion over the course of our whole lives. It is within this wider framework that the reader's grief for Virgil has value. In *Purgatorio*, X Dante describes how a work of art that depicts the suffering of a fictitious figure can prompt true empathetic suffering in the beholder:

> Come per sostentar solaio o tetto,
> per mensola talvolta una figura
> si vede giugner le ginocchia al petto,
> la qual fa del non ver vera rancura
> nascere 'n chi la vede.
>
> [As sometimes, bracing up a roof or vault,
> a figure will be seen as corbel stone
> that, bending, joins its two knees to its chest,
> at which there's born, in anyone who sees,
> from this non-truth a truly harsh distress.]
> (*Purgatorio*, x. 130–34)

The distress experienced by the viewer on seeing a painfully hunched-over caryatid is 'vera', true. The sculpted figure, of a kind commonly depicted in Romanesque and Gothic church portals and pulpits, is a fictitious depiction, but the viewer's distress — Dante emphatically declares with the 'non ver vera' juxtaposition — is real. It is a distress, Dante seems to be saying, that shares something, qualitatively, with the distress felt at witnessing non-fictitious suffering. If we read *Purgatorio*, xxx in light of this model for understanding responses to depictions of suffering in a work of art, we are offered one way in which the reader's compassion for Virgil might be understood as truthful. It is truthful in that, qualitatively, it shares something with the compassion that Dante hopes his poem as a whole will prompt us to engage in more deeply, compassion for those human beings with whom we share our lives. As such, grief for Virgil might not only teach us something of the nature of compassion, but also itself be an instantiation of the living-out of relationships of love into which the *Commedia* seeks to draw us, its readers, more fully.

A tension remains, both in *Purgatorio*, xxx and in the sermons discussed earlier: weep first for your sins and then for loved ones. Yet we might consider weeping for one's sins as itself a form of mourning, in acknowledgement of the distance that sin creates between oneself and God, of the harm done to that relationship in which, from a medieval Christian perspective, all other relationships are grounded.

Notes to Chapter 2

I thank Jennifer Rushworth for her very helpful comments on an earlier version of this essay, and the participants in the 2019 conference for such generous and productive conversations.

1. For example, *Purgatorio*, xxxii. 103–05; *Purgatorio*, xxxiii. 52–57; *Paradiso*, xvii. 124–42; *Paradiso*, xxv. 40–46; *Paradiso*, xxvii. 64–66. Scholars have recently begun investigating the strategies Dante uses to seek to prompt readers' ethical and spiritual growth; see, esp. Vittorio Montemaggi, *Reading Dante's 'Commedia' as Theology: Divinity Realized in Human Encounter* (New York: Oxford University Press, 2016); Heather Webb, *Dante's Persons: An Ethics of the Transhuman* (Oxford: Oxford University Press, 2016). Citations of the *Commedia* are from *La Divina Commedia*, ed. by Anna Maria Chiavacci Leonardi, 3 vols (Milan: Mondadori, 1991–94). Translations are from *The Divine Comedy*, trans. by Robin Kirkpatrick, 3 vols (London: Penguin, 2006–07).
2. Christian Moevs, *The Metaphysics of Dante's 'Comedy'* (New York: Oxford University Press, 2005), pp. 169–85. See also Montemaggi, *Reading Dante's 'Commedia' as Theology*, pp. 25–30, 33–35, 119–21, 152–53, 173–75, 191–95, 202–03, 250–53.

3. For an overview of preaching in medieval Italy, see Carlo Delcorno, 'Medieval Preaching in Italy (1200–1500)', in *The Sermon*, ed. by Beverly Mayne Kienzle (Turnhout: Brepols, 2000), pp. 449–560. On sermons as rich and underused resources in Dante studies, see George Ferzoco, 'Dante and the Context of Medieval Preaching', in *Reviewing Dante's Theology*, ed. by Claire E. Honess and Matthew Treherne, 2 vols (Oxford: Lang, 2013), II, 187–210; Nicolò Maldina, *In pro del mondo: Dante, la predicazione e i generi della letteratura religiosa medievale* (Rome: Salerno, 2017). On sermons as mass communication, see David d'Avray, *Medieval Marriage Sermons: Mass Communication in a Culture without Print* (Oxford: Oxford University Press, 2001), pp. 15–30.
4. Jeffrey T. Schnapp, 'Dante's Sexual Solecisms: Gender and Genre in the *Commedia*', in *The New Medievalism*, ed. by Marina S. Brownlee, Kevin Brownlee, and Stephen G. Nichols (Baltimore, MD: Johns Hopkins University Press, 1991), pp. 201–25 (pp. 211–12).
5. On Dante's rewriting of *Aeneid*, IV. 23, see Peter S. Hawkins, 'Dido, Beatrice, and the Signs of Ancient Love', in *The Poetry of Allusion: Virgil and Ovid in Dante's 'Commedia'*, ed. by Rachel Jacoff and Jeffrey T. Schnapp (Stanford, CA: Stanford University Press, 1991), pp. 113–30; Tristan Kay, 'Dido, Aeneas, and the Evolution of Dante's Poetics', *Dante Studies*, 129 (2011), 135–60, with further bibliography at n. 1.
6. The modern commentary tradition tends not to note this ambiguity; the tendency is either to give the second reading or not to give a reading.
7. On medieval conceptions of penitential tears, see esp. Piroska Nagy, *Le Don des larmes au Moyen Âge: un instrument spirituel en quête d'institution (Ve–XIIIe siècle)* (Paris: Michel, 2000).
8. Biblioteca Apostolica Vaticana, MS Vat. lat. 1255, fol. 2r: 'Eccl. 38: *Fili in mortuum produc lacrimas.* Sed heu multi plus pro morte carnis aliene quam pro morte anime proprie lacrimarentur [*sic*]. Augustinus: sciat culpabiliter se durum qui deflet dampna temporis uel mortem amici et dolorem peccati lacrimis non ostendit.' Though mostly recorded in Latin, sermons were preached in the vernacular. Translations from Latin texts are mine.
9. Ibid., fol. 40v: 'Flet homo stultus pro morte carnis aliene et non deflet mortem anime proprie. Augustinus: sciat culpabiliter se durum'.
10. Giovanni da San Gimignano, *Opus aureum sermonum quadragesimalium* (Paris: Jean Petit, 1511), fol. a2r: 'flere debent [*sic*] ad modum orbati non solum patre Deo sed etiam matre ecclesia cum non sit eorum filius'. On Giovanni, see Silvana Vecchio, 'Giovanni da San Gimignano', in *Dizionario biografico degli Italiani*, 100 vols (Rome: Istituto della Enciclopedia Italiana, 1960–), LVI (2001), 206–10.
11. Pseudo-Augustine, *De vera et falsa poenitentia*, 9, in *PL* 40:1113–30. Peter Lombard, *Sententiae*, 4 d.15 art.6.
12. Thomas Aquinas, *Scriptum super Sententiis*, 4 d.15 q.4 a.7. qc.3 expos. Latin text at <https://www.corpusthomisticum.org/snp4015.html> [accessed 6 August 2021].
13. Barolini, *Dante and the Origins of Italian Literary Culture*, pp. 151–57, discusses how Dante makes his characters 'so compelling that we invest them with our emotional concern. [...] We care about Vergil because Dante makes us care' (p. 154). Barolini warns against becoming overinvested in the question of Virgil's fate if our motivation stems from forgetting that it is only in the narrative of the poem that Virgil is in Limbo (i.e. from treating the poem as a report of how things really are in the afterlife). My analysis arises from focusing on the truth value of the *Commedia* as lying outside the poem and in the response of the reader.
14. On this vast topic, see for example, *The Poetry of Allusion*, ed. by Jacoff and Schnapp, pp. 1–156; Teodolinda Barolini, *Dante's Poets: Textuality and Truth in the 'Comedy'* (Princeton, NJ: Princeton University Press, 1984), pp. 201–56.
15. For some of these implications, see Justin Steinberg, *Accounting for Dante: Urban Readers and Writers in Late Medieval Italy* (Notre Dame, IN: University of Notre Dame Press, 2007), pp. 171–79.
16. Rushworth, *Discourses of Mourning in Dante, Petrarch, and Proust*, p. 110.
17. Dante, *The Divine Comedy*, trans. by Kirkpatrick, II, 488.
18. On the contextual resonances between *Purgatorio*, XXX, and *Georgics*, IV, see Jacoff, 'Intertextualities in Arcadia'. For a Derridean reading of Dante's, Petrarch's, and Proust's rewritings of the 'Eurydicen' lament, see Rushworth, *Discourses of Mourning in Dante, Petrarch, and Proust*, pp. 104–14.

19. Virgil, *Georgics*, IV. 523–27; *Eclogues; Georgics; Aeneid: Books 1–6*, trans. by H. Rushton Fairclough, rev. by G.P. Goold, rev. edn (Cambridge, MA: Harvard University Press, 1999), pp. 256–57.
20. Hawkins, 'Dido, Beatrice, and the Signs of Ancient Love', p. 116. As discussed above, it is also Dante-poet who acknowledges loss in these lines.
21. Explicit invitations include *Paradiso*, X. 1–27 (esp. l. 24) and *Paradiso*, II. 1–18 (esp. l. 17). On the need for research into Dante's treatment of emotions and for methodological considerations, see Zygmunt G. Barański, 'Dottrina degli affetti e teologia: la rappresentazione della beatitudine nel *Paradiso*', in *Dante poeta cristiano e la cultura religiosa medievale: in ricordo di Anna Maria Chiavacci Leonardi*, ed. by Giuseppe Ledda (Ravenna: Centro dantesco dei Frati minori conventuali, 2018), pp. 259–312 (Barański focuses on emotions as depicted in the *Commedia* rather than on ways in which Dante invites readers to engage their emotions). As discussed above (in n. 13), Barolini analyses the issue of readers' emotional concern for Virgil.
22. Dante, *Vita nuova*, XXXII. 3; *Dante's 'Vita nuova'*, ed. and trans. by Musa.
23. I borrow the term 'indwell' from David Ford's discussion of a defining feature of liturgical prayers, namely that their words can be spoken, indwelt, by diverse people in a great variety of ways: *Self and Salvation*, pp. 127–29. There are of course also differences between liturgical prayer and lament for Virgil. On the potential tension between the unique and the general created by using another's words of mourning, see Rushworth, *Discourses of Mourning in Dante, Petrarch, and Proust*, pp. 114–25.
24. With the *canzone* in *Vita nuova* XXXIII, Dante outlines a more restrictive vision of the availability of words of mourning to be indwelt by different people: while Beatrice's brother can (and Dante implies, will) use both stanzas to voice his grief, a more subtle reader would perceive that the first stanza is more fitting for the brother and the second for Dante.
25. For very different workings of compassion — compassion as reinforcing rather than bridging difference — see Katherine Ibbett, *Compassion's Edge: Fellow-feeling and Its Limits in Early Modern France* (Philadelphia: University of Pennsylvania Press, 2018).
26. Gloss on Dante, *Inferno*, II. 74.
27. On praise, see Matthew Treherne, 'Liturgical Personhood: Creation, Penitence, and Praise in the *Commedia*', in *Dante's 'Commedia': Theology as Poetry*, ed. by Vittorio Montemaggi and Matthew Treherne (Notre Dame, IN: University of Notre Dame Press, 2010), pp. 131–60 (pp. 149–58).
28. Montemaggi, *Reading Dante's 'Commedia' as Theology*, p. 230.
29. Moevs, *The Metaphysics of Dante's 'Comedy'*, p. 178.

CHAPTER 3

Mourning in and around Petrarch

Luca Marcozzi

The poetry of Petrarch is always marked by mourning. The first lines he ever wrote, when he was fourteen, were the 'Funereum cantum' for his mother, who died in 1318 or 1319 (*Epystole*, I. 7). Called home by his father while he was studying in Montpellier, the young Francesco did not get back in time and so was unable to see his mother before she died. As a result, he wrote some lines for her which he later reworked and increased in number to thirty-eight, to mark the number of years she had lived. After praising his mother, the poet consoles himself with the thought that she will live forever in the memory of posterity through his poetry. In these last lines of the poem, I would like to emphasize how the first important experience of mourning undergone by Petrarch with the death of his mother Eletta is presented without any silence or reticence; weeping and tears are allowed, before the time of consolation:

> Versiculos tibi nunc totidem, quot prebuit annos
> Vita, damus; gemitus et cetera digna tulisti
> Dum stetit ante oculos feretrum miserabile nostros
> Ac licuit gelidis lacrimas infundere membris.

> [Now in your honour I offer as many verses as you were granted years of your life. You received weeping and every other honour, until the miserable coffin was exposed before our eyes, and we were allowed to spray your icy limbs with tears.][1]

Petrarch's collection of vernacular poems, the *Rerum vulgarium fragmenta*, is, in turn, deeply marked by mourning. Petrarch begins his own romantic attachment in universal mourning, that of the Church and of the whole of humankind on Good Friday: 'onde i miei guai | nel commune dolor s'incominciaro' [all my troubles | began in the universal sorrow] (*Rvf* 3, 7–8).[2] Here, Petrarch develops a theme that owes little to lyric poetry and much more to sacred texts. The only lyric precedent of individual mourning placed in a context of general mourning is in the incipit of the *planctus* (a poem of lament) by Guittone for ser Jacopo da Leona: 'Comune perta fa comun dolore, | e comuno dolore comun pianto' [Common loss makes common pain, | and common pain makes common crying].[3] Petrarch's mourning is also in dialogue with the Book of Lamentations, as Ronald Martinez has shown.[4] Signs of weeping and of death are numerous throughout the *Canzoniere*, whose second part — with the beloved missing, with her *radical* absence — can be read as a fulfillment of this liturgical mourning. The whole of the second part of the *Canzoniere*, as Sabrina Stroppa has written, can be interpreted as an 'elaborazione del lutto', an elaboration of an experience of mourning which is announced at the beginning of the book.[5]

The previous lyric experience upon which Petrarch relies more generally for this theme of mourning, from Dante to Cino da Pistoia, and especially the latter, provided him with topical examples. For example, in the *Triumphus mortis* (another work of vernacular verse by Petrarch), death is personified as a woman in mourning enveloped 'in veste negra' [in a black garment], while Cino had described his beloved more than once as 'velata in un amanto negro' [veiled in a black cloak].[6] The death of the beloved woman was, of course, a significant and almost mandatory theme in Provençal lyric, but it entailed effects quite different in nature to those of both the early Italian lyric poets and those of the *Stilnovo*. In Dante's poetry, something very unusual happens, namely that in the *Vita nova* mourning is situated *before*, rather than after, the death of Beatrice. Dante starts crying in mourning not for *her* death, but rather for her father's death. In Chapter xiv, Dante recounts this very painful moment for Beatrice. This event is followed by his own serious illness, during which he foreshadows, in an anguished hallucination, the disappearance of his beloved lady.

His sorrow can be somehow transferred onto Beatrice, but it does not concern her, who dies 'Di necessitade' [Of necessity] (*VN*, xiv. 3), without immediately provoking in Dante extreme despair or tears. After Beatrice's death, Amore [Love] and the women who have witnessed this event all cry *before* Dante. The tragic event is exposed in a brief, almost anodyne summary, since Dante does not feel up to the task, and the pathos of the situation had already been anticipated in the poem 'Donna pietosa e di novella etate' [A lady of tender years, compassionate] at the end of Chapter xiv.[7] When the pain of the loss of the beloved lady and the torment of remembrance overwhelm every other thought, the poet finally starts weeping at the beginning of the next chapter. He writes the *canzone* 'Li occhi dolenti' [The sorrowful eyes] and he says that he places his division (that is, the prose analysis) of this *canzone* before rather than after the poem in order to let it be 'più vedova' [more widowed] at its end, so that crying and mourning are connected not only as a theme, as is obvious, but also as a means of poetic expression. The poet weeps, but his words are also widowed, so that mourning is extended from the poet to his poems.[8]

From the Sicilian poets to Petrarch, the lyric motif of mourning is pervasive. In earlier Italian lyric poetry, the reason for weeping was often, but not exclusively, related to the theme of love. In the *Rerum vulgarium fragmenta*, weeping and tears take on a fundamental material and thematic aspect. Tears are the main metaphor of the style of the *Canzoniere* from the earliest lines of the introductory sonnet: the 'vario stile' [varied *or* varying style] that Petrarch declares he has adopted for his poems and which binds together weeping and reasoning ('piango et ragiono'), *passio* and *ratio*, according to an antinomic dichotomy characterizing his style and his book of poems (see *Rvf* 1, 5). The founding text of the book, the introductory poem, immediately opposes singing and weeping, while at the same time binding them together. Weeping is also used to bear the underlying moral theme of the *fragmenta*, that of the progression of the soul towards its perfection and salvation. Tears and sighs increase at the time of Laura's death, but also before that moment (following the example of the *Vita nova*).

Petrarch owes to Cino a large part of his poetic treatment of weeping. Petrarch himself was aware of the extent to which Cino was *larmoyant*. Not only does he take from him most of his images linked to the pattern of weeping, but in the sonnet mourning the death of Cino (*Rvf* 92) he invites all the world, not only readers but poetry itself — 'donne' [women], 'Amore' [Love], 'amanti' [lovers], himself, 'rime' [poems], 'versi' [verses], Pistoia 'e i citadin' [and its citizens] — to weep for him through the use of a *figura etymologica* and the anaphora of the exhortative 'weep' ('Piangete', 'pianga'). Dante's poetry was 'widowed' without Beatrice, and in Petrarch it is poetry itself, represented as a personified perspective of the weeping poet, which is exhorted to cry for Cino's death. Petrarch's treatment of sorrow, mourning, and weeping, however, is more extensive than Cino's, linking it continuously to several other metaphors with which, potentially, the liquid matter of tears and the sound of sighs resonate.

I will give only one example of this new treatment of the theme of mourning and weeping in the *Canzoniere*. It is the well-known first incipit of *Rvf* 268, the first poem really 'in morte', after the death of Laura, and refers to the mutation of laughter into weeping:

> Amore, in pianto ogni mio riso è volto,
> ogni allegrezza in doglia,
> et è obscurato il sole a gli occhi miei.
> ogni dolce pensier dal cor m'è tolto,
> e solo ivi una voglia
> rimasa m'è di finir gli anni rei
> e di seguir colei
> la qual ormai di qua veder non spero.

[Love, all laughter is turned to crying, | all rejoicing to grief, | and the sun is obscured in my eyes. | Every sweet thought is taken from my heart, | and only there a desire | has remained: to end the evil years | and to follow her | whom I do not hope to see here anymore.]

If we look at his drafts, now in MS Vat. lat. 3196, we see that the poet replaced the beginning of this first *canzone* on Laura's death, explaining in a *postilla* in the margins that the beginning had not seemed to him sufficiently sad ('non videtur satis triste principium' is the reason given by the gloss) nor suitable to the poem that should have been the most 'lugens', the most tearful, of the whole *Canzoniere*. The incipit, although rejected, will go on to be heavily reused in the continuation of the work. The *canzone* was copied in 1349 in another folio, then changed its shape to the *canzone* that is nowadays *Rvf* 268, and takes up ff. 54v–55r of MS Vat. lat. 3195, which bear the last form of the work.

Some references to this *canzone* come down to us in MS Vat. lat. 3196, from which we can infer that a first draft, probably close in time to Laura's death, remained unfinished for over a year. On 28 November 1349, in the morning, the poet returned to his composition and annotated that he had transcribed the poem on another sheet ('Transcriptum. Non in ordine sed in alia papiro'). The poem was transformed again several years later: at least the fourth verse was reworked late at night, on 28 December 1351, and on 11 November 1356 a second copy is noted as transcribed 'in ordine aliquot mutatis' [in order, with some changes].

Here I simply transcribe the first stanza from the last version, which is entrusted to MS Vat. lat. 3195, without noting its many intermediary forms:

Che debb'io far? che mi consigli, Amore?
Tempo è ben di morire
et ò tardato piú ch'i' non vorrei.
Madonna è morta, et à seco il mio core;
et volendol seguire,
interromper conven quest'anni rei,
perché mai veder lei
di qua non spero, et l'aspettar m'è noia.
Poscia ch'ogni mia gioia
per lo suo dipartire in pianto è volta,
ogni dolcezza de mia vita è tolta.

[What must I do? What do you counsel, Love? | The time has truly come to die, | and I have lingered longer than I wish. | My lady is dead, and my heart with her: | and if I wish to follow, | I must interrupt this cruel life, | since I have no more hope | of seeing her here, and waiting galls me. | Now all my joy | has turned to weeping at her going, | all sweetness has been taken from my life.]

Why did Petrarch reject his first version and transform it into these lines? Despite the many interpretations which rely on psychological reasoning, he probably did so because he was afraid that the *canzone* might be perceived as belonging to the genre of the lament for the beloved, which was deeply embedded in the Italian lyric tradition. Elements that can always be found among texts of this tradition include: announcement of the loss, lamentations, general consideration of death (followed sometimes by an apostrophe addressed to its inopportuneness and cruelty), eulogy of the beloved (the most constant among all these features), remembrance of the past, and prayer. One such example is Giacomino Pugliese, who opposes sadness and cheerfulness in his 'Morte, perchè m'ài fatta sì gran guerra' [Death, why have you made such a great war against me], or a *Stilnovo* poet such as Lapo Gianni, who uses the same combination of crying and singing for both homage to the lady and lamentation for her death ('Donna se 'l prego de la mente mia, | com'è bagnato di lagrim' e pianti' [Lady, if the prayer of my mind, | bathed as it is in tears and weeping], and 'O Morte, fiume di lagrim' e pianto, | o nemica di canto' [O Death, river of tears and weeping, | O enemy of song]).[9]

If we look at Petrarch's rejected draft, it is hard to agree with him that it was insufficiently sad, since it contains mourning, darkness, suicidal thoughts, and desperation. The content could not be sadder, except in the poet's own view. Why? It is not easy to answer this question.[10] It is likely that Petrarch did not want to appear too indebted to the previous love lyric tradition, likely, too, that he wanted his readers to contemplate his moral turn, a turn which was accompanied by a change in form. That is why Petrarch did not want this *canzone* to be compromised by previous lamentations for the death of a beloved, which tended to be too conventional and to exhibit only limited emotional participation on the part of their authors. In his own contribution, Petrarch preferred to represent himself as a moral philosopher. In fact, the death of the woman ceases to be a lyric theme for Petrarch and becomes, in the second part of the *Canzoniere*, an opportunity to reason about death and sorrow with the few surviving readers, and to admonish them: weeping and mourning should not be considered as the same.

Another point that needs to be emphasized is the connection between this *canzone* of mourning, the first after Laura's death, and the first sonnet (as Martinez has shown).[11] *Rvf* 1, also written after Laura's death, and *Rvf* 268 both use elements from the Book of Lamentations and reinforce an idea of mourning that is much stronger than that of the previous vernacular lyric, with the exception of that of Dante who, in the *Vita nova*, had also drawn on scriptural models for poetic mourning.

This is not the only connection between the *Canzoniere* and the *Vita nova* on the subject of mourning. In the turning point of the *Canzoniere* from the first to the second part (*Rvf* 1–263 and 264–366, understood traditionally as 'in vita' and 'in morte di madonna Laura' [during the life and after the death of lady Laura]), Dante serves as a strong structural model. There is a relationship with the *Vita nova* in the passage between *Rvf* 264 and the diptych of *Rvf* 267 and 268, where a premonition occurs before the announcement of the death of Laura; the same scheme involves Chapters XIV and XIX of the *Vita nova* (in the numbering of Gorni's edition). There, Dante falls ill and has an 'ymmaginatione' (translated by Musa as 'dream') in which he foresees the death of Beatrice, which happens a few chapters later. In the same way, the death of Laura takes place in the *Canzoniere* a few poems after it had been imagined in *Rvf* 264 (with a general reflection, as in Dante, on the vanishing of earthly goods and the uncertainty of destiny for everyone).

In the passage of the *Vita nova* in which Dante foresees the death of Beatrice — as Petrarch does in his turn at the end of the first part of the *Canzoniere* — he writes:

> After thinking about her awhile, I returned to thoughts of my feeble condition and, realizing how short life is, even if one is healthy, I began to weep silently about the misery of life. Then, sighing deeply, I said to myself: 'It is bound to happen that one day the most gracious Beatrice will die.' At that, such a frenzy seized me that I closed my eyes and, agitated like one in delirium, began to imagine things: as my mind started wandering, there appeared to me certain faces of ladies with dishevelled hair, and they were saying to me: 'You are going to die.' And then after these ladies there appeared to me other faces strange and horrible to look at, who were saying: 'You are dead.' (*VN*, XIX. 3–4)

Petrarch proceeds along the same path: his premonition of Laura's death and his consideration of his own mortality in *Rvf* 264 foreshadow the account of Laura passing away. While Dante claims that he does not want to write about

Beatrice's death, Petrarch is forced to write about Laura's death, since for the poetic development of the theme of mourning he looks more to the classical tradition of consolation for sorrow (which he revitalized and bequeathed to humanism) than to the lyric tradition. He was the author of many consolatory letters written to friends, but in the *Canzoniere*, as the mourner himself, he had to be both the author and the recipient of the consolation.

While both Dante and Petrarch reject the previous lyric tradition of lamentation for the death of the beloved, Petrarch only partly follows Dante's use of scriptural imagery. Dante started the nineteenth chapter of the *Vita nova* with a quotation from the Book of Lamentations: 'Quomodo sedet sola civitas' [How doth the city sit solitary] are the opening words attributed to Jeremiah (in Lamentations 1) that Dante quotes again in writing to the 'principi de la terra' [princes of the land], in order to illustrate the miserable conditions of the city which had been as if 'widowed' at Beatrice's death.[12] The word 'widow' derives from the passage of Lamentations, from which Dante repeats the same quotation, at greater length ('Quomodo sedet sola civitas plena populo! facta est quasi vidua domina gentium' [How doth the city sit solitary that was full of people! how is the mistress of the Gentiles become as a widow!]), opening the chapter where he announces the departure of the 'gentilissima' [most noble lady].[13] But in the same chapter, with its solemn opening, Dante renounces further talk of Beatrice's death, saying: 'And even though the reader might expect me to say something now about her departure from us, it is not my intention to do so here for three reasons' (*VN*, xxviii. 2). These reasons are then distinctly and pedantically listed. However, in so doing, Dante also delays mourning, or at least the expression of his elaboration of mourning, transferring the radical absence of Beatrice to a different, mystical plane. Dante the poet heals this absence in the last cantos of the *Purgatorio* of his *Commedia*, in the earthly paradise, while in the *Canzoniere*, despite some apparitions of Laura (and the only words she speaks), mourning, though self-consoled, will never end. Petrarch, however, renounces the scriptural model; he retains some images, but addresses in the *Canzoniere* different sources, such as Boethius, Plato, and Augustine.

Even though Dante did not narrate the death of Beatrice directly, he offered to Petrarch a model for rejecting the lyric tradition of lamentation for the beloved. If Cino is for Petrarch the model for weeping, Dante is the model for mourning — albeit a problematic model, which Petrarch does not always follow. The *Vita nova* can be considered a model for Petrarch at least in terms of the structure of the narration of Laura's death in the *Canzoniere*, as I have suggested. In the *Canzoniere*, as in the *Vita nova*, many signs and premonitions of Laura's death appear, starting from the first sonnet (youthful passion as a 'breve sogno' [brief dream] that vanishes with maturity), and these are particularly intense in the narrow space between *Rvf* 264 and 267.

But Petrarch, as we have said, rejected on the one hand all the lyric tradition connected to weeping for beloved women, which seemed to him too conventional, and on the other the mystical magniloquence of the *Vita nova*, its relationship to the Bible, its prophetic aspects, and its abundance of symbolism. Petrarch's models for mourning can be found in the classical tradition instead. We should then turn to Petrarch's Latin works to find samples of mourning suitable for the moral philosopher he wanted to be, and more connected with the Stoic philosophy he wanted to follow.

In many places in the *Familiares* (Petrarch's first set of letters in Latin, *Letters on Familiar Matters*), the daily meditation on death, which is, according to Petrarch, the action that distinguishes the moral philosopher, often turns into comfort and consolation of mourning. If Dante does not want to talk about Beatrice's death, Petrarch's words of consolation flow on after the event. Weeping remains for Petrarch a pervasive lyric theme, also after Laura's death, but the moral philosopher cannot fully make use of it. In fact, crying at the death of loved ones contrasts with the teaching of the classics to which Petrarch always tends to conform. In his *De amicitia*, Cicero argues that weeping for absent friends is a mistake, and even a selfish act; nothing bad happens to those who die, so it is useless to pity them; and 'great anguish for one's own inconveniences is the mark of the man who loves not his friend but himself'.[14] Even the Church Fathers wrote against weeping in almost identical words. Petrarch recalls in a letter to Gui de Boulogne the example of Augustine, who cried for one day at the death of his mother and stopped weeping after a restorative sleep (*Familiares*, xiii. 1, 14).

On this subject, which is intertwined with that of the humanistic genre of *consolatio*, there is a rich and consolidated bibliography, ranging from Martinez's articles to Stroppa's recent *Petrarca e la morte*.[15] It is important, however, to note that the letters in the *Familiares* belonging to this consolatory genre (more than twenty in number) reach but do not go beyond the date of 1350. After this date, the task of comforting those who remain, consoling people for their sorrows, and offering solace is no longer one of the concerns of Petrarch's letters. Consolation becomes pure theory, devoid of any individual recipient, in the *Seniles* (Petrarch's second collection of Latin letters, *Letters of Old Age*).

But this is not the case for the *Canzoniere*, where the one who gives consolation and the one who receives consolation are the very same person. If Petrarch had followed the advice from the classics consistently, which he did not (advice which he distilled for his readers in another Latin work, the *De remediis utriusque fortunae* [Remedies for Fortune Fair and Foul]), he would have avoided *maeror* [mourning] and would not have complained about the bitterness of death, in particular the deaths of Laura and of friends whose names he memorialized on the page of a manuscript of Virgil (now in the Biblioteca Ambrosiana in Milan).[16] But Petrarch often runs to those imaginary tombs, even in the *Canzoniere*.

Many have noticed that the sketchbook of the *Canzoniere* presents some 'folios of mourning', in which the urgency, for the poet, to write about the death of Laura is evident.[17] The deaths of friends in 1348 and 1349 profoundly marked Petrarch's human experience; it was the *annus horribilis* which filled the guard sheets of Virgil's manuscript, a cemetery in parchment where Petrarch penned the obituary notes for those who had died. The most famous of these notes is that for Laura, which marks with the accuracy of the dates reported in it (and which are only in later years translated into the *Canzoniere*) the start and end of the romance between Francesco and Laura.[18] But all other deaths presented Petrarch with the problem of death's sudden and unexpected arrival, more than with the problem of death itself. This suddenness contrasts with the ancient philosophy of preparation for death, which views death as an event that looms over every human being, to be thought about and prepared for, rather than death as mourning, as a punishment assigned to the survivor. Petrarch moves between these two views, with the second — especially in the *Canzoniere* — proving to be the more significant.

In his lifetime, Petrarch faced many deaths, not only those of friends; he also loses a son and a grandson, and addressed to the latter a poem that was carved in stone and which can now be seen in the Musei civici di Pavia, the city where Franceschino died. The twelve lines he wrote can be considered as a *summa* or handbook of the topic of consolation, tearless and full of elements of hope. Franceschino, son of Francescuolo da Brossano and Francesca, Petrarch's daughter, was born in Venice and died in Pavia when he was little more than two years old.

> Vix mundi novus hospes iter, vitaeque volantis
> Attigeram tenero limina dura pede.
> Franciscus genitor, genitrix Francisca; secutus
> hos de fonte sacro nomen idem tenui.
> Infans formosus, solamen dulce parentum,
> nunc dolor; hoc uno sors mea laeta minus.
> Cetera sum felix, et vere gaudia vitae
> nactus et aeternae, tam cito, tam facile.
> Sol bis, luna quater flexum peragraverat orbem:
> obvia mors, fallor, obvia vita fuit.
> Me Venetum terris dedit urbs, rapuitque Papilla:
> nec querar, hinc caelo restituendus eram.[19]

> [I had just become a new host of the world; I had just set my foot in the bitter path of this fleeting life. My father was Francis, my mother Francesca, and I followed their names on the sacred source. I was a delightful child, sweet consolation of my parents, but now I am a source of pain for them, and this is the only reason for my bitterness; for the rest I am happy, since the joy of true life, the eternal one, welcomed me quickly and easily. Twice the sun and four times the moon had travelled the circumference of the world; death came to me; indeed, life came to me. The city of Venice gave life to me, Pavia tore me from the world; I do not lament, from here I returned to heaven.]

The death of his grandson is a significant moment in Petrarch's relationship with grief. In *Seniles* x. 4, he describes to Donato Albanzani his great love for his grandson who has been torn from life, and appears pleased with the patient resignation with which he is able to resist the pain of the child's death (Donato, who had lost a son, had been Franceschino's godfather). He confesses, however, that human weakness, which in the past had led him to deafen friends with his complaints, almost overwhelmed him even on that occasion:

> I confess I could not help but be upset because I have been robbed of so much sweetness of life. And if I were now of the same disposition as a few years ago, believe me, I would overwhelm all my friends, and you above all, with wailing

> and groaning; nor does it matter that I was grieving over a baby. For often such children are more deeply loved since, besides our natural instinct, the very innocence and purity of their age endear them to us, whereas, when they grow up, their superior attitude and their disobedience taint our love with resentment and turn us against them. It was, therefore, not any regard for his age, but for my own, that held me in check. [...] [I]t is unseemly for a man, and especially an old man, to weep for mortal things, since it befits him to be hardened by time and by the experience of similar misfortune, and calloused against all blows — I use my own words and Tully's.[20]

Petrarch also had to mourn the death of a son, members of the Colonna family, and the deaths of Cola di Rienzo, Azzo da Correggio, King Robert of Naples, and many, many friends, so that the whole of the second part of his life flows like that of a survivor, 'left sad and alone' ('nos solos atque inopes') by events (*Familiares*, I. I, I). For many of these experiences of mourning, he had words of solace; he wrote consolations to his Neapolitan friends, to Stefano Colonna the elder, to many friends, on the occasion of different bereavements. But from the middle of the century onwards, as we have seen, consolation tended to disappear from Petrarch's literary horizon.

If we search for a recurrent element in Petrarch's writings on consolation, we may find a contradiction within the *Canzoniere*, that is, the constant presence of weeping in his vernacular poetry in contrast to its disappearance from his moral works in Latin prose. This contradiction is more and more evident when Petrarch addresses the theme of mourning neither as a writer of letters of consolation nor as a poet regretting the absence of his deceased beloved, but rather when he deals with mourning as a matter of fact.

In one of his last texts, a letter addressed to Francesco da Carrara, Lord of Padua, Petrarch makes a plea for the regulation of funerals and of mourning. This letter is the last example of a continuous search by Petrarch for the primacy and solace of *virtus*. Petrarch asks Francesco da Carrara to prevent openly grieving women from leaving the house during the funerals of relatives or friends. This passage has been read as proof of a gendered context, since the prohibitions that Petrarch hopes for and demands are aimed only at women. Such a reading may not be far from the truth, since all the other requests made by Petrarch to his lord do not involve political or moral principles but rather simple matters of public administration. The behaviour of those attending funerals was a real problem, as evidenced by some prohibitions in statutes and regulations, for example in Venice. But it is also true that, close to his death, and at the end of the letter, Petrarch asks Carrara to use all his power to put an end to overly vociferous performances of mourning.

The letter is in itself mild and servile, and it has been interpreted in different ways. I do not dwell on it, except to recall that, addressed to Francesco da Carrara, it concerns the role and prestige of the lord and good administration, and is written at the end of 1373. Its final passage not only represents the *summa* of Petrarch's thoughts on death, but also sets out the theme of the consolation of mourning in its entirety. Beyond any interpretation one may give of this passage, it is a fact that death is treated here as an accident to be governed through any means except for tears. In this cessation of tears, Petrarch's attitude towards mourning finds its perfect fulfillment: crying and complaining should be prohibited by law. The philosopher's individual choice of moral perfection, which derives from his careful reading of the ancients and to which he has adapted with difficulty over the years, should become, by law, common practice. This was Petrarch's view a few months before his own death in July 1374:

> At first I had intended to exhort you at the end to reform your people's ways; now, in reflecting that what I attempt is utterly impossible and could never be done by force of laws or of kings, I have changed my mind. To deliberate over the impossible is certainly useless. Yet, there is one custom of your people I cannot overlook, and I not only urge you but adjure you to apply your corrective hand to this public evil and not to say, 'What you call upon me to correct is not restricted to my country, but is common to many cities.' It pertains to your own dignity, so that just as you have received many unique gifts which have made you excel among your contemporaries, your country should receive something unique from you to excel the neighboring states. You certainly know, O best of men, that in the Old Testament it is written, 'We all die', but in the New Testament it is written, 'it is ordained for men to die once'. Finally, in pagan authors it is said that 'having to die is certain, and that what is uncertain is whether it will occur on this very day'. Even though this were written nowhere, it would be no less certain, since nature tells us so over and over. Now whether it happens to us through nature or from custom turned into second nature, we can scarcely bear the death of our dear ones without grief and sobbing, and we attend their funerals often with sad lamentations, a custom which I have hardly anywhere seen so deeply rooted as in your country. Someone dies, whether he is a commoner or a noble — for that matter, it makes no difference because the spirits of commoners are stricken by emotions no less, but often even more than those of nobles, and they see less what is proper. No sooner has he breathed his last than uncontrolled grief and a torrent of tears burst forth. I am not asking you to forbid this; for it would be futile and perhaps impossible for a man [not to grieve], although the prophet Jeremiah says, 'Do not bemoan the dead, nor mourn over them with tears', while the great poet Euripides wrote in *Cresphontes*, 'Considering the evils of the present life, it is proper that we grieve at the birth of our dear ones and rejoice in their passing'; but this opinion, being too philosophical, is known to very few, and quite unheard of and unthinkable among the multitude.
>
> What then am I asking? I shall tell you. A coffin is carried out, a crowd of women bursts forth, filling the streets and squares with loud and uncontrolled shrieks, so that if anyone who does not know what is happening were to come on the scene, he could easily suspect either that they had gone mad or that the city had been captured by the enemy. Then when they have arrived at the church door, the horrible outburst doubles; and where hymns ought to be sung to Christ or devout prayers poured out for the soul of the departed in a subdued voice or in silence, there sad complaints echo and the sacred altars shake with the wailing of women, all because a mortal has died. This custom, because I consider it contrary to a decent, honorable society, and unworthy of your government, I not only advise you to reform, but if I may, I beg you. Order that no woman should set foot outside her house on this account. If weeping is sweet for those in misery, let her weep at home to her heart's content, and not sadden the public places.[21]

Contrary to what Petrarch might have hoped for, after his death he was mourned with notes of sadness that were sometimes even paroxysmal. Petrarch's mourners crowded the pages of many manuscripts, as a recent study by Romana Brovia shows.[22] Many of them follow the model of the list of great men or 'spiriti magni'. Some of them, however, applied the method suggested by Petrarch of 'mourning without tears'. According to Giovanni del Bonis, author of the eclogue 'Parnasus' on the death of Petrarch, Petrarch returned to heaven ('rediturus ad astra', l. 2); and to his friend Furens who cries for Petrarch beating his chest and tearing his clothes, the comforter Humanus replies that there is no need to cry or throw unnecessary complaints to heaven, because this would not bring his friend back to earth.[23] The model that Petrarch patiently built and developed in his moral teaching spread therefore among his first followers, testifying, also in this particular aspect, to the strength of his teaching.

Petrarch's thought spread, thanks to its exemplarity, throughout humanism and the early modern period, contributing decisively to building an ethics that seeks answers to all misfortunes by distilling these answers from the classics and conforming to their model.[24] Although that reflection has been eroded by new models and new considerations around death and its consequences, particularly around mourning and the consolation of sorrow, the deep structures of that discourse continue, in my opinion, to permeate our civilization, waiting for their deconstruction. Petrarch seems to have offered two models for the processing of mourning: first, the traditional one of consolation, and second, the more mature view which succeeded the earlier model and held that, since death is in the natural order of things, the loss of a family member or of a friend should be accepted without even the need to find relief. The latter model, rational rather than consolatory, constitutes, on the subject of mourning, Petrarch's legacy to modernity. This new system, overcoming consolation for loss, in which mourning is destined to find a rational expression, devoid of external manifestations, can be discussed nowadays looking to the past, so that we humanists of the twenty-first century distill from the past an ethics for our readers as Petrarch did for his.

Notes to Chapter 3

1. Francesco Petrarca, 'Funereum cantum', in *Epistulae metricae: Briefe in Versen*, ed. by Otto and Eva Schönberger (Würzburg: Königshausen & Neumann 2004), p. 82. Petrarch's *Epystole* (his own term) are for various reasons a neglected work whose only modern translation is in German. Therefore, the English translations are my own, as are all others in this chapter unless stated otherwise. In this essay quotations from poetry are given in the original and in translation, while quotations from prose are given only in translation.
2. Citations from Petrarch's *Rerum vulgarium fragmenta* (abbreviated to *Rvf* followed by the poem and line numbers) are taken from Petrarca, *Canzoniere*, ed. by Santagata (2010).
3. Guittone d'Arezzo, *Le rime*, ed. by Francesco Egidi (Bari: Laterza, 1940), p. 119.
4. Ronald L. Martinez, 'Mourning Laura in the *Canzoniere*: Lessons from Lamentations', *Modern Language Notes*, 118 (2003), 1–45.
5. Sabrina Stroppa, *Petrarca e la morte: tra 'Familiari' e 'Canzoniere'* (Rome: Aracne, 2014), p. 199.
6. See Francesco Petrarca, *Trionfi, rime estravaganti, codice degli abbozzi*, ed. by Vinicio Pacca and Laura Paolino (Milan: Arnoldo Mondadori, 2013), citing here from *Triumphus mortis* I, l. 31. For

the text by Cino, see *Poeti del Duecento*, ed. by Gianfranco Contini, 2 vols (Milan: Ricciardi, 1960), II, 652 (l. 4 of 'Amico, s'egualmente' [Friend, if equally]).

7. Dante, *Vita nova*, XIX. 1: 'And even though the reader might expect me to say something now about her departure from us, it is not my intention to do so here for three reasons. [...] [T]he second is that, even if this had been my intention, the language at my command would not yet suffice to deal with the theme as it deserves.' The text of the *Vita nova* is taken from Dante Alighieri, *Vita nova*, ed. by Gorni, hereafter in references abbreviated to *VN*. The English translation is *Dante's 'Vita Nuova'*, ed. and trans. by Musa (who follows the numbering of chapters by the previous ed. by M. Barbi), available online on the Princeton Dante Project <https://dante.princeton.edu/pdp/vnuova.html> [accessed 6 August 2021].
8. On the rhetorical aspects of this narration, see Martinez, 'Mourning Beatrice'.
9. For these poems by Lapo Gianni see *Poeti del Duecento*, ed. by Contini, II, 581–84, 594–97.
10. Among the scholars who have tried to answer this question, see Fredi Chiappelli, 'Non satis triste principium', *Modern Language Notes*, 100.1 (1985), 70–81; Rosanna Bettarini, *Lacrime e inchiostro nel 'Canzoniere' di Petrarca* (Bologna: CLUEB, 1998), pp. 45–83.
11. Martinez, 'Mourning Laura', pp. 17–18.
12. Citing here from the Douay-Rheims translation of the Bible in English.
13. See Vickers, 'Widowed Words'.
14. Cicero, *De amicitia*, III. 10, in *De senectute; De amicitia; De divinatione*, trans. by William Amistead Falconer (Cambridge, MA: Harvard University Press, 1923), p. 119.
15. Also relevant for the topic are: George W. McClure, *Sorrow and Consolation in Italian Humanism* (Princeton, NJ: Princeton University Press, 1991); Carol Lansing, *Passion and Order: Restraint of Grief in the Medieval Italian Communes* (Ithaca, NY: Cornell University Press, 2008), pp. 190–202; Giuseppe Chiecchi, *La parola del dolore: primi studi sulla letteratura consolatoria tra medioevo e umanesimo* (Rome & Padua: Antenore, 2005), pp. 176–263.
16. MS SP 10 27, Biblioteca Ambrosiana, Milan. For the *De remediis*, see Francesco Petrarca, *Les Remèdes aux deux fortunes/De remediis utriusque fortune (1354–1366)*, ed. and trans. by Christophe Carraud, 2 vols (Grenoble: Jérôme Millon, 2002); *Petrarch's Remedies for Fortune Fair and Foul*, ed. and trans. by Conrad H. Rawski, 5 vols (Bloomington: Indiana University Press, 1991).
17. See Laura Paolino, '"Ad acerbam rei memoriam": le carte del lutto nel codice Vaticano Latino 3196 di Francesco Petrarca', *Rivista di Letteratura Italiana*, 11 (1993), 73–102. See also Marco Santagata, 'Il lutto dell'umanista', in *Amate e amanti: figure della lirica amorosa fra Dante e Petrarca* (Bologna: Il Mulino, 1999), pp. 195–221.
18. For an English translation of the manuscript note as it concerns Laura, see Ernest H. Wilkins, *Life of Petrarch* (Chicago: University of Chicago Press, 1961), p. 77.
19. Francesco Petrarca, poem 4 of the *Carmina varia*, published many times since the sixteenth century (for the first time in 1503 in Bernardino Corio's history of Milan, *Patria historia*), and reprinted in Francesco Petrarca, *Poëmata minora quae exstant omnia nunc primo ad trutinam revocata ac recensita*, ed. by Domenico de' Rossetti, 3 vols (Milan: Societas typographica classicorum Italiae scriptorum, 1829–34), III, Appendix 1, 8. The edition cited here is that of Vittorio Rossi in 'Il Petrarca a Pavia', *Bollettino della società pavese di storia patria*, 4 (1904), 367–437 (p. 429).
20. Francesco Petrarca, *Seniles*, X. 4, in *Letters of Old Age/Rerum senilium libri I–XVIII*, trans. by Aldo S. Bernardo, Saul Levin, and Reta A. Bernardo, 2 vols (Baltimore, MD: Johns Hopkins University Press, 1992), II, 379.
21. Petrarca, *Seniles*, XIV. 1, in *Letters of Old Age*, I, 551–52. This is perhaps the longest of all Petrarch's letters.
22. Romana Brovia, 'In morte di Francesco Petrarca: consolatorie, commemorazioni, epitaffi. Primo regesto dei manoscritti', *Petrarchesca*, 8 (2020), 63–80. See also Concetta Bianca, 'Nascita del mito dell'umanista nei compianti in morte del Petrarca', *Quaderni Petrarcheschi*, 9–10 (1992–93), 293–313.
23. Giovanni del Bonis, 'Parnasus', in Maria Assunta Vinchesi, 'L'inedita egloga "Parnasus" di G. De Bonis in morte del Petrarca', *Quaderni petrarcheschi*, 9–10 (1992–93), 315–31; see in particular ll. 15–20: 'Heu doleo, et clangor iam se super aera iactat, | Et pugnis pectus atque ora reverbero palmis, | Inde genas molles, vestes mestasque rescindo, | Invius occurro solus per opaca viarum, |

Et mea damna fleo, perdens totamque salutem'; and 21–23: 'Non hoc est melius, sacrum sepelire cadaver, | Quam tantis vanis stultisque vacare querelis? | Spiritus elatus non fletibus ethera liquit' [Alas, I grieve, and a cry goes up to the sky, and I strike my chest and my face and my wet cheeks with my palms and fists, and I tear my clothes. I walk unwillingly through the darkest of roads and cry my pains, losing my life [...]. Isn't it better to bury the sacred corpse than to linger in so many vain and foolish laments? A soul has never left the sky to which it was destined thanks to tears].

24. In particular for consolation see *Forme della consolatoria tra Quattro e Cinquecento: poesia e prosa del lutto tra corte, accademie e 'solidalitas' amicale*, ed. by Sabrina Stroppa and Nicole Volta (Lucca: Pacini Fazzi, 2019). See also Chapter 6 in the present volume.

INTERMEZZO NO. 1

A Quiet Task

David Bowe

A quiet task, domestic and confined,
wound in tightly on itself, impinged
by circumstance and caution, fear and care
all held in common in uncommon times.

Even these are all in absence, screened
live, belatedly, clipped short to fit
a format too small for unspooling joys
and sufferings too broad to be contained.

The distance, the disorienting comfort,
of home when home must try to hold the world
and none of it, and none of those who give

form to days and minutes, months and years,
are here.

PART II

Lineages of Grief

CHAPTER 4

❖

Roland Barthes's Mournful Dante

Jennifer Rushworth

In his 2016 book *The Afterlives of Roland Barthes*, Neil Badmington writes persuasively that:

> Barthes, to my mind, was first and foremost a *reader* [...]. To proceed as if his body of work, posthumous or otherwise, were merely a set of ideas or theories to summarize and transmit would be to miss the point. Whether he is understood as a critic, a theorist, or an *écrivain*, Barthes wrote reading, and I see in that gesture an invitation to read with him and to write in this wake.[1]

It is Roland Barthes as a reader and one particular 'invitation to read with him and to write in this wake' that I follow in this chapter, by considering Barthes as a reader of the medieval Italian poet Dante Alighieri. Barthes is much better known as a reader of French prose, particularly that of canonical nineteenth- and early twentieth-century authors.[2] In the words of Jonathan Culler, Barthes's 'great loves' were Jules Michelet and Marcel Proust, although also the somewhat earlier marquis de Sade.[3] Barthes's interest in Italian literature, in poetry, and even in the Middle Ages seems, in comparison, to have been quite limited.[4] From this perspective, his affection for Dante is atypical, and therefore especially striking.

In a previous essay I have traced Barthes's interest in Dante to 1965, a year which saw the seven-hundredth anniversary of Dante's birth and which was celebrated in France by, amongst other matters, a special issue of the journal *Tel Quel*, led by Philippe Sollers.[5] In this essay, in contrast, I consider the presence of Dante in what has come to be called the 'late Barthes'.[6] This late Barthes includes works written after his appointment to a chair of Literary Semiology at the Collège de France (he gave his inaugural lecture on 7 January 1977) but also after the death of his mother Henriette (25 October 1977). This moment is one, therefore, of particular professional and personal significance for Barthes, and it is at this point that Dante emerges as a key interlocutor in his writings. We know that Barthes followed some of the 1965 Dantean celebrations and also made mention around that time of Dante's early prosimetrum first translated into French by Étienne-Jean Delécluze in 1841.[7] In the late Barthes, however, we see much more interest in the *Commedia* than in the *Vita nuova*, even as Barthes sets out plans to write a novel with the borrowed title *Vita nova*.[8] We also see, perhaps most significantly, Barthes's identification with Dante, on mournful grounds. This identification provides the focal point of the first part of this essay, and is most evident in a lecture first given by Barthes on 19 October 1978 under the Proustian title '"Longtemps, je me suis couché de bonne heure"'.[9]

My essay is in three parts: firstly, a consideration of Barthes's identification with Dante; secondly, an exploration of different interpretations of the 'selva oscura' (dark wood) in which Dante-pilgrim finds himself at the start of the *Commedia*; thirdly, a comparison between Barthes's mournful reading of Dante and that of an even more modern writer, Joseph Luzzi, in *In a Dark Wood: A Memoir of Grief, Healing and the Mysteries of Love* (2015). In terms of Barthes's works, I focus in particular on the aforementioned '"Longtemps"' lecture and also on the selected notes for Barthes's *Vita Nova* project published posthumously in the *Album* of unpublished material edited by Éric Marty in 2015.[10] To conclude, I consider the implications of Barthes's reading of Dante with regard to broader questions about, on the one hand, the relationship between literature and mourning and, on the other, the relationship between the medieval and the modern.

Barthes as Dante: Reading as Recognition

In her book of the same name, Rita Felski proposes 'recognition' as one of the 'uses of literature'. She asks:

> What does it mean to recognize oneself in a book? The experience seems at once utterly mundane yet singularly mysterious. While turning a page I am arrested by a compelling description, a constellation of events, a conversation between characters, an interior monologue. Suddenly and without warning, a flash of connection leaps across the gap between text and reader; an affinity or an attunement is brought to light. I may be looking for such a moment, or I may stumble on it haphazardly, startled by the prescience of a certain combination of words. In either case, I feel myself addressed, summoned, called to account: I cannot help seeing traces of myself in the pages I am reading.[11]

In support of her theory, she goes on to cite the famous statement from the last volume of Proust's *A la recherche du temps perdu* [*In Search of Lost Time*], according to which, 'In reality each reader, when he is reading, is uniquely reading himself'.[12] When Barthes turns to Dante in his '"Longtemps"' lecture, we find this same 'flash of connection' (to borrow Felski's phrase) and Proustian process of self-reading between Barthes and a select group of writers: not only Dante, but also Michelet and Proust.

Barthes's own term, however, is not recognition but identification, formulated preferably as an active, reflexive verbal form. As much is clear from his opening explanation of the lecture's Proustian title and remit:

> Does this mean I am offering you a lecture 'on' Proust? Yes and no. My subject will be, if you like, *Proust and I* [Proust et moi]. How pretentious! [...] Let me suggest that, paradoxically, the pretentiousness subsides once I myself take the stand, and not some witness: by setting Proust and myself on one and the same line, I am not in the least comparing myself to this great writer but, quite differently, *identifying myself with him* [*je m'identifie à lui*]: an association of practice, not of value. Let me explain: in figurative language, in the novel,

> for instance, it seems to me that one more or less identifies oneself with one of the characters represented; this projection, I believe, is the very wellspring of literature; but in certain marginal cases, once the reader himself wants to write a work, he no longer identifies himself merely with this or that fictive character but also and especially with the actual author of the book he has read, insofar as that author wanted to write this book and succeeded in doing so; now, Proust is the privileged site of this special identification, insofar as his *Search...* is the narrative of a desire to write: I am not identifying myself with the prestigious author of a monumental work but with the worker [l'ouvrier] — now tormented, now exalted, in any case modest — who wanted to undertake a task upon which, from the very start of his project, he conferred an absolute character.[13]

This opening paragraph is vital: firstly, for its explanation of Barthes's mode of reading, in this particular instance, as one of identification and recognition; secondly, for Barthes's interest in Proust as a struggling writer, 'the worker — now tormented, now exalted, in any case modest'. This distinction between 'the prestigious author' and 'the worker' seems also to allude to the thorny distinction between author, narrator, and protagonist of *A la recherche*.[14] Barthes situates himself as closer to the narrator, who wants to write but does not know if he can, than to Proust the published author, although there are also grounds for identifying with Proust's experience of the difficult process of writing and getting published.[15]

A similar distinction pertains to Dante, typically formulated as regards the *Commedia* through another triad: Dante-pilgrim, the character who undertakes the journey; Dante-poet, who narrates the journey; Dante, author of the *Commedia* and other works. This similarity forms the backbone of comparative readings of Dante and Proust, although there are other connections — in particular, as Barthes ultimately suggests in his '"Longtemps"' lecture, the connection, for Dante, Proust, and Barthes himself, between mourning and writing.[16] As Diana Knight notes:

> It is retrospectively obvious that Dante is as important to this lecture as Proust; indeed, the alternative title under which the same lecture was given in December in New York — 'Proust and Myself' — might well have been 'Proust, Dante, and Myself'.[17]

Halfway through the lecture, having discussed Proust's quest for a form for his writings, and the meaning of the focus on sleep at the opening of Proust's novel, Barthes turns to Dante:

> Dante (another famous opening, another overwhelming allusion) begins his poem '*Nel mezzo del camin di nostra vita...*' In 1300, Dante was thirty-five (he was to die twenty-one years later). I am much older than that, and the time I have left to live will never be half the length of my life so far. For the 'middle of our life' is obviously not an arithmetical point: how, at the moment of writing, could I know my life's total duration so precisely that I could divide it into two equal parts? It is a semantic point, the perhaps belated moment when there occurs in my life the summons of a new meaning, the desire for a mutation: to changes lives, to break off and to begin, to submit myself to an initiation, as Dante made his way into the *selva oscura*, led by a great initiator, Virgil (and for me, at least during this text, the initiator is Proust).[18]

Most striking, in this passage, is Barthes's identification with Dante, just as at the opening of the lecture he had identified with Proust. This identification relies upon a knowing rejection of biblically inspired, numerological readings of the poem, according to which the 'middle of life' is age thirty-five; hence, the journey takes place in the pre-exile Jubilee year of 1300.[19] Barthes quite bluntly rejects this reasoning, arguing that 'the "middle of our life" is obviously not an arithmetical point' and that one's life could never be neatly divided into two mathematical halves. Instead, for Barthes this 'middle' is 'semantic', a desire for what he will also call *vita nuova* or *vita nova*: new life.[20] In this way, Barthes knits more closely together Dante's *Vita nuova* and *Commedia*, despite the attempts of critics to affirm that the end of the former does not represent a promise of the latter.[21]

More radically, as we have seen, Barthes also knits together Dante and Proust, in particular through his subsequent refinement of 'the middle of life' as not merely 'the desire for a mutation' (above) but more especially a *mutatio vitae* motivated by an experience of loss:

> For Proust, the 'middle of life's journey' was certainly his mother's death (1905), even if the mutation of existence, the inauguration of the new work, occurred only a few years later. [...] [T]hough belated, this bereavement will be for me the middle of my life; for the 'middle of life' is perhaps never anything but the moment when you discover that death is real, and no longer merely dreadful.[22]

Barthes draws a parallel between Proust writing *A la recherche* after the death of his mother and Dante writing the *Commedia* after the death of Beatrice in order to ask himself what 'new practice of writing' will be possible for him after the death of his own mother.[23] To consider this question to any satisfactory degree would require an exploration of the drafts for Barthes's *Vita Nova* project, only some of which have been published.[24] Here, I will draw on these drafts insofar as they add further evidence, beyond the very choice of title, for Barthes's own *Vita Nova*.

Barthes's Dante: The Significance of the 'selva oscura'

Barthes's engagement with Dante and Proust in the '"Longtemps"' lecture is striking for its textual reduction to an engagement with incipits. In the case of the *Commedia*, this reduction means a focus on just two lines: 'Nel mezzo del cammin di nostra vita | mi ritrovai per una selva oscura' [In the middle of our life's journey, I found myself in a dark wood] (*Inferno* I. 1–2).[25] Barthes cites these lines, the whole of the first line and then the phrase 'selva oscura', in his lecture in Italian.[26] Notwithstanding, we know that Barthes accessed Dante through particular translations: firstly, the aforementioned first French translation by Delécluze of the *Vita nuova* (1841), a volume which also included Auguste Brizeux's translation of the *Commedia*; secondly, a modern translation of the *Commedia* by Alexandre Masseron (1950); thirdly, André Pézard's translation of Dante's complete works for the Pléiade series on the occasion of the Dante anniversary of 1965.[27] While these translations are, of course, interesting as translations, here I am more interested in the paratexts that accompany them.[28] In particular, the notes that guide the reader through Dante's works give us a good sense of the critical interpretations available to Barthes, and against which his own reading of the incipit of the *Commedia* is situated.

Attention to the commentary tradition has long been a staple of Dante studies, although the focus has primarily been on early modern Italian and Latin commentaries.[29] In contrast, considering Barthes's Dante means extending this commentary tradition into the twentieth century and expanding the corpus to include translations as well as editions. In Barthes's case, moreover, his commentaries on Dante include not only the paratexts of translations but also critical guides: most notably, the short chapter on Dante in Jean-Michel Gardair's introductory book on Italian writers published by Larousse in 1978 (the same year Barthes gave his '"Longtemps"' lecture).[30] One of the notes for Barthes's *Vita nova* project, dated 27 July 1979 and published in the *Album* edited by Marty, is remarkably explicit about the importance this book held for Barthes: 'Creative shock [Choc créatif], yesterday, whilst reading Gardair's short [petit] chapter on the *Divine Comedy*: I said to myself: it is the key, the (secret) guiding scheme of the Work'.[31] This quotation is fascinating for the way in which it shows that a 'creative shock' — another formulation analogous to Felski's 'flash of connection' — can come not directly from reading a work of literature but rather indirectly from reading a pedagogical guide to that same work. In his short (or 'little') chapter, Gardair first introduces Dante's life, with a particular emphasis on its political context but also affirming Beatrice's 'historical existence'.[32] Then he introduces Dante's works, eventually focusing on the *Commedia*, including brief summaries of the poem's structure and the events of each canto. It is difficult to know what particular aspect of Gardair's commentary Barthes appreciated, despite his evident enthusiasm attested in this particular index card.

I have noted above that Barthes's reading of the 'middle of life' deliberately challenges the numerological interpretation of the commentary tradition by arguing, instead, that this 'middle' is 'semantic' and signifies an encounter with death. Concomitantly, Barthes's interpretation also casts new light on the meaning of the 'selva oscura' ('dark wood') in which Dante-pilgrim finds himself at the start of the *Commedia*. Commentators have long argued over the significance of this setting, with interpretations ranging across the literal, the moral, the political, and the metaphorical. A representative sample from the commentary tradition follows, organized chronologically:

1. Ignorance	*Jacopo Alighieri (1322)*
2. The world	*Guido da Pisa (1327–28?)*
3. Vice or sin	*Pietro Alighieri (1340–42)*
4. Life	*Anonimo Fiorentino (1400?)*
5. The body	*Cristoforo Landino (1481)*
6. Error	*Alessandro Vellutello (1544)*
7. Confusion and uncertainty	*Giovan Battista Gelli (1541–63)*
8. The passions	*Baldassare Lombardi (1791–92)*
9. Exile	*Giovanni Marchetti (1819)*
10. A real 'selva'	*Raffaello Andreoli (1856)*
11. Civil war; Italy; Florence	*Brunone Bianchi (1868)*[33]

Faced with all these differing interpretations of the 'selva oscura', and therefore of the start and origin of the *Commedia*, we might almost claim for Dante what William Kennedy has claimed for Petrarch: namely, that 'From this welter of competing constructions emerges a Petrarch who could be anything and everything to all readers'.[34] In broad terms, it is evident from this list that the 'dark wood' has been interpreted in three major ways divisible by time period: firstly, in the fourteenth and fifteenth centuries, in a religious and moral light as ignorance, sin, vice, and error, by extension understood as defining characteristics of the world, life, and the body; secondly, in the sixteenth and seventeenth centuries, in a more psychological, emotional manner as confusion and the passions; thirdly, in the nineteenth century, in predominantly political terms (save for Andreoli's very literal, geographical reading). Barthes's own reading of Dante's 'dark wood' comes closest to the middle of these three periods, although he has one particular passion in mind: mourning.[35]

From Barthes's own Dante library, the interpretations put forward are quite canonical, stressing that the 'dark wood' is an experience of sin and error, with additional political implications. Most succinctly, Gardair summarizes the first two cantos of *Inferno* as follows: '*Virgil* comes to help Dante, lost in the dark, allegorical wood of sin [l'obscure forêt allégorique du péché]'.[36] Likewise, for Pézard, who translates the 'selva oscura' in a wonderfully literal fashion as 'une selve obscure': 'The forest [...] symbolizes the perils and the errors of this world [les périls et les erreurs de ce monde]'.[37] The readings of Gardair and Pézard are wholly consistent with the early commentary tradition, although Pézard gives as his more immediate source a paper by Salvatore Battaglia.[38]

In contrast, Masseron in his translation is much more verbose through the medium of a three-page introduction to the first canto of *Inferno*:

> The first canto of *Inferno*, the prologue to the whole of the *Commedia*, is probably the most difficult to understand; it is certainly the one which has been the most frantically glossed [éperdument glosé], both overall and in each of its details: to line 30 alone, for example, a small library has been dedicated. It is pointless [inutile] to add that most of these commentaries are contradictory.
>
> The least informed reader, who approaches the study of the poem for the first time, is not slow to realize that, if Dante has gone astray in a 'dark wood' [une 'forêt obscure'], the reader has likewise gone astray in a forest of symbols.[39]

This is a wonderfully Baudelairean reading of the 'dark wood', via the allusion to the 'forêts de symboles', Baudelaire's definition of 'Nature' and our place within it from his sonnet 'Correspondances'.[40] Of the 'selva oscura' in particular, Masseron goes on to explain:

> The 'dark wood' ['forêt obscure'] is the 'state of misery' ['état de misère'] to which sin leads, the state into which Dante has fallen, as a result of errors [fautes] which will be specified later, notably in cantos XXX and XXXI of *Purgatorio*; it is also the state in which humanity finds itself, abandoned by the guides which Providence had chosen for it: pope and emperor.[41]

A further note to the translation itself glosses the 'dark wood' intertextually with reference to 'the tortuous wood [selva erronea] of this life' from *Convivio* IV. xxiv, 12, and adds — in a quotation explicitly derived from the fourteenth-century commentary of Benvenuto da Imola — that 'The *wood* is said to be *dark* "because someone who does evil hates the light"'.[42]

In the context of these readings, Barthes proves to be a highly creative and idiosyncratic reader of Dante, adding a wholly new, personal, and psychological interpretation to the 'welter of competing constructions' (returning to Kennedy's phrase) already available. Barthes takes to heart Dante's invitation to the reader to participate in his journey, and consequently reads the opening of the *Commedia* as a story of grief shared by Dante and himself. In this way, Barthes renews the possible meaning and significance of the *Commedia* for a new audience. Crucially, he does so not in ignorance of the preceding critical tradition but rather with awareness of the radical nature of his reading.

Dante as a Model for Mourning: Contrasting Perspectives

That Barthes's reading of Dante has the potential to touch a chord with modern readers of Dante is further suggested by a memoir from 2015 that upholds a similar interpretation of the 'selva oscura' as mourning: Luzzi's grief memoir *In a Dark Wood*.[43] Yet while Barthes and Luzzi share this interpretation on a basic level, they also differ greatly in their understanding and explanation of their experience of grief — and therefore, ultimately, in their reading of Dante. One reason for this difference is perhaps contextual. While Barthes was an intermittent, private reader of Dante, Luzzi is a professional *italianista* and Professor of Comparative Literature at Bard College. Besides *In a Dark Wood*, his books include *Romantic Europe and the Ghost of Italy* (2008), his family biography *My Two Italies* (2014), and a forthcoming 'biography' of the *Commedia* in Princeton University Press's series 'Lives of Great Religious Books'.[44] That Luzzi knows Dante better than Barthes is beyond doubt. Yet Luzzi still shares with Barthes both an understanding of reading Dante as a process of identification and a new, personal, emotional reading of the 'dark wood' as an experience of mourning.

Luzzi's book is structured in three parts, with a prologue, modelled deliberately on the structure of Dante's *Commedia*. His prologue opens by citing the first two lines of Dante's *Commedia* in Italian and in his own English translation.[45] These lines are, of course, the same ones that Barthes had isolated in his '"Longtemps"' lecture. Luzzi initially highlights the universal significance of these lines, writing that 'We will all find ourselves in a dark wood one day, the lines suggest'.[46] Luzzi's narrative then takes an intimate turn, explaining that his own 'dark wood' was the death of his wife Katherine in a car accident on 29 November 2007. At that time, his wife was eight and a half months pregnant, and their daughter Isabel survived.

Like Barthes, though even more so given his roles as teacher and *dantista*, Luzzi is aware of the commentary tradition, yet chooses to offer his own, emotive reading of the poem. As he acknowledges, 'My reading of Dante had always been deep and personal, but when I found myself in the dark wood, his words became a matter of life and death'.[47] In particular, Luzzi reads the many references to exile throughout the poem as a reflection of his own experience of grief, writing, for instance, of Cacciaguida's prophecy of Dante's exile in *Paradiso* XVII. 55–57 that 'No other words could capture how I felt during the four years I struggled to find my way out of the dark wood of grief and mourning'.[48] For both Barthes and Luzzi, the 'dark wood' is not sin, error, Florence, or any of the other common interpretations noted above; rather, it is, in Luzzi's phrase, 'grief and mourning'.

Despite this poignant similarity, what is also striking about Luzzi's book in contrast to Barthes's account of mourning is that Luzzi charts a way out of his 'dark wood'. Perhaps Barthes did not live long enough after his mother's death to find such a path, not to mention evident differences between the death of a mother and the death of a spouse. Either way, Barthes remains stuck in the 'dark wood', for better or for worse. Notes for the *Vita Nova* project show that Barthes is interested in the idea of guide figures and the tripartite ascending structure of the *Commedia*.[49] Indeed, the '"Longtemps"' lecture, as we have seen, suggests that Proust might be Barthes's Virgil, 'at least during this text'.[50] Unlike Luzzi, however, Barthes never manages to put these structural devices into practice.

At different points in his narrative, Luzzi identifies different guides as having led him out of the 'dark wood', particularly his daughter, but also Dante:

> *The Divine Comedy* didn't rescue me after Katherine's death. That fell to the support of family and friends, to my passion for teaching and writing, above all to the gift of my daughter. Our daughter. But I would barely have made it out without Dante. In a time of soul-crunching loneliness — I was surrounded everywhere by love, but such is grief — his words helped me withstand the pain of loss.[51]

Of these two guides, the book's 'Acknowledgments' ultimately privilege one: 'I dedicate this book to Isabel because, more than anything, it was my love for her that saved me from the dark wood'.[52] Yet throughout the book Luzzi has shown the importance of Dante, while the final part of his narrative also suggests the discovery of a new Beatrice in the English violinist Helena Baillie, who will become his second wife.[53]

At the very end of *In a Dark Wood*, Luzzi encloses a short letter addressed to his daughter Isabel. This letter includes the following advice: 'it's not what lands you in the dark wood that defines you, but what you do to make it out'.[54] Luzzi is a better reader of Dante than Barthes in that he understands and follows the forward impulsion of the *Commedia*, out of the 'dark wood'. Barthes certainly read more than the first few lines of the *Commedia*, yet the '"Longtemps"' lecture encourages us to linger in our reading and to resist the poem's onward march. Juxtaposing Barthes and Luzzi reveals an 'affective turn' in readings of Dante, particularly regarding the experience of grief and a newly intimate mode of reading as identification.[55] Yet this same juxtaposition also reveals that identification with this mournful Dante can be motivated by two very different experiences and forms of grief. Dante and Luzzi both find a way out of the 'dark wood', through recourse to different guide figures and through both reading and writing. Barthes, in contrast, remains trapped within his dark wood, even as he imagines the possibility of an exit, a *vita n[u]ova*.

Concluding Thoughts: A New Dante?

Barthes's reading of Dante is partial, both in the sense that it is incomplete and unfinished and in the sense that it is skewed by personal, affective experience. Like other readers, Barthes is also fascinated more by the *Inferno* than the other two *cantiche*, and his *Inferno* is dominated by an inescapable 'dark wood'. Notwithstanding, Barthes still offers a radically new reading of the *Commedia*, one no longer moral or religious but rather darkly emotional, written under the sign of grief. Beyond this reinterpretation of the 'dark wood' and the source of the *Commedia*, Barthes finally proposes that the power of literature lies in our identification with particular stories and authors, in the way (to echo Felski) we recognize ourselves in what we read. From this perspective, the example of Barthes's mournful reading of Dante collapses any distance between the medieval and the modern, encouraging us to engage intimately with past texts.

Barthes's reading of Dante further proves to be an apt one 'for the new millennium', if we consider its resonances with Luzzi's grief memoir *In a Dark Wood*.[56] As I have suggested, Barthes and Luzzi are divided by their different experiences of grief even as they are united by their recourse to Dante in sorrow. Barthes and Luzzi are both 'Heirs of a Dark Wood' (to borrow a phrase from Luzzi's first book), although they use their inheritance in different ways.[57] A final quotation from Luzzi's text reaffirms, in a more Barthesian manner, the power of reading as identification, whilst also warning us against reducing Dante's poem to the category of 'self-help manual':

> In my grief I identified more closely with Dante than ever before, especially his story of exile, the feeling of being a pilgrim suddenly adrift in a dark wood. But *The Divine Comedy* was not a self-help manual, a means to a practical set of ends that I was able to negotiate based on Dante's advice. To say as much would do violence to the kind of poem that Dante tried to write.[58]

Literature is neither 'self-help' nor 'advice'. Yet, as the examples of both Barthes and Luzzi show, in the reader's mournful identification with character, author, situation, or language, literature can give us one way to understand ourselves better, to express our own grief, and, crucially, to feel less alone.[59]

Notes to Chapter 4

1. Neil Badmington, *The Afterlives of Roland Barthes* (London: Bloomsbury Academic, 2016), p. 110.
2. See *Les XIXes siècles de Roland Barthes*, ed. by José-Luis Diaz and Mathilde Labbé (Brussels: Impressions Nouvelles, 2019).
3. Jonathan Culler, *Barthes: A Very Short Introduction* (Oxford: Oxford University Press, 2002), p. 31. On Barthes and Michelet, see Patrizia Lombardo, *The Three Paradoxes of Roland Barthes* (Athens: University of Georgia Press, 1989), especially the assertion that 'Barthes's author, his great passion, the one he identified with, was less Proust than Michelet' (p. xi). *Pace* Lombardo, the bibliography on Barthes and Proust is extensive: see, most recently, Roland Barthes, *Marcel Proust: mélanges*, ed. by Bernard Comment (Paris: Seuil, 2020) and Thomas Baldwin, *Roland Barthes: The Proust Variations* (Liverpool: Liverpool University Press, 2019), as well as the references in Jennifer Rushworth, 'Mourning and Intermittence between Proust and Barthes', *Paragraph*, 39.3 (2016), 269–86.

4. See, nonetheless, *Roland Barthes and Poetry*, ed. by Callie Gardner (= *Barthes Studies*, 2 (2016)) <http://sites.cardiff.ac.uk/barthes/category/volume-2/> [accessed 7 August 2021]; Callie Gardner, *Poetry and Barthes: Anglophone Responses 1970–2000* (Liverpool: Liverpool University Press, 2018); Bruce Holsinger, *The Premodern Condition: Medievalism and the Making of Theory* (Chicago: University of Chicago Press, 2005), especially the chapter on 'The Four Senses of Roland Barthes', pp. 152–94; *Medieval Barthes*, ed. by Jennifer Rushworth and Francesca Southerden (= *Exemplaria*, 33.3 (2021)). On Barthes and Italy, see Guido Mattia Gallerani, 'Barthes et l'Italie: voyages, collaborations, traductions, réception, études', in *Barthes à l'étranger*, ed. by Claude Coste and Mathieu Messager (= *Revue Roland Barthes*, 2 (October 2015)) <http://www.roland-barthes.org/article_gallerani.html> [accessed 7 August 2021].
5. Jennifer Rushworth, 'Barthes as Reader of Dante: The Mediation of Sollers and the Role of Commentary', *Barthes Studies*, 4 (November 2018), 31–55 <http://sites.cardiff.ac.uk/barthes/article/barthes-as-reader-of-dante-the-mediation-of-sollers-and-the-role-of-commentary/> [accessed 7 August 2021].
6. See, for a discussion of this term, Michael Moriarty, *Roland Barthes* (Cambridge: Polity, 1991), p. 157.
7. For details, see Rushworth, 'Barthes as Reader of Dante', p. 41.
8. I will refer to Dante's *Vita nuova* with the Italian rather than the Latin spelling, sidestepping issues raised by Guglielmo Gorni's edition (Dante Alighieri, *Vita nova*, ed. by Gorni) merely in order to distinguish it from Barthes's own *Vita Nova* project (although Barthes himself is not consistent about the spelling). On the evidence for Barthes's own *Vita Nova* see below.
9. Roland Barthes, '"Longtemps, je me suis couché de bonne heure"', in *Œuvres complètes*, ed. by Éric Marty, new edn, 5 vols (Paris: Seuil, 2002), v, 459–70. Hereafter I refer to this edition by the abbreviation *OC* followed by the volume number. I cite from the following English translation: '*Longtemps, je me suis couché de bonne heure*', in *The Rustle of Language*, trans. by Howard. Unless stated otherwise, all other translations are my own.
10. Roland Barthes, *Album: inédits, correspondances et varia*, ed. by Éric Marty (Paris: Seuil, 2015), pp. xli–lxiv. An English translation of Barthes's *Album* has been published, but without translations of these index cards: Barthes, *Album: Unpublished Correspondence and Texts*, trans. by Jody Gladding (New York: Columbia University Press, 2018). Subsequent translation of this material is therefore my own. The other set of materials vital for understanding Barthes's *Vita Nova* project are the eight pages of drafts at the end of the first, three-volume edition of Barthes's *Œuvres complètes* (1995): see Roland Barthes, *Œuvres complètes*, ed. by Éric Marty, 3 vols (Paris: Seuil, 1993–95), III, 1287–94, reprinted in Barthes, *OC*, v, 994–1001 with transcription pp. 1007–18. For an English translation of these initial drafts see Roland Barthes, *The Preparation of the Novel: Lecture Courses and Seminars at the Collège de France (1978–1979 and 1979–1980)*, ed. by Nathalie Léger and trans. by Kate Briggs (New York: Columbia University Press, 2011), pp. 389–406, reprinted in Barthes, *Album: Unpublished Correspondence and Texts*, pp. 297–308.
11. Felski, *Uses of Literature*, p. 23.
12. See ibid., p. 26, and Marcel Proust, *In Search of Lost Time*, ed. by Christopher Prendergast, 6 vols (London: Penguin Classics, 2003), VI: *Finding Time Again*, trans. by Ian Patterson, 219–20.
13. Barthes, '*Longtemps, je me suis couché de bonne heure*', pp. 277–78; *OC* v, 459.
14. See Joshua Landy for a particularly clear and playful explanation, especially 'Introduction: Philosophy and Fiction (Nobody's Madeleine)', in *Philosophy as Fiction: Self, Deception, and Knowledge in Proust* (Oxford: Oxford University Press, 2004), pp. 3–49.
15. On Proust's narrator's desire to write and its relation to the book we read, see Jennifer Rushworth, 'Derrida, Proust, and the Promise of Writing', *French Studies*, 69.2 (April 2015), 205–19. On the writing of *A la recherche*, see Christine M. Cano, *Proust's Deadline* (Urbana: University of Illinois Press, 2006).
16. See Rushworth, *Discourses of Mourning in Dante, Petrarch, and Proust*, Julia Hartley, *Reading Dante and Proust by Analogy* (Oxford: Legenda, 2019), and the bibliography in each.
17. Diana Knight, *Barthes and Utopia: Space, Travel, Writing* (Oxford: Clarendon Press, 1997), p. 252.
18. Barthes, '*Longtemps, je me suis couché de bonne heure*', p. 284.
19. This calculation is reliant on an ideal lifespan of 'threescore years and ten' suggested in Psalm 90:10 (in the Masoretic numbering and the King James Version).

20. See Barthes, '*Longtemps, je me suis couché de bonne heure*', p. 286, where the phrase is also attributed to Michelet.
21. See Teodolinda Barolini, 'The Case of the Lost Original Ending of Dante's *Vita nuova*: More Notes Towards a Critical Philology', *Medioevo letterario d'Italia*, 11 (2014), 37–43, and Robert Pogue Harrison, *The Body of Beatrice* (Baltimore, MD: Johns Hopkins University Press, 1988).
22. Barthes, '*Longtemps, je me suis couché de bonne heure*', p. 286.
23. Ibid.
24. For discussion of these drafts, in addition to the primary materials outlined earlier, see Diana Knight, 'Idle Thoughts: Barthes's *Vita Nova*', *Nottingham French Studies*, 36.1 (Spring 1997), 88–98, and more recently Tiphaine Samoyault, *Roland Barthes: biographie* (Paris: Seuil, 2015), pp. 649–85.
25. The English translation here is taken from Luzzi's own translation given at the start of *In a Dark Wood*, p. 1.
26. Barthes, '*Longtemps, je me suis couché de bonne heure*', p. 284.
27. Dante Alighieri, *La Divine Comédie: traduction nouvelle par A. Brizeux; La Vie nouvelle, traduite par M. E.-J. Delécluze* (Paris: Charpentier, 1841); *La Divine Comédie*, trans. by Alexandre Masseron (Paris: Albin Michel, 1947); *Œuvres complètes*, trans. by André Pézard (Paris: Gallimard, 1965). Masseron's translation is cited in a note in Barthes, *Album: inédits, correspondances et varia*, p. lviii, while Pézard's is noted to be Barthes's 'traduction de référence' in *La Préparation du roman I et II: notes de cours et de séminaires au Collège de France 1978–1979 et 1979–1980*, ed. by Nathalie Léger (Paris: Seuil/IMEC, 2003), p. 25, n. 2.
28. For a theoretical statement of the importance of considering the paratexts of translations, see Kathryn Batchelor, *Translation and Paratexts* (Abingdon: Routledge, 2018).
29. See *Interpreting Dante: Essays on the Traditions of Dante Commentary*, ed. by Paola Nasti and Claudia Rossignoli (Notre Dame, IN: University of Notre Dame Press, 2013). In this volume, the only chapter to consider modern material is the final chapter by John Lindon, 'Notes on Nineteenth-century Dante Commentaries and Critical Editions', pp. 434–49.
30. See 'Dante Alighieri', in Jean-Michel Gardair, *Écrivains italiens* (Paris: Larousse, 1978), pp. 35–53.
31. Barthes, *Album: inédits, correspondances et varia*, p. lii.
32. See Gardair, *Écrivains italiens*, p. 35.
33. All of these references are taken from the Dartmouth Dante Project online <https://dante.dartmouth.edu/> [accessed 27 March 2020]. More generally on sylvan symbolism, see Robert Pogue Harrison, *Forests: The Shadow of Civilization* (Chicago: University of Chicago Press, 1992), especially pp. 81–87, where for Harrison Dante's 'dark forest' is 'an allegory for Christian guilt' (p. 81).
34. William J. Kennedy, *The Site of Petrarchism* (Baltimore, MD: Johns Hopkins University Press, 2003), p. 3. For a sense of the broad-ranging modern reception of Dante, see *Metamorphosing Dante: Appropriations, Manipulations, and Rewritings in the Twentieth and Twenty-first Centuries*, ed. by Manuele Gragnolati, Fabio Camilletti, and Fabian Lampart (Vienna: Turia & Kant, 2011).
35. Whether mourning can be classified as a passion in an early modern sense is a different question, although I find the connection between passion, suffering, and passivity quite apt: see Erich Auerbach, '*Passio* as Passion', in *Time, History, and Literature: Selected Essays of Erich Auerbach*, ed. by James I. Porter and trans. by Jane O. Newman (Princeton, NJ: Princeton University Press, 2014), pp. 165–87.
36. Gardair, *Écrivains italiens*, p. 48.
37. Dante, *Œuvres complètes*, trans. by Pézard, p. 883.
38. Salvatore Battaglia, 'Linguaggio reale e figurato nella *Divina Commedia*', in *Atti del Congresso nazionale di studi danteschi (Caserta, 21–25 maggio 1961): Dante nel secolo dell'unità italiana* (Florence: Olschki, 1962), pp. 21–44.
39. Dante, *La Divine Comédie*, trans. by Masseron, p. 53.
40. Charles Baudelaire, *Œuvres complètes*, ed. by Claude Pichois, 2 vols (Paris: Gallimard, 1975–76), I, 11.
41. Dante, *La Divine Comédie*, trans. by Masseron, p. 54.
42. Ibid., p. 56. Masseron himself references a nineteenth-century edition of Benvenuto's commentary: Benvenuto da Imola, *Comentum super Dantis Aldigherij Comœdiam*, ed. by Jacobo

Filippo Lacaita, 5 vols (Florence: G. Barbera, 1887). English translation of the *Convivio* from *Convivio: A Dual Language Critical Edition*, ed. and trans. by Andrew Frisardi (Cambridge: Cambridge University Press, 2018), p. 329.

43. On grief memoirs as a genre, see Chapter 10 in the present volume.

44. Joseph Luzzi, *Romantic Europe and the Ghost of Italy* (New Haven, CT: Yale University Press, 2008); *My Two Italies* (New York: Farrar, Straus & Giroux, 2014); *Dante's 'Divine Comedy': A Biography* (Princeton, NJ: Princeton University Press, forthcoming).

45. Luzzi, *In a Dark Wood*, p. 1.

46. Ibid.

47. Ibid., p. 287.

48. Ibid., p. 5. In Luzzi's translation, on the same page, these lines from *Paradiso* read '*You will leave behind everything you love | most dearly, and this is the arrow | the bow of exile first lets fly*'.

49. See, for instance, Barthes, *Album: inédits, correspondances et varia*, pp. lvi, lix.

50. Barthes, '*Longtemps, je me suis couché de bonne heure*', p. 284.

51. Luzzi, *In a Dark Wood*, p. 9.

52. Ibid., p. 297.

53. Ibid., p. 267.

54. Ibid., p. 289.

55. See *The Affective Turn: Theorizing the Social*, ed. by Patrizia Clough, with Jean Halley (Durham, NC: Duke University Press, 2007), as well as *The Affect Theory Reader*, ed. by Melissa Gregg and Gregory J. Seigworth (Durham, NC: Duke University Press, 2010).

56. Echoing here the title of *Dante for the New Millennium*, ed. by Teodolinda Barolini and H. Wayne Storey (New York: Fordham University Press, 2003).

57. This phrase is the title of Part II of Luzzi's *Romantic Europe and the Ghost of Italy*, pp. 95–159.

58. Luzzi, *In a Dark Wood*, p. 130.

59. On poetry as a way to 'feel less alone in our experience of' grief, see Don Paterson, 'Introduction', in *The Picador Book of Funeral Poems*, ed. by Paterson, p. xiii, cited by Simona Corso in Chapter 10.

CHAPTER 5

From Medieval Text to Modern Glass: Expressions of Mourning in *The Dream of the Rood* and Laurence Whistler

Susan Irvine

The artistic imagination has often over the centuries been deeply intertwined with expressions of mourning. This essay will examine two expressions of mourning — one an early medieval poem, the other modern engraved glass — far apart in terms of chronology and medium but nevertheless intimately related to one another. The earlier of the two is the anonymous Old English poem *The Dream of the Rood*; the later is an engraved glass visualization of that poem by the twentieth-century glass engraver, writer, and architectural historian Sir Laurence Whistler. By looking at these two artefacts in relation to each other, the essay will explore ways in which an expression of mourning emanating from early medieval literary culture has been received and reimagined within contemporary visual culture. In both poem and engraved glass image, I will argue, mourning becomes transfigured, through a paradoxical juxtaposition with rejoicing, into a yearning that reaches beyond the human towards the mystical or divine.

The Old English poem *The Dream of the Rood* is the earliest vernacular example of the literary genre known as the dream vision.[1] Composed probably sometime in the eighth century AD, the poem survives in one copy in a manuscript from the second half of the tenth century known as the Vercelli Book.[2] It begins in the voice of the Dreamer who records a dream that comes to him in the middle of the night. He first sees a vision of a cross, extending into the sky, enveloped in light, and bedecked with jewels. The cross's appearance fluctuates constantly, at one moment adorned with treasure, the next seeming to weep or flow with blood. The Dreamer's description of the cross gives way to the cross's own words; drawing on the classical technique of prosopopoeia (by which an inanimate or abstract thing is personified), the cross recounts the events of the Crucifixion from its unique perspective as the instrument of torture on which Christ was crucified.[3] The relationship between Christ and the cross is represented in terms reminiscent of the Germanic heroic code: the cross depicts itself as a loyal retainer of its heroic lord, Christ, ultimately, and shockingly, obliged to show its loyalty by serving as the killer of its lord. In the second half of the poem the cross recounts how it eventually became a glorious symbol of Christ's redemption of humankind. The poem finishes by returning us to the Dreamer, who offers an impassioned account of how his vision of the cross has inspired him to pursue salvation.

The expression of mourning is powerfully conveyed in the first half of the poem. The Dreamer mourns his own sinfulness, which stands out in apparent contrast to the splendour of the cross: 'Syllic wæs se sigebeam, and ic synnum fah, | forwunded mid wommum' [The victory-tree was marvellous, and I stained with sins, badly wounded with iniquities] (ll. 13–14). He explicitly recounts his mournful state a few lines further on: 'Eall ic wæs mid sorgum gedrefed. | Forht ic wæs for þære fægran gesyhðe' [I was all troubled with sorrows. I was afraid because of the beautiful vision] (ll. 20–21). But the cross too, ostensibly so splendid, displays signs that it is in mourning:

Geseah ic þæt fuse beacen
wendan wædum ond bleom; hwilum hit wæs mid wætan bestemed,
beswyled mid swates gange, hwilum mid since gegyrwed. (ll. 21–23)

[I saw that shining beacon change in garments and colours; at times it was drenched with moisture, soaked with the flow of liquid, at times adorned with treasure.]

The Dreamer's description of the cross as simultaneously bedecked with jewels and soaked with tears or blood evokes the fundamentally paradoxical nature of the Crucifixion, which simultaneously embodies suffering and triumph, defeat and victory, mourning and rejoicing.

When the cross begins to speak, it mourns in its own words the role it is obliged to undertake. It describes how it does not dare to fall down and slay those crucifying Christ, using the phrase 'ne dorste' [did not dare to] three times in close succession (ll. 35, 42, 45). Like the Dreamer, the cross laments its own guilt and fear, as well as the suffering it experiences on Christ's behalf: 'Þurhdrifan hi me mid deorcan næglum; on me syndon þa dolg gesiene, | opene inwidhlemmas. Ne dorste ic hira nænigum sceððan' [They pierced me with dark nails; on me the wounds, open malicious wounds, are visible. I did not dare to injure any of them] (ll. 46–47). Its sorrow, and that of the Dreamer, is echoed in the response of the whole of creation: 'Weop eal gesceaft,' says the cross, 'cwiðdon Cyninges fyll' [All creation wept, lamented the death of the king] (l. 56). The cross's subsequent description of itself as 'sare [...] sorgum gedrefed' [sorely troubled by sorrows] (l. 59) and 'eall [...] mid strælum forwundod' [badly wounded by arrows] (l. 62) clearly recalls the earlier description of the Dreamer as 'eall [...] mid sorgum gedrefed' [all troubled with sorrows] (l. 20) and 'forwunded mid wommum' [badly wounded by iniquities] (l. 14). After the Deposition, the cross focuses first on the mourning of Christ's followers — 'earme on þa æfentide' [wretched in the evening time] (l. 68), they proceed to sing a 'sorhleoð' [a song of sorrow] (l. 67) — and then on the mourning of the three crosses left at the site of the Crucifixion, which 'greotende' [lamenting] (l. 70) continue to stand there as Christ's body grows cold.

Ultimately, however, the poem's expression of mourning transforms itself into one of joy. The Crucifixion elicits both responses: the reasons for mourning are, the poem shows, also the reasons for celebrating. The sorrow inherent in the Crucifixion is also its joy: Christ's suffering enables humankind's redemption and eternal salvation. The mourning is resolved in the eternal bliss of heaven — imaginatively depicted in heroic terms in the last part of the poem as a group of God's people seated at a banquet, celebrating Christ's return from his glorious expedition.

The poem's contemporary audiences seem to have found it a source of inspiration, as witnessed by the inscription of parts of its text on two artefacts from the early medieval period. One of these artefacts is the eighth-century stone cross found in Ruthwell in south-west Scotland, now known as the Ruthwell Cross; it is inscribed with verses in the native runic alphabet which correspond closely to parts of the cross's speech in *The Dream of the Rood* as it mourns the death of Christ on the cross.[4] The other is a wooden reliquary cross from the late tenth or early eleventh century known as the Brussels Cross, preserved in the cathedral of St Michael and St Gudula in Brussels. This bears an Old English inscription around its sides, apparently deriving from *The Dream of the Rood* (ll. 44 and 48) and similarly giving a voice to the cross: 'Rod is min nama; geo ic ricne Cyning bær byfigynde, blod bestemed' [Rood is my name: long ago, trembling and soaked with blood, I bore the powerful king]. The words convey the same depth of grief felt by the cross as in the poem, but here, as on the Ruthwell Cross, they serve to visualize the idea of the cross speaking out and thereby create a dynamic and dramatic relationship between the viewers of the inscriptions and the artefacts themselves.[5]

Intriguing as it is to see the poem interacting with other kinds of artistic production in its own time, it is even more remarkable perhaps to find it capturing the imagination of the major twentieth-century glass engraver Laurence Whistler.[6] The Dream of the Rood window is one of thirteen engraved glass windows designed by Whistler between 1955 and 1985 for St Nicholas Church in the Dorset village of Moreton, a church built on medieval foundations whose Victorian stained glass windows had been blown out by a bomb in 1940. Whistler's replacement windows for the church are described in Pevsner's *Buildings of England* volume for Dorset as 'a stroke of genius, having the elegance and lightness of the building'.[7] The engravings, delicate and intricate, emphasize the way that the glass is both solid and yet also transparent and fragile.

For Whistler the large-scale engraving of these windows was a very different kind of enterprise from the goblets, bowls, and small glass panels that he had engraved hitherto. His career in glass engraving began in 1934 when he was twenty-two years old.[8] In keeping with his ambition at the time of being a poet, his first engraving was an inscription of a sonnet of his own on a window pane of a friend's house in Northumberland.[9] From this and other window panes followed a series of commissions for goblets, glasses, and bowls. Drawing on his own research on the work of seventeenth- and eighteenth-century glass engravers in England and Holland, Whistler developed his own take on a craft that had more or less died out in England by this time.

In his book *The Image on the Glass*, Whistler gives an account of how he came to undertake the project of engraving new windows for the church of St Nicholas in Moreton:

> In 1955 there came an opportunity to try my hand at church decoration. The small parish church of Moreton in Dorset, though remote from any town, had received a direct hit from a bomb in 1940, and had lost all its dark, Victorian stained glass, which had been inappropriate, and was not much regretted. There was War Damage money to replace it at the reconstruction, but it was thought to be a pity to redarken the church. At this moment Mr Howard Colvin, the architectural historian, visited Moreton. [...] He suggested that I might be engaged to replace the lost windows in the apse with engraved glass that would not exclude light, or spoil a pleasant view of trees all round.[10]

The five apse windows that Whistler mentions here were designed and produced in 1955. There was then a gap of twenty years, after which other engraved glass windows designed by Whistler, including the Dream of the Rood window, were added intermittently as a commemorative occasion arose or a donor came forward. Intriguingly, once he had completed twelve windows, Laurence Whistler offered to give the church a thirteenth, one that could only be seen from the outside, to be based on the theme of forgiveness and featuring the figure of Judas hanging by a noose with thirty pieces of silver falling from his hand and turning into flowers on the ground. This was initially declined by the parish council, but Whistler decided to make the engraving anyway. The panel was displayed in a local museum, until, on the eventual agreement of the council, it was installed in the church in 2014, fourteen years after Whistler's death.

The Dream of the Rood window, made in 1975, offers an imaginative recreation of the original poem. It depicts a large cross extending into the sky. One side of the cross is envisioned as shining with jewels, and smaller jewels take on wings as they flutter down from the cross-bar towards the landscape below, their shapes reflecting the design of the stone tracery in the upper part of the window. The other side, standing against a rainy background, sheds droplets, either blood or tears. At the centre of the cross is a depiction of the Alfred Jewel, an exquisite gold and enamelled object made in the late ninth century, now in the Ashmolean Museum in Oxford. Below the cross, the landscape, lit by a bright bar of light beneath an otherwise dark and cloudy sky, depicts oast houses on one side, a house nestling among trees in the centre, and on the other side wooded slopes and a body of water. An inscription referring to the person commemorated is engraved at the bottom: 'Our family rejoice in Noel Findlay 1899–1976 & his gift of happiness'. Commander Noel Charles Mansfeldt Findlay lived in Kent and it is his home and oast houses that are depicted here, along with the adjoining church.[11]

Laurence Whistler had studied English as an undergraduate at Balliol College, Oxford, in the early 1930s and probably first encountered *The Dream of the Rood* during his study of Old English there. In his biography of his brother, the artist Rex Whistler, Laurence confesses to sitting his exams 'having [...] done hardly any work on Anglo-Saxon'.[12] But in a British Library Sounds recording of June 2000, made just six months before his death, Whistler explains that he later remedied

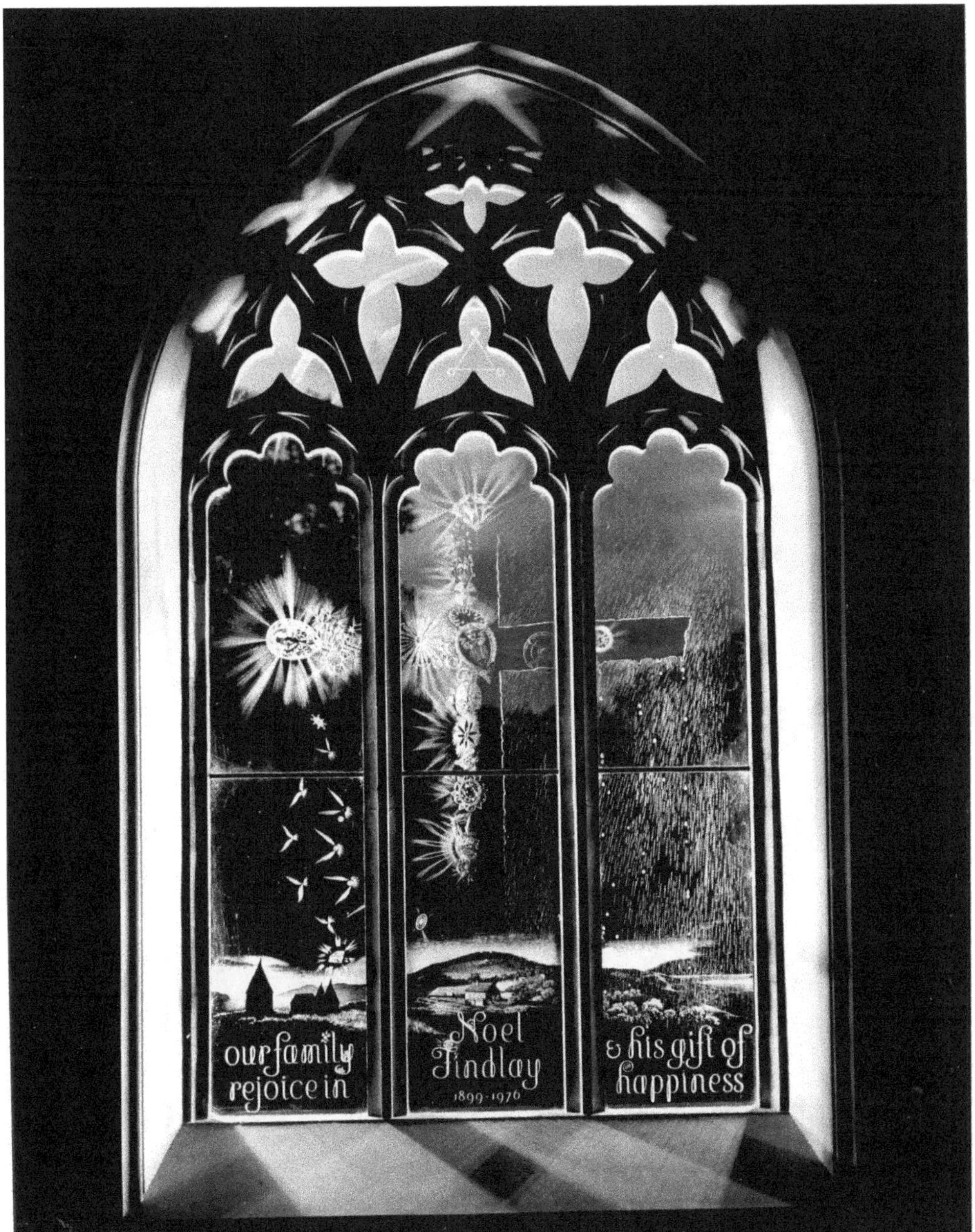

FIG. 5.1. Laurence Whistler, The Dream of the Rood window (1975), St Nicholas Church, Moreton. © Estate of Laurence Whistler. Reproduced with kind permission of the family.

FIG. 5.2. Detail from Laurence Whistler, The Dream of the Rood window (1975), St Nicholas Church, Moreton. © Estate of Laurence Whistler. Reproduced with kind permission of the family.

this, and that he came to appreciate 'the very wonderful [Anglo-Saxon] poetry', including *The Dream of the Rood* which he describes as 'beautifully written' and 'exciting'.[13] Whistler's creative visualization of *The Dream of the Rood* in engraved glass confirms that the poem made a lasting impression on his imagination. It is possible that his memories of Oxford were particularly on his mind around the time he designed this window, since just a year earlier, in 1974, he had been elected an honorary fellow of Balliol College.[14] The association in Whistler's mind between *The Dream of the Rood* and Oxford is perhaps further evidenced by a second, much smaller, visualization of the cross from the poem that he engraved later in 1975 as a memorial panel to a former principal of St Hugh's College, Oxford.[15]

Whistler was familiar with modern translations of the poem, which he would have found helpful in understanding and interpreting the original. One translation that seems to have stood out for him is that of Gavin Bone, published in 1943 in his collection of poems entitled *Anglo-Saxon Poetry: An Essay with Specimen Translations in Verse*.[16] Writing on 24 July 1978 to the Moreton parish council to express his willingness to help prepare a leaflet to accompany the Dream of the Rood window, Whistler rejects the prose translation the council has in mind, proposing instead 'this verse one by Gavin Bone, which is livelier and nearer current English, and easier to read? (I rather doubt if anyone would persevere with the prose)'.[17] Given that Bone's poetry seems to have been little known by the mid-1970s, this is perhaps a surprising choice on Whistler's part.[18] It is possible that Whistler's and Bone's paths crossed at Oxford through their shared interest in writing poetry: Bone was a Fellow of St John's College at the same time that Whistler was up at Balliol (1930–34), and two of Whistler's early volumes of poetry were published during this period, the second of which earned him the award of the Royal Gold Medal for 1935.[19] More likely, though, Whistler's interest in Bone's poetry developed later through his conversations with Bone's brother, Stephen, who studied at the Slade School of Fine Art with Laurence's brother Rex. Stephen Bone was consulted by Laurence as part of the latter's research for his biography of Rex. In that book Laurence records Stephen's account of Rex's arrival at the Slade: '"He burst in upon us," Bone told me, "and shocked and impressed us all."'[20] Both Stephen and Laurence shared the experience of losing talented brothers at a young age (Gavin Bone died in 1942 at the age of thirty-four, and Rex Whistler in 1944 at the age of thirty-nine). Stephen Bone might well have brought Gavin Bone's translations of Old English poems to the attention of Laurence Whistler in the course of their discussions.

Drawing on the poem, Whistler's Dream of the Rood window expresses the paradox of simultaneous suffering and joy through the image of the Crucifixion. The flashing jewels on one side and the rain and droplets on the other reflect the Dreamer's vision in the poem of a cross shifting between glittering with gems and flowing with blood or tears. The way in which suffering and joy are intertwined is represented in the presence of jewels on both sides of the cross-beam. In depicting one of the jewels on the bleeding side of the cross as an embossed shield, moreover, Whistler may be responding to the idea expressed in the poem that the ancient hostility of wretched ones is visible through the gold: ‘Hwæðre ic þurh þæt gold ongytan meahte | earmra ærgewin’ [However through the gold I could perceive the ancient hostility of wretched ones] (ll. 18–19). Whistler adds a further dimension to the imagery of the poem by connecting the jewels and blood to sunshine and rain respectively: the brightest jewel shines out like the sun on the far left of the window, and the drops of blood merge with the rainy backdrop on the right. Meteorological phenomena thus become implicated in the paradox of the Crucifixion.

In Whistler's engraving, as in the poem, the cross hovers in the sky, expressing the universality of its significance as an emblem of both mourning and celebration across time and space. The vastness and abstract conception of the cross contrast with the detailed representation of the earthly landscape beneath: they are both separate from one another and yet intrinsically bound up with one another. The words in the lower part of the window imply loss and mourning in the name and dates of the person commemorated but they also celebrate his life in referring to the gift of happiness he gave.

In the poem *The Dream of the Rood*, the distinction between the cross and Christ is blurred: it is the cross, for example, that takes on Christ's sufferings at the Crucifixion: ‘on me syndon þa dolg gesiene’ [on me the wounds are visible] (l. 46). In his engraved glass visualization Whistler gives an intriguing interpretative twist to this blurring. There is no figure of Christ on the cross. But Whistler uses the image of the Alfred Jewel as a way of suggesting the head of Christ.[21] Its size, shape, and position together hint at the idea of Christ's bowed head on the cross. Moreover, the half-length portrait of a man holding flowers in each hand on the front of the Jewel itself — most plausibly interpreted as either Christ as Wisdom, or a personification of Sight[22] — becomes in Whistler's engraving an ambiguous image, an optical illusion capable of being perceived in two different ways.[23] From one perspective it is, as in the original, a figure holding two flowering rods. From the other it is the features of Christ's face, his brow ridges formed by the hands of the figure and his nose and nostrils formed by the tubular stems of the flowers. To enhance further the suggested association between the Alfred Jewel and Christ's head, Whistler places at the top of the engraved jewel a circular gem with pin-shaped spokes that recalls the crown of thorns placed on Christ's head prior to the Crucifixion to heighten his suffering.

The conceit of using the Alfred Jewel to suggest Christ's head is a highly inventive one and gives rise to other possible layers of meaning. If the Alfred Jewel suggests Christ's head, then the cross itself serves visually as his body, with the cross-beam as his outstretched arms and the upright serving as the rest of his body. The figures of Christ and the cross become blurred with one another, just as they do in the poem. By this means Whistler also seems to gesture towards a personification of the cross, brilliantly incorporating the poet's depiction of the cross as an inanimate object which can nevertheless speak.

The idea of an inanimate object with a speaking voice is, moreover, implied by the Alfred Jewel itself. Like a number of other Anglo-Saxon objects, the Alfred Jewel refers to itself in the first person. In intricate gold lettering around the edge of

Fig. 5.3. The Alfred Jewel (871–99 AD), Ashmolean Museum, Oxford.
Image © Ashmolean Museum.

its enamelled centre, are inscribed the words: 'AElfred mec heht gewyrcan' [Alfred had me made]. Whistler has engraved these words in his representation of the jewel. The shape of the Alfred Jewel on the cross, and the reminder through the lettering that this is an inanimate object speaking out, seem to allude ingeniously to the personified cross of the original poem.

It is possible that the decision to depict the Alfred Jewel also held a more personal meaning for Laurence Whistler, in light of his ongoing mourning for his brother Rex's untimely death in the Second World War. In *The Dream of the Rood*, Christ is referred to three times as 'cyning', or king (ll. 44, 56, 133). Whistler's depiction of an object commissioned by King Alfred to suggest Christ's head alludes implicitly to this 'kingly' aspect of Christ in the poem. Whistler, though, may also have had another *rex* [king] in mind. Laurence's relationship with his elder brother Rex had been a close one: it was Rex who gave Laurence his informal artistic education, and continued to be an important influence on the development of his work.[24] After Rex was killed in action in 1942, Laurence devoted much time to publishing books promoting his brother's work and reputation. The meaning of Rex's name is punned on by Laurence in his biography of his brother, where he describes him as 'a child of promise only partly fulfilled, christened Rex to be kingly, and at least regal in generosity'.[25] In depicting a jewel which was commissioned by one king (Alfred the Great, called 'Alfred Rex' on contemporary coinage), and served to suggest the head of another (Christ), Laurence may have had Rex, the 'kingly' one, in mind. If Laurence did build a memory of Rex into the window through his engraving of the Alfred Jewel, then it was presumably because for him the idea of sacrifice was indelibly associated with the death of his brother in the Second World War.

The Alfred Jewel and the other gems engraved by Whistler on this window shine out brightly as an image of light against the darkness behind them. The contrast of dark and light in the window resonates with the significance of imagery of dark and light in the original poem: there, for example, Christ's body is described as a shining radiance against the darkness of the clouds:

> Þystro hæfdon
> bewrigen mid wolcnum Wealdendes hræw,
> scirne sciman; sceadu forð eode,
> wann under wolcnum. (ll. 52–55)

[Darkness had covered with clouds the Ruler's body, its shining radiance; a shadow went forth, black under the clouds.]

The poet here creates a poetic envelope structure, with the radiance of Christ's body shining out from the darkness of clouds which precede and succeed the moment of his death. For Whistler, even more than for *The Dream of the Rood* poet, the contrast between light and dark was integral to his work. The medium of engraved glass depends upon this very contrast: the process of engraving sets the light of the engraved glass against the darkness of what is left unengraved. In his book *The Image on the Glass*, published in the same year as the Dream of the Rood window was made, Whistler said of engraving that 'the light needs the dark to be intelligible'.[26] The symbolic implications of the inextricable link between the two were fully explored by Whistler. In his Dream of the Rood window, the brilliance of the gems is just one part of a design in which the darkness of the sky behind and of the body of the cross itself are equally conspicuous. Through his use of light and dark, he probes the depth of human experience: the inevitable intertwining of joy and melancholy, gain and loss, celebration and suffering, life and death. Most importantly of all, perhaps, he uses light and dark to suggest a contrast between the known and unknown: in the darkness is all that is most mysterious about the universe and its relationship with humanity. The way that Whistler envisions the cross plays an important role in this. Its uneven, almost tentative, outline hints at something that is not quite real and this intangible quality is intensified by the way its dark body merges with the darkness of the sky. The complex and unknowable relationship between the human and the divine is powerfully visualized in the window.

In capturing the visionary quality of the cross, Whistler is of course responding to the Old English poem's dream vision genre and the poet's own evocation of this through dream-like blurring and blending in imagery and narrative. In conception and design, though, it arguably bears comparison too with a more modern artistic rendering of the Crucifixion. In 1951 Salvador Dalí painted an extraordinary depiction of Christ on the cross known as Christ of St John of the Cross. It is a painting that Whistler was no doubt aware of, if only through the controversy it generated amongst modern art critics from the moment it went on display at Glasgow's Kelvingrove Art Gallery and Museum (where it is currently housed) in 1952. Although Whistler does not show any particular interest generally in Dalí's work, he does mention him as an influence on Rex who in 1942 painted (apparently at the request of fellow officers) a surrealist landscape in the style of Dalí.[27]

Salvador Dalí's painting of Christ of St John of the Cross depicts Christ on the cross against a dark sky and hovering over a landscape with hills and a body of water. Dalí attributed the inspiration for the painting to a dream. At the bottom of his studies for the painting he wrote:

> In the first place, in 1950, I had a 'cosmic dream' in which I saw this image in color and which in my dream represented the 'nucleus of the atom'. This nucleus later took on a metaphysical sense; I considered it 'the very unity of the universe', the Christ![28]

The resemblances between the composition of Dalí's painting and Whistler's engraving are worth remarking: the huge visionary cross hovering above the earth, the darkened sky behind it, the band of bright sky below, and the precisely drawn landscape with hills and water at the bottom. Their perspectives on Christ, though, are very different. Dalí's alienating overhead angle shows Christ looming ominously over the landscape; Whistler's front-facing view encourages close engagement with the stylized and complex intertwining of Christ and cross.

If the influence of Dalí played any part in the composition of the window, it would only be as one of a host of sources contributing to the final design. For Whistler, the influence of other writers and painters was an essential element in his own artistic development. With glass engraving he found his own individual

FIG. 5.4. Salvador Dalí, *Christ of St John of the Cross* (1951), Kelvingrove Art Gallery and Museum, Glasgow. Image © CSG CIC Glasgow Museums Collection.

medium: as he puts it in *The Image on the Glass*, 'I had found, by purest chance, a small untrodden lawn of snow to write my name on with the point of a stick'.[29] But he never left behind his earliest artistic influences and constantly found new ones too. The nineteenth-century painters Samuel Palmer and Edward Calvert, he writes, were 'the first after my brother Rex to influence me strongly,' but, he goes on to add, 'since then I have gone to school with other masters'.[30] The Old English poet, the modern English poet Gavin Bone, and the maker of the Alfred Jewel are some of the masters whose influence can be firmly felt in Whistler's visualization in glass of *The Dream of the Rood*. The power of the window is inherently linked to the many different kinds of sources that inspired it.

Creatively reinterpreting an Old English poem, and with recourse to other sources as well, Whistler's engraved glass Dream of the Rood window magnificently visualizes the complexities of human experience where mourning can also be rejoicing, where death can also be life, and where the past, despite its linguistic and cultural distinctiveness, can also be the present. Whistler, just like the poet of *The Dream of the Rood*, expresses the idea of mourning in ways that link it intrinsically to other contrasting elements of human experience. For both poet and glass engraver, medieval and contemporary respectively, the experience of mourning ultimately becomes a means by which human apprehension of the divine can be explored. Through often paradoxical juxtapositions, powerfully conveyed in visual symbols, our relationship to something more mysterious and unknowable is brought to the fore.

Notes to Chapter 5

1. For an important and accessible edition of the poem, see *The Dream of the Rood*, ed. by Michael Swanton (Manchester: Manchester University Press, 1970). Quotations from the poem are cited from this edition. Translations are my own unless otherwise stated.
2. Vercelli, Biblioteca Capitolare, CXVII. See N. R. Ker, *Catalogue of Manuscripts Containing Anglo-Saxon* (Oxford: Clarendon Press, 1957), p. 460, no. 394; Helmut Gneuss and Michael Lapidge, *Anglo-Saxon Manuscripts: A Bibliographical Handlist of Manuscripts and Manuscript Fragments Written or Owned in England up to 1100* (Toronto: University of Toronto Press, 2014), no. 941.
3. See Margaret Schlauch, '*The Dream of the Rood* as Prosopopoeia', in *Essays and Studies in Honour of Carleton Brown*, ed. by P. W. Long (New York: New York University Press, 1940), pp. 23–34.
4. See *The Dream of the Rood*, ed. by Swanton, pp. 94 and 96, for a transliterated rendering of the verses on the Ruthwell Cross. On the relationship between the poem and the Ruthwell Cross, see for example, Jane Roberts, 'Some Relationships between *The Dream of the Rood* and the Cross at Ruthwell', *Studies in Medieval English Language and Literature*, 15 (2000), 1–25.
5. See John Hines, 'The Ruthwell Cross, the Brussels Cross, and *The Dream of the Rood*', in *Transitional States: Change, Tradition, and Memory in Medieval Literature and Culture*, ed. by Graham D. Caie and Michael D. C. Drout (Tempe: Arizona Center for Medieval and Renaissance Studies, 2018), pp. 175–92.
6. See Robin Ravilious, 'Whistler, Sir (Alan Charles) Laurence (1912–2000)' (23 September 2004; rev. 8 October 2009), in *Oxford Dictionary of National Biography* (Oxford: Oxford University Press, 2020) <http://doi.org/10.1093/ref:odnb/75009> [accessed 7 August 2021].
7. Michael Hill, John Newman, and Nikolaus Pevsner, *The Buildings of England: Dorset*, Pevsner Architectural Guides (New Haven, CT: Yale University Press, 2018), p. 426.
8. The art of point-engraving consists of scratching or tapping a glass with a point; it differs from etching on glass in that it involves no use of acid.

9. See Laurence Whistler, *The Laughter and the Urn: The Life of Rex Whistler* (London: Weidenfeld & Nicolson, 1985), p. 93 and passim. For a concise analysis of the range of Whistler's talents, see Jim McCue, 'Laurence Whistler: An Oxford Artist', *Oxford Poetry*, 16.2 (2016), 36–39.
10. Whistler, *The Image on the Glass*, p. 37.
11. The family home of Commander Findlay and his wife, Lady Mary Findlay (who commissioned the window), was Court Lodge in the village of Hastingleigh near Ashford. The family's connection with Kent may also be reflected in some of the Anglo-Saxon jewels that Whistler chose to incorporate in his engraving (for example, the jewelled disc brooch found in Sarre, Kent, and the circular brooch found in Canterbury (both held in the Ashmolean Museum, Oxford) and the disc brooch found at Priory Hill, Kent, now in the British Museum). I am grateful to Dr Michael Bintley (Birkbeck College, London) and Dr Eleanor Standley (University of Oxford) for discussions on this point.
12. Whistler, *The Laughter and the Urn*, p. 186.
13. British Library Sounds, Whistler, Sir Laurence (1 of 5) National Life Stories: Crafts Lives, C960/04 <https://sounds.bl.uk/Oral-history/Crafts/021M-C0960X0004XX-0001V0> [accessed 7 August 2021].
14. I would like to thank Dr Bethany Hamblen, Archivist and Records Manager, Balliol College Library, Oxford, for giving me access to the relevant correspondence.
15. See Laurence Whistler, *Scenes and Signs on Glass* (Woodbridge: The Cupid Press, 1985), plate 26. I would like to thank Robin Ravilious for drawing my attention to this memorial panel. It was presumably made later than the window at Moreton Church since, unlike the latter, it is not included in the 'Check List: Glasses Engraved by Laurence Whistler' published in 1975; see Whistler, *The Image on the Glass*, p. 166 (see also pp. 168–69). The two engravings have interesting similarities and differences; for the purposes of this essay I will focus on the window at Moreton Church.
16. Gavin Bone, *Anglo-Saxon Poetry: An Essay with Specimen Translations in Verse* (Oxford: Clarendon Press, 1943).
17. I would like to thank the Whistler family for making this letter available to me, and for their generous and helpful responses to my enquiries.
18. I am indebted to Professor Tony Edwards for information and helpful discussions about the life and work of Gavin Bone. See now his 'Gavin Bone and his Old English Translations', *Translation and Literature*, 30 (2021), 147–69.
19. Laurence Whistler, *Armed October* (London: Cobden-Sanderson, 1932) and *Four Walls* (London: Heinemann, 1934).
20. Whistler, *The Laughter and the Urn*, p. 54.
21. Whistler, *Scenes and Signs on Glass*, p. 161 and caption to plate 11.
22. For the identification of the figure as Christ as Wisdom, see D. R. Howlett, 'The Iconography of the Alfred Jewel', *Oxoniensia*, 39 (1974), 44–52; for its identification as a personification of Sight, see Egil Bakka, 'The Alfred Jewel and Sight', *Antiquaries Journal*, 46 (1966), 277–82 (endorsed convincingly by Charles D. Wright, 'Why Sight Holds Flowers: An Apocryphal Source for the Iconography of the Alfred Jewel and Fuller Brooch', in *Text, Image, Interpretation: Studies in Anglo-Saxon Literature and its Insular Context in Honour of Éamonn Ó Carragáin*, ed. by Alastair Minnis and Jane Roberts (Turnhout: Brepols, 2007), pp. 169–86).
23. The technique recalls the *Reversible Faces* which Rex Whistler drew for Shell (1931–32), later published separately by Laurence Whistler, where the same features form two distinct characters. See Whistler, *The Laughter and the Urn*, pp. 128–29, and Hugh and Mirabel Cecil, *In Search of Rex Whistler: His Life and His Work* (London: Frances Lincoln, 2012), p. 141.
24. Ravilious, 'Whistler, Sir (Alan Charles) Laurence (1912–2000)'. See also Cecil, *In Search of Rex Whistler*, pp. 246–47.
25. Whistler, *The Laughter and the Urn*, p. 299.
26. Whistler, *The Image on the Glass*, p. 43.
27. Laurence Whistler: 'a Dalí, in which, unevasive as always, he [Rex] included a tank far-off in flames' (*The Laughter and the Urn*, p. 253).
28. Cited in Robert Descharnes, *Dalí* (New York: Harry N. Abrams, 2003), p. 114.
29. Whistler, *The Image on the Glass*, p. 24.
30. Ibid., p. 31.

CHAPTER 6

The Poet's Mourning and the Philosopher's Consolation: René Descartes's Letter of Condolence to Constantijn Huygens

Jürgen Pieters

I

On 10 May 1637, the Dutch poet and diplomat Constantijn Huygens (1596–1687) lost his wife. Like many other women of her time and age, Suzanna Van Baerle fell victim to a fatal infection incurred after having given birth to her first — and, as it turned out, sole — daughter. The little girl had been born two months earlier; she was named after her mother.[1] As we know from the author's Latin diary, Huygens's wife died at five thirty in the afternoon. Six days later, she was buried. The day after the funeral, the grieving husband and his five young children moved to their new house in The Hague, the construction of which Suzanna had supervised in person. 'Alas,' the poet wrote in his diary, 'without my pigeon' ('sine mea turture').[2]

Huygens and his wife had been married for nearly ten years when Suzanna died. They had been wed on 6 April 1627. Suzanna was not Huygens's first love, but she was definitely his most steadfast one.[3] The day of their wedding had been carefully selected: it was scheduled to take place exactly three hundred years after Petrarch had first laid eyes on his Laura in the church of Saint Clare in Avignon. Like many early-modern poets, Huygens was fascinated by Petrarch's work, whose illustrious example he once hoped to emulate.

The closest Huygens ever came to writing a 'genuine' Petrarchan sonnet — as opposed to a number of mere imitations which he produced, destined to remain forever in the great precursor's shadow — was the poem that made his wife immortal, to Dutch ears, at least: 'Op de dood van Sterre' [On the Occasion of Stella's Death]. Huygens wrote his well-known sonnet on 24 January 1638, eight and a half months after Suzanna died.[4] In true Petrarchan vein, Huygens conceived of Suzanna as a 'star' that had been shining in the sky ever since God had called for her. Here is the poem, followed by my own translation, in which I have not attempted to recreate the original sonnet's sound-structure (rhymes, alliteration, meter), nor Huygens's numerous puns:

Of droom ick, en is 't nacht, of is mijn' Sterr verdweenen?
Ick waeck, en 't is hoogh dagh, en sie mijn' Sterre niet.
O Hemelen, die my haer aengesicht verbiedt,
Spreeckt menseche-tael, en seght, waer is mijn' Sterre henen:

Den Hemel slaet geluyt, ick hoor hem door mijn' stenen,
En seght, mijn' Sterre staet in 't heilige gebied,
Daer sy de Godheit, daer de Godheit haer besiet,
En, voeght het lacchen daer, belacht mijn ydel weenen.

Nu, Dood, nu snick, met een verschenen en verby,
Nu doorgangh van een' steen, van een gesteên ten leven,
Dun schutsel, staet naer by; 'k sal 't u te danck vergeven;

Komt, Dood, en maeckt my korts van dese Cortsen vry:
'k Verlangh in 't eewigh licht te samen te sien sweven
Mijn Heil, mijn Life, mijn lijf; mijn' God, mijn' Sterr, en my.[5]

[Might I be dreaming? Has night come, or could it be that my Stella is gone? | I'm wide awake, it's the middle of the day, and I cannot see my Stella. | O heavens, who are forbidding me to see her face, | Speak to me in a language that man can understand, and tell me, where has my Stella gone? | I can hear Heaven's sound through my complaints, | It is telling me that my Stella is in the holy region | Where she can see God and God can see her. | If laughter is allowed there, she must be laughing at these idle tears of mine. | Now, death, now, final sigh, at once appearing and gone, | Now, stony grave, allow me my death-throes, the passage to eternal life, | Thin cover, stand by me: I will give you thanks for it, | Come, death, and release me as soon as possible from these feverish thoughts | I long to see together, suspended in the eternal light, | My fate, my love, my body; my God, my Stella and myself.]

Unfortunately, Huygens was not dreaming. Suzanna had really gone. His children had lost their mother and he himself needed urgently to resume his busy professional occupation as secretary to Stadtholder Frederick Henry, the 'Prince' of the Dutch Republic, who urged his first man in charge to return to court as soon as possible after his wife's funeral.[6] Huygens was given little time to grieve and the harsh reality of her absence would definitely not have been easy to process, as his sonnet on her death makes clear. Added to the poem's title is a Latin phrase that in several reflections on the poem has actually come to take the place of the Dutch title: 'Cupio dissolvi' [I long to be dissolved]. The phrase is borrowed from St Paul, who in his Epistle to the Philippians famously talks about his 'longing to be dissolved' (1:23–24), that is, the longing of his soul to be released from his body and to rise up to God. In Huygens's poem, that longing is at its clearest in the desperate apostrophe to death in line 12.

In the passage from his epistle that contains the phrase to which Huygens alludes, Paul refers to his own desire to exchange life on earth for a higher existence and to be with God ('esse cum Christo') forever. However, in the ensuing line that desire is balanced and eventually overturned by the realization that one can also be with Christ on earth. Moreover — and this is the part of the epistle that will *also* have spoken to Huygens — there are people on earth who are in need of Paul's presence: the Philippians, for one, to whom Paul needs to deliver Christ's message:

> For to me to live is Christ, and to die is gain.
> But if I live in the flesh, this is the fruit of my labour: yet what I shall choose I wot not.
> For I am in a strait betwixt two, *having a desire to depart*, and to be with Christ; which is far better:
> Nevertheless to abide in the flesh is more needful for you.
> And having this confidence, I know that I shall abide and continue with you all for your furtherance and joy of faith;
> That your rejoicing may be more abundant in Jesus Christ for me by my coming to you again. (Epistle to the Philippians 1:21–26, my emphasis)

Like St Paul, Huygens also knew that he was needed on earth. His now motherless children needed to be taken care of and his country, still waging what at that point seemed to be an everlasting war against the Spanish king, also needed his attention. Even though the poem does not refer to Huygens's earthly obligations, their presence is felt in the ambivalent allusion of the Latin title. As Huygens knew all too well, the desire to be taken to Heaven had to be tempered with a reasonable awareness of the tasks that God has given us in life. Without that balance, 'the longing to dissolved' came dangerously close to a mere plea for suicide, a blasphemous one at that.

St Paul's 'Cupio dissolvi', as Huygens will have known — possibly from John Donne's sermons or Montaigne's *Essais*[7] — basically refers to a longing for the Day of Judgement, when God would call unto him the souls of the faithful. The closing lines of Huygens's poem envision that moment at which the poet is convinced he will be reunited with his departed wife. Until that eagerly awaited moment comes, Huygens realized that he needed to fulfill the tasks on earth that his Creator had designed for him. He needed to rest assured and be patient, praying, like Donne (who lost his wife in similar circumstances), that God would be willing to grant him the strength to bear what had to be borne.[8] In one of the sermons in which he reflects upon Paul's 'Cupio dissolvi', Donne ends by saying:

> Enlarge our daies, Lord, to that blessed day, prepare us before that day, all the daies of our life, an assurance in that Kingdome, which thy Son our Saviour hath purchased for us, with the inestimable price of his incorruptible bloud, To which glorious Son of God&c.[9]

II

Around the end of May 1637, a couple of weeks after Suzanna Van Baerle's death, Huygens received a touching letter of condolence, sent by his good friend René Descartes, who had been living in the Dutch Republic since 1629.[10] The letter contains a message of consolation that seems to be steeped in Descartean philosophy. While it teaches us something of Descartes's thinking, it is also quite revealing of the deep friendship that Huygens and the author of the *Discours de la méthode* felt for each other. Even though Descartes's message of comfort is clear, it may sound somewhat crude to twenty-first-century ears. Now that Huygens has finally had to give up hope of Suzanna's recovery, the philosopher writes, he also has to bid leave of the despair that may lead other people, weaker minds than his, to heartache and other destructive emotions. Descartes is convinced that Huygens needs to restart living the life of reason; that is, he needs to understand that whatever happens in life is necessary. Suzanna did not just die, she died because God decided that her time had come, and because bodily mortality is a necessary component of human life. Here is the central passage in Descartes's letter, which I want to relate in what follows to the vision upon which Huygens's sonnet ends:

> I am in no way doubtful that you will allow yourself to be entirely directed by reason. Which is why I am convinced that it will be much easier for you to find your own comfort and to regain your habitual ease of mind, now that there is no more remedy in sight, in contrast to the time when you could still find occasion to live in fear and hope. It is, after all, a fact that, when all hope is gone, our desire also declines — at least, it releases its grip and diminishes in strength. When we have but little desire (or none at all) to regain what we have lost, there is little room left for strong regret. It is true that those who are of a weaker spirit cannot appreciate this logic at all. Without realizing what they are telling themselves, they imagine that what has been different before can still be the case, and that God is, as it were, under a loving obligation to do for them whatever it is that they want. But a strong and generous soul such as yours, who is aware of the workings of our nature, always submits herself to the necessity of nature's law. And even though it takes considerable effort for this to happen, I value friendship so highly that I think that everything from which we suffer out of friendship is pleasant in itself, to the extent even that those who die for the wellbeing of the people they love, to me seem to be happy to the very last moment of their lives.[11]

Descartes is praising Huygens in this letter for what he labels the generosity of his friend's soul. But what exactly does he mean by this? And how on earth could this injunction be at all consoling? As he was to make clear, twelve years later, in his *Passions de l'âme* (1649), generosity, to Descartes, is the quality of a person who is humbly aware of their own possibilities and limitations, able to find a balance between their powers of volition and their determination to think and act rightly. 'True Generosity,' as we can read in Descartes's definition of the concept in Article 153 of the *Passions de l'âme*, 'makes a man esteem himself as highly as he can legitimately esteem himself'. It consists, as Descartes goes on to write:

> Partly in his understanding that there is nothing which truly belongs to him but this free control of his volitions, and no reason why he ought to be praised or blamed except that he uses it well or badly; and partly in his feeling within himself a firm and constant resolution to use it well, that is, never to lack the volition to undertake and execute all the things he judges to be best — which is to follow virtue perfectly.[12]

What generosity boils down to, as Descartes puts it in a later article, is 'the volition we feel within ourselves always to make good use of our free will'.[13]

In Article 155 of his treatise ('What virtuous Humility consists in'), Descartes couples the quality of generosity to the Christian ideal of *humilitas*: 'the most

Generous are usually the most humble', Descartes claims. After all:

> Virtuous Humility just consists in this: our reflection on the infirmity of our nature and on the errors we may previously have committed or are capable of committing — which are no less than those which may be committed by others — causes us not to prefer ourselves to anyone, but to think that since others have their own free will just as we do, they can use it too.[14]

The opposite of generosity is 'pride', as we can further read in Article 157 of the *Passions de l'âme.* Those who are blessed with a generous soul, Descartes writes, 'are entirely masters of their Passions, particularly Desires, Jealousy, and Envy'.[15] Descartes's discussion of the opposition between generosity and pride makes clear that, in the end, those who excel in the former quality are not only in control of their free will and their passions, but also of their faculty of reason. Generous people not only behave and act in the proper way, they also *think* rightly. The 'vice' of pride is 'so unreasonable and so absurd,' Descartes writes, 'that I would hardly have believed there were men who gave themselves up to it'.[16]

Later in his treatise, Descartes also discusses the two passions which he urges Huygens to give up in his letter of condolence: hope and fear — or 'Apprehension', as the latter is labelled in the treatise. According to Descartes, the two passions are of a pair. As he writes in Article 165 ('About Hope and Apprehension'):

> Hope is a disposition of the soul to be convinced that what it desires will come to pass, caused by a particular movement of the spirits, namely by that of Joy and Desire mingled together. And Apprehension is another disposition of the soul, convincing that it will not come to pass.[17]

The fact that hope and apprehension are opposites does not mean that they never coincide in the emotional economy of an individual. Descartes writes:

> Although these two Passions are opposites, we can nevertheless have both of them at once, namely when we simultaneously represent different reasons to ourselves, some making us judge that the fulfillment of the Desire is easy, the others making it appear difficult.[18]

In the course of the weeks before Suzanna Van Baerle's death, Huygens may well have found himself in the conflicting sort of situation that Descartes is describing here, torn between two passions that moved him in opposite directions. The philosopher's suggestion that Suzanna's death put an end to this difficult situation may sound, if not cruel, then at least cold to us, but it is entirely in line with the classical regime of consolation to which Descartes's letter is clearly related.[19] Consolation can be found in rational reflection, which means that those who wish to bring comfort need to argue, first and foremost, against the blinding force of our emotions. This is exactly what Descartes does at the beginning of his letter: he urges Huygens to regain his rational composure, the 'tranquillité d'esprit' that is so characteristic of 'generous' people. Once he has been able to steer away from the emotional turmoil in which his wife's illness has left him, Huygens will be able to find comfort for himself (consolation, for Descartes, seems to be self-consolation, primarily).

III

Now that Suzanna is gone, Descartes is effectively arguing, Huygens can come back to his reason. And in that reason, he will see the comforting logic that his wife's death was inevitable. What happened, needed to happen, Descartes decides, not only because God wanted it to happen, but also because this is how nature functions. Obviously, we do not know what Huygens felt when he read Descartes's letter. Maybe he was touched by the wisdom of his friend's words. Maybe he considered them as distant and cold as we might be inclined to.

At first sight, it would seem that in his sonnet Huygens is doing the exact opposite of what his friend suggests he should do. The desire to keep 'Sterre' (Stella) at his beck and call (a desire that Descartes ascribes to 'des esprits faibles' [weak spirits]) seems to have grown stronger by the end of the poem, especially if we relate it to the desire to which the poem's Latin title alludes. Huygens will have wrestled with the logic that Descartes tries to instill in him. This we can surmise from the copy of Descartes's letter that was preserved and later edited by Leon Roth. In the margin of Descartes's consolatory reflection that the grieving husband's desire would decrease along with his hope, Huygens wrote a line from a poem by Petrarch that may as well be taken to express the very opposite of what Descartes meant: ''l desir vive, et la speranza è morta' [desire is alive and hope is dead]. The line is taken from the sonnet *Rvf* 277 of the *Canzoniere*, one of the poems 'after the death of Laura'. Like Huygens's Stella, Petrarch's beloved is a star in heaven, 'from where she shines brighter than ever in the heart'. In Anthony Kline's translation, the entire sonnet reads as follows:

> If Love does not bring me new counsel,
> my life must change, unwillingly:
> the sad heart's anguished so with grief and fear,
> now desire still lives, but hope is dead:
>
> so my life's confused, discomforted,
> completely, and I weep night and day,
> weary, rudderless in a stormy sea,
> on an uncertain course with no true pilot.
>
> An imaginary guide leads me, since my true
> one is under the earth, or rather in heaven,
> from where she shines brighter than ever in the heart:
>
> but not to my eyes, because a sad veil
> conceals that longed-for light from them,
> and makes my hair white before my time.[20]

In Petrarch's original text, the third and fourth lines of the poem are related to each other in a different way from the English translation: 'tanta paura et duol l'alma trista ange, | che 'l desir vive, et la speranza è morta'.[21] What the couplet says is that the poet's fear ('paura') and pain ('duol') are such ('tanta') that his desire continues to live while his hope has gone. In Huygens's version of the line, the first word ('che') has disappeared. In isolation from the original context of the poem's opening stanza, the singled-out line gives the impression of denying Descartes's consolatory reason rather than subscribing to it. Read in the context of the opening stanza — and, indeed, of the entire sonnet — the line is closer to Descartes's message of comfort: if the poet allows himself to remain under the spell of his emotions, he will never be able to (re)find comfort's calm reassurance. After all, as Petrarch's poem makes clear, those who are driven by the storm of their emotions, find themselves 'rudderless', 'on an uncertain course with no true pilot'.

Like Huygens, Petrarch is torn by the absence of his love, whom he can no longer see with the eyes that he mentions in the poem's closing stanza. His longing for her is still alive, even though the hope that he will be able to see her in this life has gone forever. In the poems that follow *Rvf* 277 in the composition of the *Canzoniere*, the poet's awareness that the light of true love cannot be seen by his mortal eyes grows steadily. True love comes from the spiritual light that radiates from Laura in heaven. It is the light which the poet will only be able to experience when he meets her in the beyond, face to face, 'in the eternal light' to which Huygens refers in the penultimate line of his sonnet. 'To see her once again I have to die,' Petrarch exclaims in the sonnet *Rvf* 291: the line can be seen as his variant of the 'Cupio dissolvi' motif. Interestingly, in the sonnet *Rvf* 302, Petrarch's beloved Laura addresses the poet, in anticipation of the moment when they will meet again: 'She took my hand, and said: "If my desire | is not in error, you will be with me again in this sphere"'. In the sonnet *Rvf* 290, desire and hope, the two emotions that Descartes singled out in his letter to Huygens, are qualified as 'sempre fallace' [always deceiving], but it is clear that in heavenly Laura's case, 'desir' (the desire of divine Love) can never be mistaken.

There is a final poem by Petrarch that I want to single out in its entirety, because it echoes not only the final vision of Huygens's sonnet 'On the Death of Stella', but also Descartes's urging, in the letter of condolence, that his friend find comfort for himself. The sonnet is *Rvf* 345, which in Kline's translation reads as follows:

> Love and grief drove my tongue astray
> where it should not go, in its lamenting,
> to say of her, for whom I sang and burned,
> that which, even if true, would be wrong:
>
> her blessedness should calm my sad state,
> and console my heart, seeing her
> so at home with Him who was
> always in her heart when she was living.
>
> And I do calm and comfort myself:
> not wishing to see her in this inferno,
> wishing rather to die or live alone:
>
> whom I have seen in the mind's eye lovelier
> than ever, flying, on high with the angels,
> to the feet of her, and my, eternal Lord.

'Anzi voglio morire': Petrarch's tenth line calls to mind the Pauline 'longing to be dissolved', but the poem's closing stanza marks an important difference with the vision that is presented at the end of Huygens's sonnet. In Petrarch's poem, the vision of the poet's 'occhio interno' is such that he sees Laura in the heavenly vicinity of God. His own perspective remains that of a mere mortal, imagining his true Love from what is still a sublunary position, 'in questo inferno'. Huygens's final vision gives the impression of being more complex. The closing lines of his sonnet can be taken to suggest that he is longing for a place where not only is he able to simply be together with Stella in heaven, but where he can also see himself, together with her and the God they both serve. The lines indicate that he is on the lookout for a dual perspective, so to say, a different 'dissolution', as it were. In the world of our regular senses that is simply impossible and in the world of the imagination it is a mere fiction. But the final vision of Huygens's sonnet does not involve the 'seeing' of the imagination: it is the 'seeing' of meditation, far superior to the two types of looking that Huygens introduces in the opening line of his sonnet: dreaming and waking.

IV

Earlier in this text, I related Descartes's efforts to bring comfort to what I labelled the classical regime of consolation. Huygens was sufficiently schooled in Cicero and Seneca to recognize the humanist background of his philosopher-friend's arguments. His familiarity with Boethius's *De consolatione philosophiae* made him aware, furthermore, how these arguments could be made subservient to the basic consolatory axiom of Christian thinking: the faithful need to take comfort in the wisdom of God, of whose grace that wisdom is the very foundation. In 1647, ten years after his wife's death, Huygens published a long consolatory poem that was addressed to a good friend of his who was slowly turning blind. In the poem, which he also discussed with Descartes, he made ample use of Boethius's *Consolation of Philosophy* as well as of the third book of the *Tusculanae disputationes,* which contains Cicero's eclectic reflections on the diverse classical 'schools' of consolation.[22] The central underlying argument of the consolatory text marks the difference between the classical and the Christian regimes of comfort: while in the former regime the woman's predicament could be taken as a whim of fate that needed to be borne with equanimity and rational understanding, it is now presented as the outcome of God's providential design. God wanted this to happen, so Huygens's friend needs to have faith in the right(eous)ness of his decree.

The same idea lies behind both Huygens's sonnet on his wife's death and Descartes's letter of condolence — and Petrarch's poems, for that matter. In my monograph on the historical interrelationships between literature and consolation, I have tried to show that the modern regime of consolation differs significantly from the classical and Christian regimes. The most marked difference, in my view, is this: while both the classical and Christian regimes of consolation are supported by what one could call the self-evidence of consolatory success, in the modern regime of consolation the fundamental impossibility of being consoled ('Untröstlichkeit', as Hans Blumenberg calls it) is the norm rather than the exception.[23] In the classical and Christian regimes, words and acts of consolation only fail if the person who is being consoled fails to understand their intention and effects in the proper way. In the modern regime, that failure is a given, as it were, not something to be avoided. Whereas in classical and Christian thought, the successful act of consolation involves the return of the suffering individual to the collective from which their suffering resulted in a temporary exile (a return to the *sensus communis*, in the classical regime, and to God in the Christian one), the modern notion of consolation is founded on an altogether different idea of suffering: the loss for which we need to be consoled cannot really be repaired in this regime; after that loss there is in no way a 'before' to which to return.

The decline in the importance of religion in Western modernity is obviously an important aspect in this specific development. The largely secular perspective that marks the modern regime of consolation goes a long way towards explaining why we find it difficult to see the intrinsically comforting value of God's providential design. The inhuman endurance of Job, the iconic figure of Christian consolation, is alien to many of us, I would think. Similarly, whenever we read a classical *consolatio* — Plutarchus's letter to his wife on the death of their daughter, for instance — we are usually struck by these writings' strong (and, to our ears, strange) belief in the sheer comforting force of rational argumentation.

Judging by the case that was central to this chapter, however, the basic difference (if not opposition) between pre-modern and modern ideas of consolation does not necessarily hold for conceptions of mourning. At the risk of drawing an all-too-hasty conclusion, I am tempted to hear in Descartes's analysis of the process in his letter to Huygens an echo of Freud's description of mourning in 'Trauer und Melancholie' [Mourning and Melancholia]. As Freud sees it, those who succumb to the latter fail to get a sound grip on their desire for the loved one, whose passing away these frustrated mourners just do not seem to be able to accept. In Freud's view, the lasting force of that desire inevitably results in the unsound form of mourning that melancholy is. Describing the difficulty of the process and the dangers of excessive mourning to Ludwig Binswanger in 1929, Freud writes:

> Although we know that after such a loss the acute stage of mourning will subside, we also know we shall remain inconsolable and will never find a substitute. No matter what may fill the gap, even if it be filled completely, it nevertheless remains something else.[24]

In his letter of condolence to Huygens, Descartes sounds even more apodictic: now that all hope has gone, his friend will surely be able to avoid the despair that accompanies an all too lengthy loss of one's reason. Excessive grief is unreason, as Descartes knew. Not that he knew Shakespeare's play, but he would surely have agreed with Hamlet's murderous uncle:

> It shows a will most incorrect to heaven,
> A heart unfortified, a mind impatient,
> An understanding simple and unschooled.
> (*Hamlet*, 1.2.95–97)

Huygens would also have agreed, but that did not stop him from grieving properly. On the very day that he wrote his sonnet 'On the Death of Stella', he also wrote a brief Latin poem in which he reproached a friend who had urged him to consider remarrying. However amicable, the very suggestion went against the nature of the grieving poet's commitment to his love, in life as well as in his poetry. Like Petrarch's Laura, Suzanna remained the one who could not be replaced, even — and maybe even more so — 'in morte'. Huygens never remarried: he died on 28 March 1687, just under half a century after his beloved Stella.

Notes to Chapter 6

This chapter is based on several paragraphs taken from Jürgen Pieters, *Op zoek naar Huygens: Italiaanse leesnotities* (Gent: KANTL/Poëziecentrum, 2014), pp. 44–55. It also contains new material.

1. Mart J. van Lieburg, 'Constantijn Huygens en Suzanna van Baerle: een pathobiografische bijdrage', *De zeventiende eeuw*, 3 (1987), 171–78.
2. *Dagboek van Constantyn Huygens, voor de eerste maal naar het afschrift van diens kleinzoon uitgegeven*, ed. by J. H. W. Unger (Amsterdam: Gebr. Binger, 1885), p. 30. For another account of Suzanna's death see Jacob Smit, *De grootmeester van woord- en snarenspel* ('s Gravenhage: Nijhoff, 1980), pp. 191–92, and Elizabeth Keesing, *Het volk met lange rokken: vrouwen rondom Constantijn Huygens* (Amsterdam: Querido, 1987), pp. 85–86.
3. For a full account of their courtship, see Frans R. E. Blom and A. Leerintveld, '"Vrouwenschoon met Mannelicke reden geluckigh verselt": de *perfect match* met Susanna van Baerle', in *Vrouwen rondom Huygens*, ed. by E. Kloek, F. Blom, and A. Leerintveld (Hilversum: Verloren, 2010), pp. 97–114.
4. For fuller analyses of the poem see, among others: J. J. M. Westenbroek, 'An Anatomy of Melancholy: Huygens' "Op de dood van sterre" en de afsluiting van "Dagh-werck"', *Spiegel der Letteren*, 13.3 (1970–71), 161–73; D. M. Bakker, 'Huygens' Op de dood van Sterre: analyse van interpretaties van de eerste regel', in *Opstellen door vrienden en vakgenoten aangeboden aan Dr. C. H. A. Kruyskamp*, ed. by H. Heestermans ('s-Gravenhage: Nijhoff, 1977), pp. 15–24; R. Lievens, 'Huygens' Op de dood van Sterre', *Handelingen van de Koninklijke Zuidnederlandse Maatschappij*, 26 (1972), 325–33; F. L. Zwaan, 'Repliek' [on the former contribution by R. Lievens], *Handelingen van de Koninklijke Zuidnederlandse Maatschappij*, 27 (1973), 152–56; Sonja Witstein, 'Huygens en Petrarca', in *Een Wett-steen vande Ieught* (Groningen: Wolters-Noordhoff, 1980), pp. 111–14; L. Strengholt, '"Of droom ick?" Over de eerste regels van *Op de dood van Sterre*', in *Huygens Studies: Bijdragen tot het onderzoek van de poëzie van Constantijn Huygens* (Amsterdam: Buijten en Schipperheijn, 1976), pp. 101–13.
5. Constantijn Huygens, 'Op de dood van Sterre', in *Korenbloemen*, ed. by Ton van Strien (Amsterdam: Querido, 1996), p. 21.
6. 'Redeo in Aulam a Principe vocatus', Huygens notes in his diary on 19 May 1637 [I am returning to Court, upon the Prince's request]: *Dagboek van Constantyn Huygens*, ed. by Unger, p. 30.
7. We know that he was familiar with both works. For his use of Montaigne's *Essais*, see Jürgen Pieters and Christophe Van der Vorst, '"Cui Dono Lepidum Novum Libellum?": Huygens' *Ooghen-troost* door een nieuwe bril', *Nederlandse letterkunde*, 14.1 (2009), 49–76. For Montaigne's reference to the 'Cupio dissolvi' motif, see M. A. Screech, *Montaigne & Melancholy: The Wisdom of the Essays* (London: Duckworth, 2000), pp. 45–46. As we know from his autobiography, Huygens met Donne in person in 1624. Later, he translated several of Donne's poems into Dutch. From the auction list of his personal library, we know that he had a 1622 copy of Donne's sermons. See: <https://adcs.home.xs4all.nl/Huygens/varia/catal.html> [accessed 8 August 2021]. For the details of his meeting with Donne, see Constantijn Huygens, *Mijn leven verteld aan mijn kinderen*, ed. by F. R. Blom, 2 vols (Amsterdam: Prometheus/Bert Bakker, 2003), I, 127, and II, 220–21.
8. John Stubbs, *Donne: The Reformed Soul* (London: Viking, 2006), p. 318.
9. John Donne, 'Sermon Preached at Whitehall March 3 1619', in *The Sermons of John Donne*, ed. by G. R. Potter and E. M. S. Simpson, 10 vols (Berkeley: University of California Press, 1953–62), II, 363.

10. The letter is dated 20 May 1637. See *Correspondence of Descartes and Constantyn Huygens: 1635–1647*, ed. by Leon Roth (Oxford: Clarendon Press, 1926), pp. 45–48. All translations are my own.
11. Ibid., p. 46.
12. René Descartes, *The Passions of the Soul*, trans. by Stephen Voss (Indianapolis, IN, & Cambridge: Hackett, 1989), p. 104 (Article 153).
13. Ibid., p. 106 (Article 158).
14. Ibid., p. 105 (Article 155).
15. Ibid., p. 105 (Article 156).
16. Ibid., p. 106 (Article 157).
17. Ibid., p. 110 (Article 165).
18. Ibid., pp. 110–11 (Article 165).
19. For an outline of that regime, see Chapter 1 in Jürgen Pieters, *Literature and Consolation: Fictions of Comfort* (Edinburgh: Edinburgh University Press, 2021), pp. 23–61. See also Chapter 3 in the present volume.
20. Petrarca, *The Complete Canzoniere*, trans. by Kline. Subsequent references to Petrarch's poems in translation are to this edition.
21. Francesco Petrarca, *Canzoniere*, ed. by Marco Santagata (Milan: Mondadori, 1996), p. 1122. Subsequent references to Petrarch's original poems are to this edition.
22. The poem's title is 'Ooghen-troost' [Comfort for the Eyes]. See Pieters, *Op zoek naar Huygens*, pp. 97–118.
23. Hans Blumenberg, 'Trostbedürfnis und Untröstlichkeit des Menschen', in *Beschreibung des Menschen* (Frankfurt: Suhrkamp, 2006), pp. 623–55.
24. *Letters of Sigmund Freud 1873–1939*, ed. by Freud and trans. by Stern, p. 386.

INTERMEZZO NO. 2

Tufts in Straggling Thunder: On Kristina Carlson, *Mr Darwin's Gardener*, translated by Emily Jeremiah and Fleur Jeremiah

Timothy Mathews

Part of a set chronicling a passage of time, this piece seeks to bridge subjective and communal experience. Like Walter Benjamin wandering through the arcades of Paris in the 1920s and 30s, it's driven by the intuition that art matters among all the wares on offer. But also that it speaks indirectly, as an accompaniment to the traumas and hopes of life, like a silent song for which I'm trying to find some words with which to speak to you.

> It is the mind that was woven, the mind that was jerked
> And tufted in straggling thunder and shattered sun.
> — WALLACE STEVENS*

There are any number of reasons for a person to pick up a book and begin to read it. I was struck not only by the profile of the Peirene Press but the word 'Peirene' itself, the sound of it, and also the mental decisions as to how to pronounce it which went on in the voices in my own head. I've never known anyone called Irene, perhaps that's why the word Peirene transports me to another time in the past, a different generation now transported back to me in some way by the sound in my ear. The prospect of irenic reconciliation instead of conflict also murmurs away, reconciliation between generations as well as attitudes, and instead of everyday indifference and violence bubbling away too. But Peirene is the name of a nymph, daughter of a river god though it's unclear which, and who knows whether a mother was needed? But she became a mother herself, and when her child by the sea god Poseidon died, she was so overcome by grief, her tears were so unending that they transformed her into a fountain. It can still be seen in Corinth. Or the imaginary one known to people familiar with classical mythology, closely or distantly, and caught up in some other way in its fraying seams. In any case, if you imagine a fountain now it'll have some connection to a real one you've known, and in this story of water, water everywhere, are you hearing loss or renewal?

* Wallace Stevens, 'The Dwarf', in *Parts of the World* [1942], in *The Collected Poems of Wallace Stevens*, ed. by John N. Serio and Chris Beyers (New York: Vintage Books, 2015), p. 221.

Peirene Press books are short, the boundary between immersion in them and in the ephemera of the rest of life quite unsteady. The press supports the Maya Centre, a counselling group offering psychotherapy for women in London on low incomes, the purchase of each book triggers a donation, and I couldn't help feeling a connection perhaps never to be made with that psychic fragility, known if at all to individuals alone. The book is not only a linguistic translation from Finnish to English, but also between generations, mother and daughter working over distances dividing them but with the same languages. It seems to transport the reader back and forth between a kind of Nordic desolation and the home counties of England. A tenuous sense of community hovered over the book as I began to read it and just as I began to discover how much the community inside it was under stress.

It begins with a congregation, which extends upwards and sideways to weave the fabric of the book. It is made from many characters, or rather voices, which emerge from under the cloud of a 'we' and which gradually individuate. But their voices never quite do become distinct, some have very similar names, like Henry and Harry, and the proximity of those two isn't any less troubling when I discover that one is the father of the other and also the nature of the relation between them. The 'we' sit in the church 'smelling of wet dog and the hard church pew is not easy on the bum'. There's a sense of a frozen and desolate piety shrouding the opening pages, perhaps it's generated by free association with the Finnish life and language I imagined the translators trying to convey. The congregation smells neither good nor bad, and it is neither good nor bad, 'when we clasp our hands in prayer we bring both sides of ourselves together', who could ask for anything more humane or humble, and devout? And yet what are those two sides so blithely or even brutally reconciled in the cold and the wet? What a tangled web we weave, and what an entangled bank there is as well in these opening pages, there's a sense of tension simmering away but also a wealth and variety of plant life sprouting everywhere — by contrast, or compensation? Or secret affiliation? 'Weeds are the stuff of parables' we hear someone say as anyone there might, 'just like in the Bible, and God had a hell of a job weeding out the rushes, thistles and couch grass'. To me it seemed like the voice of a woman.

But the book has many voices all lost in one another, and reading it is like watching a play with many characters played by many fewer actors, perhaps a play by Bertolt Brecht where the actors come and go taking various parts and attitudes, and viewers start looking at the issue in different places, if they can find it. Or like watching a play by Complicité and getting tied up in the web of its pressure points. Gradually different voices do settle, and the lines in the sand of the British class system begin to re-appear. There's a doctor, there's a family of shopkeepers, it seems like a general store, there's also an inventor, his design for an adjustable funnel doesn't seem to be getting anywhere for him, and there's a book club for women and women writers. One of these voices belongs to Mr Darwin's gardener, in the village of Downe near Bromley in Kent, where Charles Darwin moved with his family in 1842 and lived until his death in 1882. Finland has landed south of London; quite some time before London and Bromley grew into each other.

The novel opens with an image of the village idiot, Edwin, and somehow I knew I was being mesmerized not by a dramatic announcement but the fabric of the book, the way the details of life can lead anywhere and disclose or confuse what people show. Many of the opening pages give barely perceptible clues of things to come. An accident. An assault. A birth. But mostly the sense of a confused or broken language. There's a relation waiting to be formed, it includes the human and the animal, also the human and the vegetal. This is how Carlson evokes chickens clucking in the mind of someone, a voice in a voice:

> jack-daws rabb-le grey coats think they are bet-ter than ver-ger and vic-ar when the bell tolls the who-le crowd dis-per-ses and all souls burst into soot flakes.

The communication of animals is differently translated in all human languages, and rings differently in the mother-tongue of anyone. Memory gives way to constraint before you know it, and right here the translation of animal sounds translates into pressure and resentment, who's better than whom in the pecking order, before it all goes up in smoke. Or soot, with its associations of the industrial revolution, or the warm middle-class fireside with children sweeping the chimneys. All vapourized now anyway, it seems, but with what damage to the souls of those who come later? Connections continue to teeter, the narrative unfolds along the loosest of associations, metaphor and its sense of purpose collapses and spreads sideways.

All God's creatures have hearts on the left side of their breasts, though I'm not sure about fish and snakes and lizards. Thomas's wife died and the daughter, now eleven was not right from birth, and the son aged six, is small and frail and strange and not good at fighting.

I'm reminded of a prose poem by Charles Baudelaire, not because poetry beautifies, but on the contrary because Baudelaire is also trying to give voice to the fits and starts of consciousness, especially the way intimate and commonplace thoughts seep into each other until the difference dissolves and it's unclear who is talking to whom, or how violence and indifference become so commonplace themselves. An incipient sense of trauma emerges in the weave of these voices, it's brutal, it envelops them all, across all the sliding differences between them, and between reader and writer and translators. Lurking resentment and the crimes that found a society begin to show.

Margaret, the daughter of Harry and Elaine Rowe the shopkeepers selling general goods, and the sister of Henry, Margaret has had an illegitimate child and is to be sent away to avoid the scandal. The father is Daniel, the verger who steals from the donations box and drinks the communion wine. The same Daniel who is said to have conversations with Charles Darwin, but who publishes a fabricated account of them in *The Edinburgh Review*, in which he attributes to Darwin the idea that the weak should be allowed to wither with no precious resources given them. Daniel is set upon and left for dead by the men in the community of church-goers, believers or not; attacked in a road from the village, a sack put over his head, kicked and beaten and left for dead. But Elaine Rowe finds him, patches him up and sends him on his way. With the result that neither the all-but murder nor the act of Christian charity can be mentioned, both are crimes against the laws of society and this society. Who knows from what distance or proximity as readers we imagine them? Illegitimacy, abjection, silenced by social stability, but silenced in return.

Why is Darwin embroiled with trauma and violence? Why does this short novel in which everything disperses explore grief through Darwin and Darwin through grief?

Thomas the gardener plants seeds according to the seasons and according to Mr Darwin's plans. His wife died a slow death leaving him with their mentally disabled daughter and son with a growth defect. He wonders why they should all survive, the three of them. But the time comes when Thomas stops shouting his despair at the wind and the rain. A time to banish God and get on with his life; the God that has haunted him since childhood, voices of fire and brimstone that fill his head still and overwhelm him. But he sees a different God. And hears only his silence. He hears 'what silence sounds like when even the wind fails the bare branches and the snow falls down. God passed but left Tom his daughter and his son, the soft reinforcement of the four-stranded rope'. What does reinforcement sound like or feel like that comes from things, from objects like this twined rope that entwined things together, and someone to others, and perhaps it still does, but how can it now? The looseness of the metonymies all over the writing seems to confirm the fragility of connections, attachments hover over their own disintegration, and relations seem to have lost their weave: the daughter who can't think right, the son who can't grow right, the wife whose death is felt like a skin.

God has passed, and yet the sound of passing is left, the signs of signs, insignia and features, and the voices of voices. All of them show all we can know of evolution and the life that it gives. Has Thomas the gardener reconciled spirituality and Darwinism? The world he inhabits is overcrowded with box trees, magnolias, brilliant bougainvillea, fragrant lilies in different colours, hundreds of different roses, narcissi and hyacinths, there seem no seams or sacks or beds or borders or containers at all. In his fantasy butterflies of silver and gold float on the branches of real trees with a mechanism to make their wings flutter. It's their beauty that flutters over his mind, and now between readers and their shadow. He can see beauty at work, how it works, how life has come to be, in its vast independence from him and in which he is also included. The workings of his mind return to him in the workings of the world, each leaving its imprints in the magic of the other.

Purged of exploiting the weak in the name of progress, Darwin describes the unpredictable wonder of life. Purged of vengeance God offers a house of generosity, where voices echo without drowning each other out. Has Thomas found one in the other? Or when he hears the silence of God everywhere is he suffering a psychotic episode, drowning in his own exile? At the end, no-one can tell whether he's demented with grief or integrated with life and family. On the verge of a mad and brutal act of violence to purge his pain and the world of imperfect beings. Or accepting life and its melancholy; but also its community.

The book's confusing pathways have drawn me into the violence of people to each other; immersed me at the same time in the healing people offer each other, and the poetry needed to understand it. Minds shattered are also woven, beaten like a brass shield refracting the light of others. Worn out, worn, waiting to be worn, loose congregations of people may find the freedom to speak. A book to make us wonder at life and work at life.

PART III

The Politics of Mourning

CHAPTER 7

❖

'I did it. I do not deny it': Mourning, Tragedy, and the Law in Contemporary Philosophy

Uta Staiger

grief, *n.*
Deep or violent sorrow, caused by loss or trouble. *In modern use.*
A wrong or injury which is the subject of formal complaint or demand for redress. *Obsolete.* (*OED*)

Ash
is astounding.
Made out of death yet
sort of offhand.
— Anne Carson[1]

There could hardly be a more excruciatingly subjective experience than grief. By definition, mourning is neither transferable nor repeatable: it is how we, as individuals, attempt to deal with the immensity of personal loss. Even so, it has always been subject to constraints that are socially or clinically determined. Just as Freud originally compared a regular, temporary reaction to loss with a pathological variant 'that is absorbing [the mourner] so entirely',[2] Claudius cautioned Hamlet that once the 'filial obligation' of 'obsequious sorrow' was done, it had better stop:

To persevere
In obstinate condolement is a course
Of impious stubbornness. 'Tis unmanly grief.
(*Hamlet*, 1.2.92–94)

Hamlet of course does nothing but persevere until he brings about his own death, and that of the entire royal house of Denmark. Unconstrained grief, it appears, may not only run up against prevailing norms of health, morality, and gender. It also easily spills over into areas that are political or legal in nature. As with Hamlet, mourning can lead to a singular preoccupation with rectifying the injury that is associated with loss — even where such redress would lead to (further) transgressions of the law. It is in this sense, certainly, that mourning becomes Electra.[3] To grieve, as Bonnie Honig puts it, carries a double meaning which we overlook at our peril: 'it means both to express grief and to litigate or seek redress for a wrong'.[4]

Mourning clearly has an uneasy relationship with the 'body of rules [...] which a particular state or community recognises as binding on its members or subjects', as the *OED* defines 'law'. But it may also have a surprisingly close correlation with how a political 'community recognises [rules] as binding' in the first place — and by extension, defines itself *qua* community. As we shall see, this nexus played a not insignificant role in shaping the democratic *polis* in the fifth century BCE, and it has proved a source of fascination in the history of thought ever since. This fascination, of course, is fuelled by the fact that, not least since German idealism, philosophy engaged with this nexus by way of *aesthetic* source texts that were themselves a historically circumscribed representation of mourning: Greek tragedy. Indeed, as Miriam Leonard put it, 'the history of thought and the meaning of tragedy today are inextricably linked'.[5] But, in another twist of the story, it is some strands of philosophy themselves that are now coming under scrutiny for being excessively mournful. Lamenting the very losses (of rationalism, universalism, sovereignty) they have striven to do away with, do some thinkers now reinstate universalism through the backdoor of shared human suffering — and if so, does this mitigate their critical efficacy?

This chapter will trace some of these twists and turns in the relationship between mourning, philosophy, and the law. Teetering somewhat perilously on the brink of disciplinary decorum, it will touch on texts, stagings, and paintings in order to examine if, and if so how, mourning may retain a political and critical force to be reckoned with.

Antigone Revisited

Where else would we start this journey but with the most iconic of mourners, Antigone? Central to Western philosophy especially from the late eighteenth century onwards — Hegel to Heidegger, Kierkegaard to Lacan, Nietzsche to Žižek — she holds an unrivalled place in our political imagination. Hers of course is quite the story. Recall that Oedipus's sons Polynices and Eteocles, brothers to Antigone and Ismene, vie for the Theban throne following their father's banishment. Polynices leads an army against Thebes to claim the throne from Eteocles — both die. The now king of Thebes, Creon, the siblings' maternal uncle and father of Antigone's husband-to-be Haemon, decreed that Eteocles was to be given proper burial, while the attacker was 'to be left unwept, unburied' (l. 35).[6] Antigone defies this prohibition and buries Polynices twice, confirms it twice ('I did it. I do not deny it', l. 492), a crime for which she is ultimately condemned to death.[7]

Hegel used Antigone's mourning in *The Phenomenology of Spirit* to describe a fundamental conflict of law. On one side of the Hegelian scale falls divine law, represented by womankind and the home, associated with the earth-dwelling *chthonic* gods and characterized by intuition. Divine law becomes manifest primarily by the women's task of tending to the family's dead, which reaffirmed each member as belonging to a common universal. On the other side is human law, associated with the Olympian *Tagesgötter*, characterized by consciousness and represented by man who, by moving across the threshold to the public realm, has become a citizen. The *polis*, embodied in the citizenry, exercises its authority by constraining individual acts. Importantly, the opposition is such that, when in conflict, the woman will see human law as nothing but 'the violence of human caprice', while the man will see only the 'disobedience of the individual' to said law.[8] Against procedural reason of state, the 'rebellious principle of pure individuality' sows its internal seed of destruction. But at this stage in the realization of ethical life — and for Hegel it is a crisis to be overcome by a different order — neither can prevail over the other. Both Creon and Antigone are partially right; both are blinded to the legitimacy of the other's view.

It is this abstraction of Antigone into a symbol of ethical resistance against a potentially unjust law that has proven so alluring to philosophy (and art) over time.[9] 'Wherever the strength of a man's intellect, or moral sense, or affection brings him into opposition with the rules which society has sanctioned, there is renewed the conflict between Antigone and Creon,' as George Eliot put it.[10] From Hölderlin to Nietzsche, Kierkegaard to Heidegger, Lacan to Irigaray, philosophers have often approached Antigone by engaging with Hegel's reading, or by recasting the myth for their own interpretive objectives. Judith Butler, to take one of the most recent examples, sees Antigone's defiant agency at work redefining kinship and the (heteronormative) state from within. Born of incest, prioritizing loyalty to brother over husband and appropriating the language of the law she rebels against, Antigone is here not outside and prior to the law, as Hegel had it, but inscribed in it: a figure not of 'oppositional purity' but of the 'scandalously impure'.[11]

All texts quoted, though at a significant historical and philosophical remove from each other, illuminate the nexus between mourning and the law as the place where political action is possible as well as constrained. However, they also commit *the* 'basic humanist fallacy': they read Antigone as a modern character.[12] By so doing, they ignore the historical and material conditions of the text they work from: a tragedy first performed in Athens in 442–41 BCE, part of Sophocles' Theban trilogy.[13] Yet it is precisely the historical performance conventions and institutional functions of tragedy that offer radically enhanced insight into the contested relationship between mourning and the law — as well as ensuing philosophical appropriations thereof. They are thus worth exploring in some detail.

Tragedy as an art form emerged in late sixth- and fifth-century BCE Athens as part of a historical shift in attitude towards mourning; a shift closely linked to what the historian of ancient Greece Nicole Loraux called the 'invention of Athens' itself.[14] Until the late sixth century, mourning practices traditionally took the form of predominantly female, oral lamentations marked by loud keening, *threnos* and *goos*. In the process of Athenian democratization, however, these traditions began to be increasingly regulated, then channelled into two new rhetorical conventions. One was the *epitaphios logos*, the funeral oration, which Thucydides in the *History of the Peloponnesian War* singles out as instrumental for the consolidation of the democratic *polis*. Restricting passionate female lamenting of loss, this Periclean invention instead sought to reclaim the (war) dead for the purposes of the *polis*: their death was 'overshadowed by the city, the ultimate authority of all Memory'.[15]

The second substitution for traditional mourning practices was tragedy. Appearing in the fifth century BCE, it too was performed, and watched, only by citizens: no foreigners, no slaves, and (probably) no women. In the words of classicist and poet Anne Carson:

> Why does tragedy exist? Because you are full of rage. Why are you full of rage? Because you are full of grief. [...] Grief and rage — you need to contain that, to put a frame around it, where it can play itself out without you or your kin having to die.[16]

The regulation of mourning was thus important both for the creation of the *polis*'s laws and for tragic form.[17] The tensions between traditional and newly sanctioned modes of mourning are certainly reflected in the Sophoclean play itself. As such, Eurydice's exit from the stage, having been informed of Haemon's suicide, makes the messenger fret that:

> she finds it unbecoming to mourn in public.
> Inside, under her roof, she'll set her women
> to the task and wail the sorrow of the house. (ll. 1377–79)[18]

It is also borne out in Antigone's final dirge for herself, which could count as a skilful citation of the Periclean *epitaphios logos*. As with her laments for Polynices, however, Antigone here too invokes pre-democratic, heroic forms of memorialization, while clearly prioritizing kin over *polis*. Mourning practices were associated with defining as well as questioning the limits of the democratic *polis*, who pertained to it, and what was permissible in this community.

As Honig argues persuasively, this tension on stage will have resonated with the elite concern of the audience that the democratic *polis* sent soldiers to battle with only a poor substitute of memorialization awaiting them, compared to what the kin could have and previously would have provided.[19] Indeed, not even Creon himself may be able to reign in traditional lament — he, who had announced at the beginning of the play that 'you cannot know a man completely [...] till he's shown his colours, ruling the people | making laws' (ll. 194–95), and whose very first decree had been the prohibition to bury Polynices.[20] As he is informed of his wife's suicide, he wails loudly, seemingly performing the very Homeric mode of mourning he had proscribed. However, he also departs from this mode in key ways, thus suggesting in a rather unsettling manner that perhaps 'no economy of mourning and membership [...] is up to the task of voicing and managing the grief'.[21]

Foreign Bodies

Tragedy may well, as Carson had it, seek to put a frame around grief and rage — yet frames have the infuriating habit of inciting what they are meant to contain. Indeed, in a fifth-century Athens that was politically conflictual, repeatedly violent, and threatened by war, tragedy was rather 'more than a controlled self-representation that the city-state chooses to reveal'.[22] Quite the contrary: tragedy brought to the stage issues which citizens would likely have chosen to disregard or reject. The theatre of Dionysus, which like the assembly had moved from the Agora to just outside the spaces the city assigned to public life, also received civic assemblies that 'openly deviated' from the norms governing the emerging city-state.[23] Like the god himself, who is characterized by excess and madness, a proximity of *eros* and *thanatos*, the theatre constituted spatially and dramatically an '"alien" enclave inside the territory of the city into which it [was] nevertheless fully integrated'.[24]

This notion of tragedy as one of internal foreignness in the body politic is a productive one to examine the relationship between mourning and the law. Antigone, far from standing in for a political community striving for just laws, represents this foreignness acutely. Herself 'unmourned', her mourning practices estrange her from both law and kin. In fact, in her dirge, she self-identifies twice as *metoikos*, a stranger — or in a more precise technical sense: a resident foreigner who did not possess rights of citizenship.

> unmourned by friends and forced by such crude laws
> I go to my rockbound prison, strange new tomb —
> always a stranger [*metoikos*], O dear god,
> I have no home on earth and none below,
> not with the living, not with the breathless dead.
> [...]
> I go to them [my parents] now, cursed, unwed, to share their home —
> I am a stranger [*metoikos*]! (ll. 938–42, 955–56)[25]

Through this invocation, Antigone is characterized as being entirely outside any law (human or divine) and any community (living or dead). Indeed, the chorus address her as representing 'a law to yourself | alone, no mortal like you' (ll. 912–13).[26] She is literally auto-nomos (*autonomos*), acting according to her very own laws. These attributes mirror those of her father. In *Oedipus at Colonus*, which was the last performed of the Theban plays but in terms of narrative precedes *Antigone*, the banished king awaits his end on the sacred grounds of the Eumenides. This is a region just outside Athens, which is both described as the bulwark of the *polis* and the threshold to the netherworld. Oedipus's connection with the site immediately sets him apart as a foreigner: 'no native, a stranger | else he'd never set foot where none may walk' (ll. 149–50).[27] Like his daughter, he has arrived at the hour of his death at a place entirely foreign to law and community. Yet unlike his daughter, he pleads *not* to be seen as such: 'I beg you, don't look on me as an outlaw [*a-nomon*]' (l. 164).[28]

Indeed, burial sites are richly significant in the Theban trilogy's economy of space. Just as Polynices was denied burial within the city, Antigone's fate is not 'stoning to death inside the city walls', as Creon originally intended, but entombment 'in a rocky vault' outside (ll. 43 and 873).[29] It is a liminal site, external to yet important for the fate of the city, and one which will keep much of Western philosophy in thrall for centuries. Similarly, Oedipus's grave acquires importance well beyond his death. Welcomed by the Athenian king Theseus, the banished Oedipus arrives at Colonus a supplicant with apparently empty hands. Yet he comes with the greatest of promises: 'a blessing to the hosts I live among, | disaster to those who sent me, drove me out' (ll. 113–14).[30] This is because the battle between Athens and its rival Thebes, Apollo predicted, will be won on the site of Oedipus's grave — so long as its location remains a secret. Given the two city-states' enmity in the Peloponnesian War, which Athens had lost by the time *Oedipus at Colonus* was performed (401 BCE), this carried unsettling overtones for Athenians. The first extant tragedy, Aeschylus's *The Persians* (472 BCE), already asked them to mourn for their enemies, specifically their keening, barbarian queen. But not unlike Euripides's *Medea*, where Theseus's father Aegeus offers murderous Medea refuge in Athens on the promise she would cure his sterility and thus guarantee a lineage of Athenian aristocracy, the Theban plays end by linking the future of the city-state to the burial site of a non-citizen who had transgressed both moral and state laws. We will return to this.

Furthermore, foreignness also seeps into the language of grief itself, as Loraux describes in a wonderfully evocative passage.[31] Traditional female laments *threnos* and *goos* were characterized precisely by unmediated, non-verbal, prolonged expressions of grief that stood diametrically opposed to the reasoned discourse of *logos* that was to characterize the emerging city-state. Tragedies often rendered such lament — see Elektra, or Creon's laments — with the interjection *aiai*. Concerned with tragic form, Aristotle criticized the excessive use of such practice as *xenikon*: as an effect of strangeness or as an offence against discourse itself. But if one were 'to eliminate every strange or foreign element, *xenikon*, in the tragedies that we know, what would remain of the tragic genre?' Loraux goes on to ask.[32] What indeed?

In addition, the (unrelated) adverb *aei* [always], was used in political speeches to describe the city both as ever loyal to its founding laws and in continuous renewal, perpetual recreation. In tragedy, however, the term acquires a rather different meaning. There, it serves to signpost a never-ending, excessively performed grief and anger. Just as Antigone doubly affirms her deed, Elektra doubly negates the possibility of relinquishing her object of grief: 'there is no question that I may ever forget'. Here, 'the *aei* of perpetual recreation is diverted to mourning, the nourishing and procreative feminine force is diverted to the service of sorrow, an endlessly revived and rejuvenated sorrow'.[33]

Tragedy thus gives us a host of things to think about as we reconsider the relationship between mourning and the law. Performed in an 'alien enclave' in the city, tragic theatre not only gave the stage to figures who, often themselves non-citizens, transgress moral and legal norms and threaten the ideology of the *polis* in which they speak. It also does so often in a language of ineffable grief that chafes with reasoned discourse, and in a repetitive, indeed performative manner that runs counter to the civic institutional order in which it is nonetheless fully incorporated. These stubborn acts of mourning are lodged uncomfortably, if fascinatingly, in mythical Thebes, in the play, and in the *polis* itself — but also, by extension, in the very tradition of Western political thought.

Mourning/Melancholia

The regulation of mourning thus tells us something about the rise of the democratic *polis*. Via Greek tragedy, it has also informed thinking about politics and the law — from Hegel to Hölderlin, Nietzsche to Kierkegaard, Benjamin to Heidegger, Lacan to Irigaray, Butler to Honig. More recently, however, mourning has also entered the debate about philosophy as such.

Nowhere else perhaps is the conjunction between mourning and philosophical critique as present as it is in the work of Jacques Derrida. Throughout his work, Derrida returned again and again to the question of mourning, exploiting its resonance with friendship, fidelity, and finitude. As part of a text on foreignness and mourning, *De l'hospitalité* [Of Hospitality], he also revisits *Antigone* and *Oedipus at Colonus*.[34] Here, he refers to both places of burial beyond the city walls with the term *chora*. Originally understood to designate sites within the circumscription of the ancient Greek city-state yet outside the *polis* proper, the notion has a rich philosophical heritage going back to Plato, who describes it as a formless interval, a receptacle or abyss, part of the process of creation. For Derrida, Oedipus's secret grave or crypt is an abyss that represents both a promise and an obligation. As such, it is structurally similar to the dynamics of hospitality. Because hospitality is reciprocal, Derrida argues, the host depends on the guest granting their presence in order to be able to be host. The guest ends up holding the host hostage: Oedipus, the foreigner and outlaw, has ancient Athens in a bind.

But, in a further move, Derrida also makes 'politics' more generally contingent upon mourning.

> There is no politics without an organisation of the time and place of mourning, without a topolitology of the sepulchre, without an anamnesic and thematic relation to the spirit as *ghost*, whom one holds, just as he holds us, hostage.[35]

What is more, he likens mourning to the process of thinking itself, pointedly substituting the Cartesian notion: 'I mourn, therefore I am'.[36] The teleology of the Hegelian spirit deconstructed, lamenting the excesses of rationalism, Derrida's thought constructs itself upon a sort of empty crypt, a foundational absence. Like Antigone, who is bereft of her father's grave, this mournful thought operates ceaselessly: 'without a determinable *topos*, mourning is not allowed [...]. The only possible mourning is the impossible mourning'.[37] You might say that mourning holds Derrida's philosophy hostage.

This is precisely the point of departure for British philosopher Gillian Rose. In a slim but powerful book, *Mourning Becomes the Law*, she posits a causal relationship between philosophical mourning, effective philosophical critique, and an inauguration and preservation of law. Drawing on a distinction between tragedy/mourning and baroque *Trauerspiel*/melancholia, and taking explicit recourse to *Antigone*, Rose is concerned about excessively performed philosophical grief, which she believes detrimental to critique. Aiming squarely at postmodern philosophy for its renunciation, as she puts it, of the possibility of truth, reason, and power, she argues that it remains caught in an eternal 'nostalgia for presence'.[38] It is an opposition cast in theatrical terms: 'Instead of producing a work, this self-inhibited mourning produces a play, the *Trauerspiel*, the interminable mourning play and lament, of post-modernity. [...] This is no work of mourning: it remains baroque melancholia'.[39] Rose calls postmodern philosophy an endless aberrated lamentation, bewailing the lost stability of the notions it has itself deconstructed:

an inconsequential, melancholic refusal to let go. By contrast, a successful and 'inaugurated' philosophical mourning that completes and overcomes the lost object would return, she argues, to participate in and actively configure politics, authority, and law: ready to take on the injustices of the city.

Rose performs two analytical manoeuvres here, one of which is difficult to sustain; the other, however, is productive as a way of rethinking the relationship between mourning, philosophy, and the law. First, her critique draws upon a fundamentally incomplete reading of Freud's theory of mourning. As others in this volume have analysed in greater detail (see especially the Introduction), the early Freud distinguished between successful mourning (*Trauer*) and pathological melancholia. In mourning, the ego will not be impoverished by the death of a loved one; any excessive emotional investment in the absent object can and will eventually be withdrawn. This, as Nicolas Abraham and Maria Torok describe it, is 'introjection', or maintaining a moderate dwelling for the deceased within the subject.[40] Excessive mourning or melancholia, by contrast, proceeds through identification with the lost object towards a narcissistic 'incorporation' of the other; a process Freud had described in terms of eating, devouring, swallowing.[41] Loss is denied, the lost object encrypted in the body.

Post-war, however, Freud revised his account substantially. In *The Ego and Id*, he recognizes that identification with the lost one may not be pathological but indeed the condition for successful mourning.[42] Only by internalizing the lost other, preserving and reconstituting it within oneself, Freud now argues, does one become a subject. Collapsing the difference between mourning and melancholia, successful and pathological grief, this account speaks less of consolation and overcoming. Instead, Freud now thinks, mourning may never be fully completed: working through grief may mean preserving the lost object within one's self. This of course is the reading Derrida picks up on, when he describes mourning in terms of a prothesis, a graft within a divided self, as well as in terms of fidelity to the other.[43] It is also reminiscent of Butler, who writes that the ties we maintain with one another 'constitute what we are', indeed 'compose us'.[44] This fundamental interdependence brings with it a vulnerability, Butler argues, as we impinge upon each other in ways that are neither entirely foreseeable nor controllable. And with this vulnerability, which loss and mourning expose more than anything else, comes an ethical responsibility towards the other.

By following the early Freud, then, Rose's critique is based on a reductive understanding of the process of mourning. The strict separation between 'inaugurated' mourning and ineffectual melancholia is difficult to sustain; the unfinished nature of the work of mourning not necessarily a reason for rejection. However, her underlying critique of what she calls 'postmodern philosophy' (and which Honig names 'mortalist humanism') remains forceful. Theorists and critics seeking to renounce or dismantle universalist notions of reason, power, sovereignty, she argues, often end up replacing these now discredited notions with a new turn to ethics: an invocation of our common human mortality, our shared exposure to loss. Grieving the absence of securities that proved none such, mourning itself 'steps in to take the place of the very thing whose loss we lament: universalism', as Honig writes nearly twenty years after Rose, but in virtually the same words.[45] Yet by so doing, this 'despairing rationalism without reason', as Rose had it, struggles to attend to the actual, intractable, contested workings of power and sovereignty that politics necessarily entails.

In their own practices, Rose and Honig seek to approach philosophy differently. The former does so, in her own words, 'aporetically'; that is, by stressing the gaps between the universal and the particular, by focusing on the 'irruption of thought: [...] galvanising the difficulty of thinking in the wake of disaster, without generating any fantasy of mending the world'.[46] It is an approach that understands itself as precarious but active, imperfect but worth the risk. Honig similarly stresses interruptions — certainly in her *Antigone, Interrupted* — of the play, of its reception history, of the messy politics of mourning, of thought itself. Interestingly, though, the two thinkers choose different paths. Honig, in her dramaturgically focused counter-reading of the Greek tragedy, proceeds by teasing out unsuspected elements — the conspiracies, plots, linguistic manipulations usually associated, since Benjamin, with the baroque *Trauerspiel*. In her own words, she attends to the 'Hamletization' of Antigone.[47] It is a move Rose is unable to perform, given her strict differentiation between mourning/tragedy and melancholia/*Trauerspiel*. Instead, Rose turns to another female mourning figure, the wife of Phocion, as represented in a 1648 painting by the French baroque artist Nicolas Poussin.

Ash/Ismene

Phocion (402–318 BCE) was a highly regarded Athenian statesman and, as Macedonia's agent, a temporary ruler of Athens. During a time of unrest, he was condemned and executed by his political enemies, who denied him burial within the city walls, leaving his ashes unconsecrated outside the city walls. As Rose (following Plutarch) recounts it, and Poussin represents pictorially, Phocion's unnamed wife furtively visits the site to gather his ashes and give him a clandestine burial. So far, so Antigone. Rose interprets this and Antigone's act as 'finite act[s] of political justice' — expressing opposition not against law per se, nor against the presumed unjust *nature* of the law, but against the arbitrary *abuse* of the law.[48] Poussin's architectural backdrop does not represent the unjust sovereignty of the *polis* and the law, Rose says, but the institutions which, due to finite acts of civic opposition, will again and again return to justice. The city wall, protruding just off-centre into the separation of inner and outer, is neither breached nor closed. With Rose we might read it as an *aporia*, at once a difficult path and a puzzlement, critiquing the relationship between inclusion and exclusion, legitimacy and illegitimacy, past devastation and future action. The act of gathering ashes, foregrounded yet diminutive against the towering city, does not oppose but oscillates between the *polis* and its beyond.

Two angles are worth pursuing in our context, as they open up different avenues to explore mourning, politics, and the law. The first is to note that in her defiant act of mourning, Phocion's wife is not alone. She is accompanied by a servant, whose apprehensive posture in Poussin's painting signals the risk both women are taking as they infringe the law. It is less the vulnerability of the grieving wife, the gesture of love that opposes the unjust city, and rather the vulnerability of two risk-takers, which is at issue here. As with Antigone's sister Ismene, who is traditionally portrayed as impassive, pliant, deficient in political courage, where she is not directly silenced ('written — spoken — out of the family line', as Simon Goldhill puts it), we would do well to pause with the servant.[49] To cast our conceptual net wider, rather than hone in on the sacrificial heroine alone. Indeed, in a radical re-reading concentrating on elements usually more at home in the baroque *Trauerspiel*, Honig encourages us to see Ismene as her sister's co-conspirator and plotter, responsible, even, for the first of the two forbidden burials. By so doing, Honig revaluates action over passivity, solidarity over suffering: she reads the sisters as 'partisan sororal actor[s] in concert'.[50]

This very phrasing points toward an Arendtian conception of political action, which, of course, was rooted, too, in a theoretical obsession with ancient Greece. To act, in Hannah Arendt's sense, is to take an initiative, to begin, via the ancient Greek *archein*, which is both to begin and to lead, to set something in motion and to rule.[51] But action is not only an individual's 'insertion in the world' by word and deed. Action perforce needs to happen in response to others — and by provoking their response in turn. It cannot occur in isolation. The complicity of Phocion's wife's companion, like Ismene, helps shift the emphasis from a tragic towards an agonistic conception of agency. Between the pairs of them, political action is not purely sacrificial nor heroic. It mobilizes and solicits, publicly. One could even go further and add that servant and sister build bridges to the spectator of both painting and play: extending our own gaze towards the cityscape and men representing the law, they open up, teasingly almost, the possibility of partaking in their delegitimate acts of mourning.

This brings us to the second angle worth exploring. Almost unnoticeably, Rose lets slip how Phocion's wife buries her husband's ashes in her home. In fact, he is buried by the hearth, in the heart of the *oikos*, the heart of kinship: dedicated to the household gods. Fascinatingly, although Rose does not choose to comment on it, this brings us back to the distinction between domestic and public, *oikos* and *polis*, which has so dominated the history of political thought. Hegel, we recall, was intrigued by how Antigone's delegitimate tending to the dead brought *oikos* and *polis* into open conflict. Arendt, not dissimilarly, cast the relationship between *oikos* and *polis* as one that foregrounds the tensions between necessity and freedom. In Arendt's reading, there is no true political action — and thus freedom — without turning our back on the *oikos*. Love, for Arendt, had no place in politics. And Rose, so astutely rejecting an account of infinite love, a new ethics to replace the law, so astutely, too, making a case in favour of critical rationality, fails to be alert to the distinction when she speaks of Phocion and Antigone as 'returning the soul to the city'.[52]

Yet just as we have read Antigone as a figure of internal foreignness that questions the arbitrary use of power while herself remaining partially incognisant of the legitimacy of sovereignty as a principle, the ash Phocion's wife buries by the hearth is productively unsettling. Indeed, according to an apocryphal account Rose mentions but does not further pursue, Phocion's wife may even have consumed his ashes. This of course points us back to the (originally pathological-melancholic) idea of Freudian 'incorporation': the devouring, encrypting of the other within the self, which Rose struggled to legitimate, and which rather surreptitiously reappears in her text. There is something relentless, excessive in this domestic enactment of fidelity. It just might suggest that, while we should indeed be wary of reinstating a new ethics of mourning as a premise for political thought, preserving, claiming, and returning critically to the injuries that result from loss can be politically productive.

Neither Antigone nor Phocion's wife, perhaps, are ultimately as suitable as it seemed for a narrative of overcoming, their acts at once an expression of ineffable grief and the result of a virtually baroque, conspiratorial wrestling with the law. Yet because, not despite this, both acts retain a thoroughly political, perilous force. The key to their critical force may lie precisely in their capacity to resist closure, just as they insist on reworking the law. Whether kept in the human body or the communal *polis*, the divided self or the divided city, it is not just the lost one but the mourner who is maintained in, and continues to reshape, the structure within which they are lodged.

Conclusion/Carson

In the 2015 paperback translation-cum-recreation of Sophocles' play, *Antigonick*, poet and classicist Anne Carson prefaced the text with a translator's note in the form of a letter, or ode, to Antigone.[53] It is a note that ponders the power and problem of language; how to arrive at and carry over what cowers behind it. It references Antigone's faith in 'a deeply *other* organization that lies just beneath what we see' and her status as *autonomos*, which 'sounds like a kind of freedom | but you aren't interested in freedom'.[54] Skating over translations, adaptations, interpretations, and stagings from Hegel to Brecht, Butler to Žižek, Carson acknowledges the difficulty of approaching Antigone today: 'there was never a blank slate'.[55] But as she comes to the end of the preface, she hones in on her own. Referencing one of Ingeborg Bachmann's late poems, which begins 'I lose my screams', Carson ends with a mission statement:

> dear Antigone,
> I take it as the task of the translator
> to forbid that you should ever lose your screams.[56]

We continue to be fascinated by the dilemmas that arise when grief comes into conflict with the body of rules that a political community recognizes as binding. At times of crises, which also call into question the way we make our laws and the way in which these laws represent us, mourning easily spills over into rage, and from there to civil disobedience and protest. As we seek to address utterly contemporary questions of justice and political community — such as Black Lives Matter of 2020 — we still turn for explanatory models to ancient Greece and often ancient Greek tragedy, which seem so eloquently to ponder the relationship between mourning and the law. Yet rather than turning mourning into the basis for a new ethics, or seeking to overcome grief in order to accept the law, we need to constantly assess, and where necessary redress, the shortcomings of the law that so affect us. How then to define the nexus of philosophy, mourning, and the law? Well, we could do worse than paraphrasing another of Carson's texts, where she cites the scholar B. M. W. Knox, who said of Euripides what Thucydides wrote about what the Corinthians said of the Athenians: that they were made never to live in peace with themselves and to prevent the rest of humankind from doing so.[57]

Notes to Chapter 7

1. Anne Carson, '*The Designated Mourner* by Wally Shawn, Final Production, NYC, June 2013', *London Review of Books*, 35.21 (7 November 2013), p. 12. Also included as one of the chapbooks in Anne Carson, *Float* (London: Jonathan Cape, 2016).
2. Freud, 'Mourning and Melancholia', p. 246.
3. A nod to the play cycle by Eugene O'Neill, *Mourning Becomes Electra: A Trilogy* (New York: H. Liveright, 1931), based on the *Oresteia* and focusing on the obsessively vengeful mourner Electra.
4. Honig, *Antigone, Interrupted*, p. 119.
5. Miriam Leonard, 'Tragedy and the Seductions of Philosophy', *The Cambridge Classical Journal*, 58 (2012), 145–64 (p. 154).
6. Sophocles, *Antigone*, in *The Three Theban Plays: Antigone, Oedipus the King, Oedipus at Colonus*, trans. by Robert Fagles (London: Penguin Classics, 1984), pp. 55–128 (p. 60).
7. Ibid., p. 81.
8. G. W. F. Hegel, *Phenomenology of Spirit*, trans. by A. V. Miller (Oxford: Clarendon, 1977), p. 280.
9. George Steiner, *Antigones: The Antigone Myth in in Western Literature, Art, and Thought* (Oxford: Oxford University Press, 1986) brings together a great many examples of Antigone's far-reaching legacy.
10. George Eliot, 'The *Antigone* and Its Moral', *Leader*, 7 (29 March 1856), 306.
11. Judith Butler, *Antigone's Claim: Kinship between Life and Death* (New York: Columbia University Press, 2000), pp. 6–9. For an excellent counter-reading that recalls the all-male performance conventions in homosocial Athens, see Olga Taxidou, *Tragedy, Modernity and Mourning* (Edinburgh: Edinburgh University Press, 2004).
12. Taxidou, *Tragedy, Modernity and Mourning*, p. 33. I am greatly indebted to Taxidou for first drawing my attention to the topic, including the reference to Gillian Rose.
13. This, of course, is a long-standing bugbear of classicist scholarship, which often resists the philosophy of the tragic — the 'naturalized' reading of Greek tragedy in the wake of eighteenth-century German idealism — because it a-historically universalizes Greek tragedy. For Jean-Pierre Vernant and Pierre Vidal-Naquet, in *Myth and Tragedy in Ancient Greece*, trans. by Janet Lloyd (New York: Zone Books, 1988), tragedy literally dies at the hands of philosophical rationalization — a curious alignment, as Leonard has pointed out, with Nietzsche's view, who otherwise of course exemplifies precisely the reading they oppose ('Tragedy and the Seductions of Philosophy', p. 150).
14. Nicole Loraux, *The Invention of Athens: The Funeral Oration in the Classical City* (Cambridge, MA: Harvard University Press, 1986).
15. Ibid., p. 3.
16. Anne Carson, 'Preface. Tragedy: A Curious Art Form', in *Grief Lessons: Four Plays by Euripides* (New York: NYRB Classics, 2006), pp. 7–9 (p. 7).
17. Taxidou, *Tragedy, Modernity and Mourning*, pp. 8–9.
18. Sophocles, *Antigone*, p. 123.
19. Honig, *Antigone, Interrupted*, p. 97.
20. Sophocles, *Antigone*, p. 67.
21. Honig, *Antigone, Interrupted*, pp. 116–17.

22. Nicole Loraux, *The Mourning Voice: An Essay on Greek Tragedy* (Ithaca, NY: Cornell University Press, 2002), p. 14.
23. Ibid., p. 23.
24. Ibid., p. 25.
25. Sophocles, *Antigone*, p. 103.
26. Ibid., p. 102.
27. Sophocles, *Oedipus at Colonus*, in *The Three Theban Plays: Antigone, Oedipus the King, Oedipus at Colonus*, trans. by Robert Fagles (London: Penguin Classics, 1984), pp. 279–388 (p. 291).
28. Ibid., p. 292.
29. Sophocles, *Antigone*, pp. 60 and 100.
30. Sophocles, *Oedipus at Colonnus*, p. 289.
31. Loraux, *The Mourning Voice*, pp. 40–41.
32. Ibid., p. 41.
33. Ibid., p. 33.
34. Jacques Derrida, *Of Hospitality*, trans. by Rachel Bowlby (Stanford, CA: Stanford University Press, 2000).
35. Jacques Derrida, *Aporias*, trans. by Thomas Dutoit (Stanford, CA: Stanford University Press, 1993), p. 61.
36. Jacques Derrida, *Learning to Live Finally: The Last Interview. An Interview with Jean Birnbaum*, trans. by Pascale-Anne Brault and Michael Naas (New York: Palgrave Macmillan, 2007), p. 17.
37. Derrida, *Aporias*, p. 61.
38. Gillian Rose, *Mourning Becomes the Law: Philosophy and Representation* (Cambridge: Cambridge University Press, 1996), p. 11.
39. Ibid., pp. 64, 69.
40. Nicolas Abraham and Maria Torok, 'Introjection-Incorporation: Mourning or Melancholia', in *Psychoanalysis in France*, ed. by Serge Lebovici and Daniel Widlöcher (New York: International Universities Press, 1980), pp. 3–16.
41. Freud, 'Mourning and Melancholia', pp. 249–50.
42. Sigmund Freud, *The Ego and the Id*, in *The Standard Edition of the Complete Psychological Works of Sigmund Freud*, ed. and trans. by James Strachey, 24 vols (London: Hogarth Press, 1953–74), XIX (1961), 12–66.
43. Jacques Derrida, *Memoires for Paul de Man*, trans. by Cecile Lindsay, Jonathan D. Culler, and Eduardo Cadava (New York: Columbia University Press, 1986), pp. xiii, 56.
44. Butler, *Antigone's Claim*, p. 21.
45. Honig, *Antigone, Interrupted*, p. 1.
46. Rose, *Mourning Becomes the Law*, p. 9.
47. Honig, *Antigone, Interrupted*, p. 147.
48. Rose, *Mourning Becomes the Law*, p. 25. Indeed, although Rose does not mention it, shortly after the execution of Phocion, Athenians reversed the judgment, decreed a public burial, and bestowed public honour on Phocion.
49. Simon Goldhill, 'Antigone and the Politics of Sisterhood', in *Laughing with Medusa: Classical Myth and Feminist Thought*, ed. by Vanda Zajko and Miriam Leonard (Oxford: Oxford University Press, 2016), pp. 141–62 (p. 157).
50. Honig, *Antigone, Interrupted*, p. 155.
51. Hannah Arendt, *The Human Condition* (Chicago: University of Chicago Press, 1998), p. 176.
52. Rose, *Mourning Becomes the Law*, p. 36.
53. Anne Carson, 'The task of the translator of *Antigone*', in Sophocles, *Antigonick*, trans. by Anne Carson (New York: New Directions Books, 2015), pp. 3–6.
54. Ibid., p. 5.
55. Ibid., p. 6.
56. Ibid.
57. Carson, *Grief Lessons*, p. 8.

CHAPTER 8

Musical Language and Remembering the Tragic in Dmitri Shostakovich's String Quartet no. 8

Luca Aversano

> The first stories, the first declamations, the first laws were in verse; poetry was discovered before prose; it had to be so, since the passions spoke before reason. The same was true of music; at first there was no music other than melody, nor any other melody than the varied sound of speech, accents formed the song, the quantities formed measure, and people spoke as much by sonorities and rhythm as by articulations and voices. To say and to sing were formerly one, says Strabo; and, he adds, this shows poetry to be the source of eloquence. He should have said that both sprang from the same source and were initially but the same thing. In view of how the first societies united was it surprising that the first stories were set to verse and that the first laws were sung? Was it surprising that the first grammarians subordinated their art to music and were at one and the same time teachers of both?
>
> A language that has only articulations and voices is therefore in possession of only half its resources; it conveys ideas, it is true, but in order to convey sentiments, images, it still needs rhythm and sounds, that is to say a melody.[1]

The capacity of musical language to narrate and represent emotional experience effectively, about which Jean-Jacques Rousseau writes, is a subject that recurs throughout the Western philosophical tradition. This characteristic had already been pointed out by the Greeks, for whom music lay on the boundary between pure expression of sentiment and the greatest representation of composed order, the norm, and the canon. If Dionysius enlivened Bacchic festivals with the sound of the aulos, liberating the passions of the soul in unrestrained sensual enjoyment, Apollo let the strings of his cithara resonate according to a pre-existent tuning system which fixed these strings in mathematical relations which were certain, distinct, and measurable. The dialectic between Dionysius and Apollo, in more specifically musical terms, was also manifested in the contrast between the wind instrument's free continuum of sound and the cithara's 'discrete' manner of tone production, that is, its production of specific, separate, distinct sounds. The traces of this dialectic are discernible even today in the distinction between fixed pitch instruments (like the piano) and variable pitch instruments (such as wind or string instruments), where the former can be connected to music's clearly rational, arithmetical nature, while the latter can be made to correspond to the demand for freedom and escape from measured control which constitutes the 'dark' side of the world of sound.

From this perspective, musical language has always tended towards the reconciling of these two opposites, as if to constitute itself, in other words, within a system of norms which make emotional expression intelligible. Just how embedded in ancient Greek culture was the need to establish a relation between the order of sounds and their emotional effect is confirmed by the 'promulgation' of musical *nomoi*: melodies conceived for different occasions and which — according to the Greek poet Terpander (seventh century BCE) — were deemed to produce different effects on the human mind according to their circumstances and context and, naturally, as a consequence of the disposition of the sounds of the melodies themselves.

The *nomos*, a word which in Greek means 'law', was what regulated musical composition, in a system of correspondences between melodies (as the succession of intervals organized rhythmically) and immediately relatable emotional reactions, which meant that each piece of music was imbued with an *ethos*, with a recognizable and thus infinitely repeatable character.

The legacy, in modern times, of these ancient ideas can clearly be found in the Baroque theory of musical affects (*Affektenlehre*), according to which it was possible to represent, evoke, and express moods and emotions through specific melodic, rhythmic, harmonic, and tonal features. The primary objective of opera — which was born in the Baroque period — was indeed the representation of the affects and passions, which through music would journey from the realm of the individual to embrace absolute, objective contexts, *sub specie aeternitatis.* On the other hand, the powerful capacity of musical language to move and to represent emotion has never been called into question; if anything, at different moments in time, this capacity has been trapped in various rational codes of communication which can be interpreted, as intimated above, as the overcoming of the opposition between music's mathematical and emotional sides, or better as *coincidentia oppositorum* [the unity of opposites].

In the economy of this essay, the function of this overture on the nature of musical language is to frame the topic of remembering the tragic, as manifested in Shostakovich's String Quartet no. 8 in C minor, op. 110, within the broader perspective of the relationship between subjective expression and a collective dimension that is interwoven into a musical composition. I will return to these aspects in the conclusion to my contribution, after having given some indications as to the genesis and context of the work and a brief analysis of its structure.

In July 1960 the Soviet government asked Shostakovich to go to East Germany, in order to follow the group of cinematographers occupied with the production of the film *Five Days, Five Nights*, for which the composer was to write the music. The shooting, led by the director Leo Arnštam, took place in Dresden, since the film focused on the Allied bombing of the city. On his return, Shostakovich wrote the following to his friend Isaak Glikman on 19 July, describing the small town of Görlitz some forty kilometres from Dresden where he had stayed:

> A place of incredible beauty — as it should be, the whole area being known as 'the Switzerland of Saxony'. The good working conditions justified themselves: I composed my Eighth Quartet. As hard as I tried to rough out the film scores which I am supposed to be doing, I still haven't managed to get anywhere; instead I wrote this ideologically flawed quartet which is of no use to anybody. I started thinking that if some day I die, nobody is likely to write a work in memory of me, so I had better write one myself. The title page could carry the dedication: 'To the memory of the composer of this quartet'.[2]

In contrast, in Dresden the composer was also able to witness the consequences of Nazism and the Second World War for himself: a devastated city, razed to the ground by English and American bombings supported by the Soviet Union. His memory turned to images of war and, in all likelihood, to the first period of strained relations with Soviet power. Shostakovich had certainly been linked by ties of friendship to Stalin, as is attested by various letters of a familiar nature, as well as by his being granted economic privileges, places to live, and cash prizes. Nonetheless, there had also been difficult moments: in 1936, on the occasion of the premiere of *Lady Macbeth of Mtsensk*, the Soviet newspaper *Pravda* tore the opera to shreds with its famous article entitled 'Muddle Instead of Music'. Evidently, the experimental language of *Lady Macbeth* — which called for, amongst other things, a sex scene on stage during which the glissandi of the trombones proved to be unequivocally suggestive — went beyond the limits permitted by Stalinist rhetoric, so much so that the opera was forbidden in theatres until 1963. Some of Shostakovich's symphonies were also subjected to boycott and remained unperformed for a long time despite their success with the public.

A further moment of crisis and shock throughout the intellectual world occurred shortly after the composition of Quartet no. 8, in 1961, when Khrushchev pushed Shostakovich to join the Party in order to present him as an ambassador of Soviet music in the West. At this time, the composer was in fact considered in Europe and the United States effectively to be a dissident, and for this reason his adherence, however late, to communism provoked understandable concern amongst public opinion in the West. Another fraught moment, in the opposite direction to this earlier incident, took place in 1962, with the performance of Symphony no. 13 (*Babiy Yar*), op. 113, based on poems by the poet Yevgeny Yevtushenko. These poems recall the massacre of Jews at Kiev by Nazis during the Second World War, in the context of the composer's marked interest in Yiddish culture. Soviet antisemitism, which was widespread at this time, tended to target any non-aligned intellectuals, many of whom were Jewish, so that the *Babiy Yar* symphony was interpreted as unpatriotic and was therefore boycotted from its very first performance.

Further in the light of his personal and political past, the experience of the trip to Dresden evidently upset him, inspiring him to channel his own emotional state into a musical composition. The quartet took form under the sign of that cry of personal grief and suffering that is characteristic of so many of Shostakovich's works, and was sealed by the important dedication 'To the victims of fascism and war', which, however, would seem to distance the work from its original intention of celebrating the memory of its creator. Yet this dedication does not appear in the original manuscript, but was added later, and it is not clear who authorized such an addition.[3] In any case, regardless of the official dedication and in apparent contradiction to it (as we will see in due course), Quartet no. 8 arises from an essentially individual and autobiographical experience. The various self-citations of musical themes from earlier works, which Shostakovich himself enumerates in the already-quoted letter to Glikman, confirm as much:

> The quartet also uses themes from some of my own compositions and the Revolutionary song 'Zamuchen tyazholoy nevolyey' [Tormented by grievous bondage]. The themes from my own works are as follows: from the First Symphony, the Eighth Symphony, the [Second Piano] Trio, the Cello Concerto, and *Lady Macbeth*. There are hints of Wagner (the Funeral March from *Götterdämmerung*) and Tchaikovsky (the second subject of the first movement of the Sixth Symphony). Oh yes, I forgot to mention that there is something else of mine as well, from the Tenth Symphony. Quite a nice little hodge-podge, really.[4]

The other clear element of biographical individuality, with reference to the composer's emotional, mournful situation, lies in the structure of the opening theme of the quartet, formed of four notes which constitute the underlying motif of the work:

> He was still in mourning for his first wife, and his unhappy second marriage had just come to a sour end. The composer's bleak state of mind seems to find its reflection in every note of the quartet, which is plagued with repetitive motifs, sobbing melodies, dogged drones and jabbing chords. With an insistence that verges on obsession, the music repeats a four-note lament: D, E flat, C, B natural. This chromatic cluster, which the composer often embedded in his music, is a kind of signature, a musical transliteration of his name based on German musical notation. (In German, the notes spell DEsCH, pronounced DSCH, the first letters in the German spelling of his name: Dmitri Schostakowitsch.) In essence, the music repeats the words 'me, me, me, me'.[5]

According to Richard Taruskin, what is distinctive about Shostakovich's eighth quartet is precisely its unusual wish to determine its meaning: 'This is the one composition of his that does ask expressly to be read as an autobiography, the one time Shostakovich did put an explicit note in a bottle'. The repetition of the musical motif D-S-C-H and the numerous self-citations, Taruskin continues, show that 'Shostakovich was clearly identifying himself as a victim. The point is made over and over again'.[6] On the other hand, as Natalia M. Naiko has highlighted, the circumstances of Shostakovich's life contributed to the fact that the theme of death fixed itself very early on in his mind, acquiring an important, if not a central, position within his artistic production.[7]

Starting with the autobiographical connection and in accordance with what is a typical feature of Shostakovich's music, ideas of the tragic and of grief permeate the whole of Quartet no. 8, which is structured in five movements (*Largo, Allegro molto, Allegretto, Largo, Largo*) to be performed without a break.[8] The four opening notes, arranged according to the interval of a tritone (D-S-C-H, in German nomenclature, i.e. D-E flat-C-B natural), immediately create that atmosphere of gravitas and tension which signal the nature of the whole work. Introduced by the cello, the dark *Largo* turns from a fugato into a fanfare, with quotations from the First Symphony (op. 10) followed by a quotation from the Fifth (op. 47). The movement suddenly explodes into the *Allegro molto*, in which the first violin's pounding quadruplets recall the 'battle music' of the Eighth Symphony (op. 65). A violin solo, from the Piano Trio no. 2, op. 67, announces the third movement, *Allegretto*: a spectral waltz which seems to express the futile attempt to flee from the horrors of the war. The melody in the violin (the same motif D-S-C-H) insists on the B natural characteristic of the scale of G major, and this clashes with the B flat of the accompaniment in the viola, which is characteristic instead of the scale of G minor. The result is a tonal ambiguity, between major and minor, which is typical of Shostakovich's musical style.

In the transition to the fourth movement, *Largo*, the first notes of the *Dies Irae* are heard, then quotations from the Cello Concerto no. 1, op. 107, and from the opera *Lady Macbeth of Mtsensk*, present in the cello's melody. A series of fast, low chords, repeated three times, evokes a sequence of gunshots or, if a reference to the tradition of classical music is desired, the famous 'destiny which knocks at the door' of Beethoven's Fifth Symphony. The fifth movement, *Largo* again, reprises the fugal section from the opening movement. Alongside the motif D-S-C-H, the first themes of the quartet are echoed, before a conclusion which ends by fading into silence.

From the more specific perspective of musical language, the theme of the tragic and the idea of mourning are represented in sound through a series of stylistic features and models which stem from the ancient musical tradition mentioned at the start of this essay. As Olesya A. Osipenko notes, in his quartets 'the composer chooses certain genre models to implement the images of death that act for him as the carriers of mourning semantics (the funeral march, chant, elegy and ancient dances of Spanish origin: sarabande, chaconne, passacaglia)'.[9] In Quartet no. 8 the most important traditional reference is that of the funeral march, a type of music originally created to accompany funeral rites and which composers subsequently introduced into oratorios (for example Handel's *Saul*), into operatic works (Wagner's *Götterdämmerung*), and into symphonic and chamber works as a means of creating a sorrowful and intense expressive atmosphere.

In the second episode of the fourth movement of the Quartet, based on the Revolutionary song 'Zamuchen tyazholoy nevolyey', Shostakovich revisits the original model of the march, changing the metre, slowing the tempo down significantly, eliminating any distinctive sign of the melody (dotted rhythms, accentuation, other rhythmic motifs), and leaving only the initial rising fourth in the upbeat. In addition, the composer introduces the rhetorical figure of the so-called *passus duriusculus*, an ascending or descending melodic line formed of chromatic semitones and used in the Baroque period to represent and intensify the expressivity of words such as 'suffer', 'die', 'sorrow', 'pain', and so on. The melody's movement in octaves, marked *fortissimo* and entrusted to the second violin, viola, and cello, reveals, moreover, an affinity with the first theme of the sixth movement of String Quartet no. 11 in F minor, op. 122, a theme which likewise represents the solemn step of a funeral march.[10] A further musical sign that is characteristic of the 'tragic' is the choice of the key of C minor for the structure of the quartet, a key traditionally used for funeral marches and to recall the idea of death, along with the characteristic use of string instruments to recreate the sound of drums.

In short, Shostakovich includes rhetorical figures and elements of the Western musical tradition in the musical fabric of his composition, reworking them in order to achieve his own expressive aims. The relationship within the quartet between the semantics of a musical language that has become codified over time and the individual solutions adopted by the composer seems to reflect, by way of analogy, the relationship between historical memory and the memory of individual, lived experience. The relationship with historical memory in the form of musical tradition is, moreover, very present across the whole corpus of Shostakovich's quartets:

> Themes of Shostakovich Quartets are varied in terms of genre models they contain, which are enshrined in the historical memory [...]. The composer uses primary genres as the basis: song, romance, sarabande, waltz, baroque aria, polka, gallop, serenade, march, and genres that have emerged in the professional works: humoresque, scherzo, nocturne, elegy.[11]

The same procedure of musical self-citation, which permeates in particular the quartet under discussion, is, after all, based on an exercise of memory.

The apparent contradiction inherent in the dedication of Quartet no. 8 ('To the victims of fascism and war') is thus resolved, in a manner which in a certain sense coincides with the composition's markedly autobiographical character: Shostakovich's tragic individual destiny is an integral part and at the same time the result of historical destiny. Moreover, it is even thanks to history and to the memory of musical language — understood as the collection of semantically codified stylistic features that is handed down — that the emotional individuality of the composer and his composition is able to find a representational form that can be understood and shared publicly. This rhetorical device of signifying the tragic through the projection of individual memory in collective memory is probably at the basis of Shostakovich's choice to have none other than his Quartet no. 8 played at his own funeral, in 1975. Two comments by Shostakovich corroborate this reading. As we have seen in the quoted letter of 19 July 1960 to his friend Glikman, Shostakovich wrote that the quartet could serve as his personal epitaph and be dedicated 'To the memory of the composer of this quartet'. On the same topic of death, suffering, and burial, Shostakovich also declared:

> I feel eternal pain for those who were killed by Hitler, but I feel no less pain for those killed on Stalin's orders. I suffer for everyone who was tortured, shot, or starved to death. [...]
>
> The majority of my symphonies are tombstones. Too many of our people died and were buried in places unknown to anyone, not even their relatives. [...] Where do you put the tombstones [...]? Only music can do that for them. I'm willing to write a composition for each of the victims, but that's impossible, and that's why I dedicate my music to them all.[12]

The death of Shostakovich in music is, at heart, the death of all those who have suffered.

Notes to Chapter 8

1. Jean-Jacques Rousseau, 'Essay on the Origin of Languages', in *The Discourses and Other Early Political Writings*, ed. by Victor Gourevitch, 2nd edn (Cambridge: Cambridge University Press, 2018), pp. 292–93. The translator adds after sounds in the final line of this quotation: [or sonorities].
2. Dmitry Shostakovich, *Story of a Friendship: The Letters of Dmitry Shostakovich to Isaak Glikman, 1941–1975*, ed. by Isaak Glikman and trans. by Anthony Phillips (Ithaca, NY: Cornell University Press, 2001), pp. 90–91.
3. David Fanning, *Shostakovich: String Quartet No. 8* (Burlington, VT: Ashgate, 2004), p. 12.
4. Shostakovich, *Story of a Friendship*, p. 91.
5. Marina Harss, 'Running Like Shadows', *The Nation*, 16 July 2013 <http://www.thenation.com/article/running-shadows/> [accessed 15 November 2020].
6. Richard Taruskin, *Defining Russia Musically: Historical and Hermeneutical Essays* (Princeton, NJ: Princeton University Press, 1997), pp. 493, 494–95.
7. Natalia M. Naiko, *Poznavshii tainu zvuka: stat'i o muzyke i muzykantakh* [Understanding the Secret of the Sound: Articles about Music and Musicians] (Krasnoyarsk: Krasnoyarsk Academy of Music and Theater, 2012), p. 79.
8. See Olesya A. Osipenko, 'Mourning Themes in the Music of Dmitri Shostakovich', *Journal of Siberian Federal University. Humanities & Social Sciences*, 7.3 (2014), 404–15.
9. Ibid., pp. 404–05.
10. Ibid., pp. 409–10.
11. Ibid., p. 404. The question of historical memory is also discussed in Olga A. Bozhchenko, 'Faktory formirovaniia istoricheskoi pamiati' [The Factors Forming Historical Memory], *Voprosy kul'turologii* [Issues of Cultural Study], 9 (2012), 57–62.
12. *Testimony: The Memoirs of Dmitri Shostakovich*, ed. by Solomon Volkov and trans. by Antonina W. Bouis (New York: Limelight Editions, 1995), pp. 155–56. For discussion of the authenticity and accuracy of the *Testimony*, see *A Shostakovich Casebook*, ed. by Malcolm Hamrick Brown (Bloomington: Indiana University Press, 2004).

CHAPTER 9

The Ontology of Mourning

Aarathi Prasad

Mortuary Contexts

> People did not know yet what death was and therefore tried to warm up the body.
> (Proposition offered in explanation of the choice of hearth burials.)
> — P. M. Küsters[1]

At a fundamental level, mourning the dead assumes an ability to contemplate abstractions: to remember the past, and to imagine a future, including one in which the mourner too will no longer be present.[2] Such an ability to parse information symbolically — that is, through a thought process in which a person's 'external environment and internal mental states are deconstructed' to envision multiple potential realities 'not only as it is directly perceived by the senses, but as it *might* be' — is thought to have been the result of a major cognitive reorganization for our species.[3] When exactly that point arrived is still debated. Both a gradual evolution over the two million years since our multiple human antecedents first appeared — and an epochal event that would have occurred inside a few generations of the first modern humans (*Homo sapiens sapiens*) some 200,000–300,000 years ago — have been proposed.

Our archaeological record, which tells of the lives and activities of *Homo sapiens*, but also of our extinct relations, supplements the 2.5 million-year-old fossil record we have of our deepest history. In amongst this, funerals are one of the most frequently encountered classes of cultural feature observed, and include a variety of practices through which our ancient relations have been sent off: cremations, inhumations, disarticulations, disaggregations, as well as combinations of any of these.[4] Such treatment of bodies after death has been identified 'as a strong social statement and as a metaphor for social organisation',[5] but it is also recognized that in interpreting the deposited remains of a human body, any analysis of a burial is an analysis of a symbolic action; that 'a burial is part of a funeral, and a funeral is part of a set of rituals by which the living deal with death'.[6]

Before the appearance of engraved or painted rock art — considered material evidence of activities pointing to the emergence of symbolic thinking in the human lineage — it has been funerary practice that offers 'one of the few opportunities to address the deepest elements of the psyche of Palaeolithic humans'.[7] The oldest identified burials of morphologically modern humans date from the Middle Palaeolithic, between *c.* 120,000 and 90,000 years before the present. Found at Qafzeh, a large cave at the flank of a hill near Nazareth, these are burials of a minimum of twenty-seven individuals: adults, children, and babies, including a new-born, as well as a double burial of an adult with a child. Although the intentionality of the placement of these remains has been called into question by some researchers, they appear to be true burials, in that they consisted of placing the corpse in a prepared pit which was then back-filled, in some cases, after the insertion of grave goods into, or near, the grave. These antlers, incised flakes, objects covered with scraped red ochre, and possibly also seashells indicate 'rites' that went beyond simple prevention of scavenging of the dead or even a basic provision of dignity, and may or may not allude to some kind of belief in an afterlife.[8]

In the study of the archaeology of death, the body of the deceased, and its treatment, serves as a direct reflection of the past society to which it belonged.[9] Many inferences have been made as to the relationship between the diverse forms of mortuary custom and beliefs throughout recorded history, and preceding it, from cave burials and exposure, to sky burials and cremation. The fact that suitable caves existed did not always mean they were appropriated for burials, for example, so explanations for the choice of where graves were located have sought to reconcile rituals of mourning with assumptions about the fears or desires of those who were left behind. 'The dead are buried near, or in, their old homes, because they are wanted back again, in the form of babies born of women of their own clan, tribe or family,' says one proposal, for example;[10] or, in citing the burial of children under house floors:

> It is not impossible that we have here one of the ways in which the fear of the dead may have been gradually dispelled. May we not imagine that one of the first steps was the refusal of the mother to allow her dead child to be banished from the house?[11]

Globally, contemporary funerary rituals reflect those across human histories, in which a diversity of practices is evident. Depending on cultural perspectives, some mourning customs that keep the dead near are deeply affecting, like those of the Torojan people of Sulawesi, Indonesia, said to have the most complex funerary rituals in the world. Observing their contemporary practice — which is rooted in pre-Christian traditions (*Aluk To Dolo*, or 'Way of the Ancestors') — from an attachment-based bereavement model, these might be interpreted as an expression of 'complicated grief', which in modern, Western psychiatry is considered a prolonged grief disorder which includes ongoing difficulty comprehending the death, intense yearning and longing for the person who died, preoccupation with thoughts and images of the deceased, and debilitating 'avoidance behaviours'.[12] Mummified with a solution of formaldehyde and water, Torojan dead are referred to as *to makula* [one who has fever] or *to mama* [a person who is asleep], and, as such, are kept and cared for at home for weeks, months, or even years after their death. Expressions of not being ready to let loved ones go are common. 'I'm not sad, because she's still with us,' one Torojan woman said of her seventy-three-year-old mother, who had lain dead in the family house for more than a year.[13] The delay is often so that sufficient funds can be gathered for the funeral ceremony, which will cost between USD 50,000 and 500,000, primarily due to the requirement to purchase up to twenty-four buffalo (expensive animals) for public ritual sacrifice. The buffalo go with the deceased to the next world, to ensure their wealth. Until that first sacrifice of the mortuary rites has taken place, the dead are not seen as dead. After that, every three years they are removed from their graves, in ever-progressive states of decay, to be cleaned, given new clothes, shoes, eye glasses, food, and drink.[14] In this way, mourners are able to continue to care for those they have lost, and Torojan youth are able to share a meal or even a cigarette with relatives who had died long before they were born.

Peculiar though they may seem, such funerary rituals — which over time, and space, have included defleshing, re-burying and cannibalizing bodies, burying ancestors under the floor of one's own home, plastering, carving or decorating skulls — kept loved ones close in some way. In the human treatment of our dead we changed our practices of where, and how, we parted with our dead, even as we were changing the way we lived, from agrarian settlements to cities, for example, so that mortuary practice began to reflect our increasing social complexity, augment our social memory, and reflect our cosmological beliefs.

Creatures Like Any Other?

> If man wants to set up a contest in resembling himself and award himself the prize, no one will quarrel with him. — MARY MIDGLEY[15]

Francesco d'Errico and Chris Stringer's 2011 paper, 'Evolution, Revolution or Saltation Scenario for the Emergence of Modern Cultures?', opens with an interesting premise:

> It is too easy to argue that since we are the only hominin species left on the planet we must be unique and special in some respect. This proposition does not tell us what were the paths that our ancestors took to become so distinctive and to what extent we share partially, or entirely, this supposed uniqueness with our present or past relatives.[16]

Hominins refers to a group consisting of extinct human species, all our immediate ancestors, and modern humans (*Homo sapiens*), who originated within the past 300,000 years. D'Errico and Stringer describe three scenarios, all proposed to account for the origin of cultural modernity: that modern cognition is unique to our species and the consequence of a genetic mutation that took place approximately 50,000 years ago in Africa among already evolved anatomically modern humans; that cultural modernity emerged gradually in Africa starting at least 200,000 years ago in concert with the origin of our species on that continent; or else, that innovations indicative of modern cognition are not restricted to our species, but appear, and disappear, in Africa and Eurasia between 200,000 and 40,000 years ago, before becoming fully consolidated.

In marrying the acts of mourning with the capability of complex language acquisition and communication — these markers of cultural modernity, including the development of symbolic thinking that is considered a differentiator between humans, *Homo sapiens*, and other animals, including other primates, to whom we are genetically closely related — archaeologists and anthropologists have not failed to note that ritual, defined as a repeated pattern of behaviour performed at specified times, often involving tangible inclusion of symbols, and composed of rites or actions that may serve to uphold social goals, is anything but exclusive to us, specifically, or even to human beings at all.[17]

At the Qafzeh Cave, that site of the most ancient known *Homo sapiens sapiens* burials, were also found inhumations of another human, now extinct: *Homo sapiens neanderthalensis.* Morphologically different but archeologically very similar human groups, these more muscular Neanderthals, with their distinct skulls and faces, and our own ancestors, early modern *sapiens*, existed at around the same time, populated the same spaces, and used typologically and technologically similar toolkits, although, as a proxy for their manual abilities, analysis of their hand anatomy seems to suggest that they both must have displayed significant behavioural differences, at least in their physical engagement with the material world.[18] However, in a 2002 report on the excavation of Qafzeh, paleoanthropologist Bernard Vandermeersch made note of the fact that the proximity of the two types of humans, and of their practices there in West Eurasia in the middle Palaeolithic would have:

> forced researchers to reconsider the possible ties between these two groups, a problem that to this day has not received a satisfactory explanation. Second, the relationship between one human genus and another and between cultures, the relationships between the biological and the cultural had to be viewed in a different way. The problem of a possible correlation between 'levels' of biological development of taxons who preceded us and their degree of cultural 'maturation' is a recurrent one in all research in prehistory and anthropology. [...] [I]t is worth pointing out that the Qafzeh discoveries showed that these correlations no longer hold when dealing with the relationships between Neanderthal and Modern man.[19]

Dating from around 60,000 years ago, the Qafzeh Neanderthal burials, much like those of the *sapiens*, appear to be intentional interment: although deliberate placement of bodies (or parts of them) into unmodified locations in an environment has also been found, in several cases Neanderthal graves had been dug into, and covered with the same pre-existing strata. That is to say, these were not just abandoned bodies that simply became covered over with the passing of time. Over the last decades, questions as to whether Neanderthals actually possessed the cognitive capability to bury their dead have attracted criticisms and doubts. But some Neanderthals did bury their dead, at least some of the time.[20] It is unclear as to whether those who did so learned this behaviour from humans, or developed it independently; after all, recent studies demonstrate that we and they interbred, with genomic evidence suggesting gene flow from early *Homo sapiens* to (eastern Altai) Neanderthals *c.* 100,000 years ago and flow from Neanderthals to *Homo sapiens* between *c.* 60,000 and 50,000 years ago.[21]

But even without any *Homo sapiens* interaction, the fact that Neanderthals treated their dead in socially meaningful ways should not be surprising, given that there is good evidence that they cared for their sick and elderly, and used pigments, coloured shells, as well as falcon, vulture, and other feathers as jewellery to decorate themselves — all taken as signs that they were capable of symbolic, and complex, thought.[22] There is also recent evidence from three sites in Spain demonstrating that the earliest cave art to emerge in Iberia (older than 648,000 years) predates the arrival of modern humans in Europe by at least 20,000 years, implying that this art must have been the work of Neanderthals.[23] In a funereal context, Neanderthals may have also placed flowers in graves, at least those found in northeast Iraqi Kurdistan, where pollen has been identified in the soil of a burial dating to 70,000 years ago.[24] Although a hypothesis that a rodent species had brought this pollen in through tunnels had been posited,[25] robust evidence for this may be lacking, and how these flowers got into the burials remains under investigation.[26] Nonetheless, there have been other elements of interest found in Neanderthal interments that are notable. In 1933, at La Ferrassie cave in France, for example, 'burial 6' dated to around 60,000 years ago and which contained the grave of a three-year-old Neanderthal child, was found to be covered with a large limestone slab, whose underside was decorated with arrangement of cupule-art, circles cut into stone, in a pattern of two larger hollows with eight pairs of smaller holes. Apart from finds like these, no convincing example of actual grave goods is known from the Neanderthals, although, interestingly, archaeologist Paul Pettitt notes that 'grave goods may or may not relate to metaphysical notions of an afterlife or bodily extension; they probably speak more of self-expression and concepts of ownership. It may well be that neither existed in Neanderthal societies'.[27]

Hundreds of thousands of years before any known *sapiens* or Neanderthal burials, the placement of the remains of *Homo naledi* also poses questions about how our more ancient forebears grieved for their dead. *Homo naledi* lived around 300,000 years ago, of whom more than 1500 articulated and disarticulated fossils representing at least fifteen individuals were unearthed from the narrow 3 by 5 m 'Dinaledi' chamber deep inside the Rising Star cave system in South Africa between 2013 and 2014, with further exploration of the far separated 'Lesedi' chamber leading to the discovery of 131 further specimens.[28] Found thirty metres deep underground, these *Homo naledi* fossils form the largest collection of a single species of an ancient human-relative discovered in Africa. Its bones show that there is a distinct similarity between the hands, wrist, and feet of *Homo naledi*, of *Homo sapiens*, and of those belonging to Neanderthals. But its brain, which was small, and its upper body shape are considered more 'primitive', in that they reflect instead the very early human species *Homo habilis*, and even the pre-human australopithecines.[29]

A significant question around the discovery of *Homo naledi* is exactly why so many of their remains were there in that specific location at all. How did they come to rest so far into a difficult to access cave system? In a similar vein to those arguments used to challenge the intentionality of Neanderthal burials, a number of possible explanations have been offered in respect of *naledi* too: perhaps *Homo naledi* simply lived in those caves, rather than just dying there; or that their remains had been washed in by a flood — both of which have now been ruled out. Others argue that the evidence is largely consistent with intact bodies being deliberately disposed of in the cave and then decomposing, as 'detailed analyses of the taphonomy and distribution of the hominin bone accumulations suggested at least some of the bodies were deposited while still fleshed'.[30] Another point worthy of note is that, unlike the Qafzeh and Es Skhul Caves in Israel, where both *Homo sapiens* and Neanderthals were found, Dinaledi appears to have been the domain only of *Homo naledi*. The caves exclusively contain the bodies of these hominins, with no remains of other ancient humans, or their relatives yet found there.

In respect of the capacity for symbolic thought, that enigmatic prerequisite of mourning ritual, the observation of *Homo naledi*'s diminutive brain size, at around 465–560 of the 1082–1832-millilitre volume of modern *Homo sapiens*, versus its more modern-human-like appendicular anatomy is an interesting one.[31] *Homo habilis* — 'handy' or 'skilful' man, who lived around one to two million years before *Homo naledi*, and who is the earliest known member of the genus *Homo* — had a brain volume range of 500 to more than 700 millilitres. But the idea that identical total brain volumes imply identical internal organization does not always follow. Instead, it is how brains are organized within whatever volume an animal's skull contains that holds more pertinent information in terms of social cognition and differing abilities to cope with cultural maintenance, as Pearce and co-authors (2013) noted in a study in which they investigated differences in brain organization of Neanderthals compared to anatomically modern humans:

> The differences in the partitioning of brain tissue might have substantial implications for cognitive processing in Neanderthals compared with contemporary anatomically modern humans. For instance, there is a well-established relationship between brain and bonded group size across anthropoid primates, as well as between specific areas of the frontal lobe and active social network (total number of personal contacts) size at the within-species individual level in both macaques and, more importantly, humans. In addition, neuroimaging studies have shown that this relationship between key brain region volumes and group size is mediated by mentalizing (theory of mind) competences. [...] The mean size of the active network for living humans predicted by cross-primate neocortex ratio comparisons has been corroborated across not only historical and modern traditional subsistence societies, but also in online social environments. This suggests that throughout human evolution, brain structure and cognitive function have placed a constraint on bonded group size and social complexity.[32]

As such, the kind of social complexities which would have seen *Homo naledi* returning to a difficult-to-access, communal burial chamber, if that is what the Dinaldi and Lesedi collection of fossils indeed represents, may not pose as significant a conundrum as first it may appear. For the brain of *Homo naledi* has been reported to contain structural detail similar to those of bigger-brained members of the genus *Homo*, including us, with recent research suggesting that such common, persistent structures emerged early in the story of *Homo*, potentially permitting more advanced cognitive functions, regardless of overall brain volume differences.[33]

Responses Towards the Dead: Tales from the Animal World

> Then the Elephant's Child grew all breathless, and panted, and kneeled down on the bank and said, 'You are the very person I have been looking for all these long days. Will you please tell me what you have for dinner?'
> 'Come hither, Little One,' said the Crocodile, 'and I'll whisper.'
> — RUDYARD KIPLING[34]

Humans, extant and extinct, represent, of course, just one broad type of animal, but grief-like reactions to death in a range of other animals have also long been noted, including by Charles Darwin, as being expressed in a number of species as altered patterns of behaviour, and/or apparent distress. Subsequently, however, the issue of anthropomorphism as the projection, or subjective interpretation of human emotions onto other animals became a concern in the absence of robust studies. But animals, both human and non-human ones, do attend to deaths and display altered behaviours around them. Routines of normal behaviour become markedly different; forms of visible emotional distress are articulated through social withdrawal, the failure to eat or sleep, with visible postural changes, or vocalizations. From ducks to turtles, bison to whales, some animals have been recorded to display altered behaviours only at the loss of those to whom they are attached; others, also towards dead strangers of their own type; yet others, to other kinds of animals entirely. Not surprisingly, much of the literature has been dedicated to observations of the first, and particularly with respect to the maternal response to deceased young, and those of the young towards their mothers. In her 1990 book, *Through a Window*, primatologist Jane Goodall describes the death of an eight-year-old chimpanzee, Flint, following a period of what she describes as depression at the death of his mother, Flo:

> Never shall I forget watching as, three days after Flo's death, Flint climbed slowly into a tall tree near the stream. He walked along one of the branches, then stopped and stood motionless, staring down at an empty nest. After about two minutes he turned away and, with the movements of an old man, climbed down, walked a few steps, then lay, wide eyes staring ahead. The nest was one which he and Flo had shared a short while before Flo died. [...] [I]n the presence of his big brother, [Flint] had seemed to shake off a little of his depression. But then he suddenly left the group and raced back to the place where Flo had died and there sank into ever deeper depression. [...]
>
> Flint became increasingly lethargic, refused food and, with his immune system thus weakened, fell sick. The last time I saw him alive, he was hollow-eyed, gaunt and utterly depressed, huddled in the vegetation close to where Flo had died. [...] The last short journey he made, pausing to rest every few feet, was to the very place where Flo's body had lain. There he stayed for several hours, sometimes staring and staring into the water. He struggled on a little further, then curled up — and never moved again.[35]

As animals that are also highly socially complex — a factor which may play a significant role in the development of mourning behaviours — elephants have also been widely reported to have a general interest in death, and to investigate carcasses including and beyond those to whom they are related. In a recent paper, Rutherford and Murray further previous observations by describing interesting nuances to the grief behaviours evident following the deaths of herd members. Changes to their personality and affiliative behaviours (those social interactions that function to reinforce social bonds), the researchers found, were not uniform, but age- and relationship-related:

> Overall, the herd spent less time socializing and engaging in affiliative behaviours following the death of the adult female when compared to baseline data, yet spent more time engaging in these behaviours after the death of two calves. The death of the central female had a dramatic impact on her infant calf, resulting in increasingly withdrawn behaviour, yet had the opposite effect on her adult daughter, who subsequently established a more integrated role within the herd. Emotional stability fell in the motherless calf but rose in an adult female, who had lost her adult daughter, but had a new calf to care for.[36]

These two, differing responses to the death of a parent could easily be very recognizable to human families too. As such, perhaps, as animals, some of our grief-related behaviours could be called zoomorphic, as much as theirs might reasonably, rather than fancifully, seem anthropomorphic. But what about animals to whom we are more evolutionarily distant, like ants? A great deal about the chemistry and underlying mechanisms of how animals deal with their dead, or, more bluntly put, their modes of corpse management, have been learnt from the study of insects. Within this class, many of the Hymenoptera (which include ants, but also bees and wasps), are known as 'eusocial' insects, meaning they display a number of peculiar characteristics. Their adults live in groups, in which there is an overlap of generations. Their juveniles are cared for cooperatively, but not all individuals get to reproduce. There is a deeply altruistic element to eusociality, with evolutionary biologists tracing its origins through a pathway that started with solitary organisms acquiring benefits from group behaviour, something that may be further elucidated through the recent field of sociogenomics, which studies the molecular basis of social life through an integration of molecular biology, genomics, neuroscience, behavioural biology, evolutionary biology, and bioinformatics.[37]

In his review of responses to death and dying in primates and other mammals, primatologist James Anderson — who with archaeologist Paul Pettitt and zoologist Dora Biro had proposed the creation of a new field of interdisciplinary research called 'evolutionary thanatology' to more fully capture the breadth of the topic[38] — describes the fundamental involvement of chemical signals from corpses in the response of eusocial insects around death.[39] The production and perception of such chemicals holds a fundamental place in the question of what aspects of the 'death concept' might be common across animals, in terms of how they differentiate between what is alive and what is dead. Called necromones, these chemicals elicit 'necrophoric' behaviours that underlie insect corpse management strategies, including avoidance of, discarding, ingesting, and burying the dead. The 'smell of death' chemicals — putrescine and cadaverine — were also found to be involved in the burial of dead rats by living, laboratory rats who used bedding material for the purpose. Anderson writes:

> The smell is often repugnant enough to initiate action to get relief, either by moving away from the smell, or locating the corpse and disposing of it. Surprisingly, the first experimental study of the ability of putrescine to elicit 'escape' behaviours in humans was published relatively recently, and it demonstrated effects even when the putrescine presented was below the threshold of conscious awareness.[40]

How chemically imprinted, and, therefore, shared, might our responses to death be? Added to the necromones, an endocrinological approach, in which fluctuations to the levels of a number of hormones in those who are bereaved (both human and non-human) are examined, has been instructive in elucidating our 'emotional' response to deaths. These include: oxytocin, implicated in mother-infant bonds, as well as other social bonds, like those between sexual partners/mates; and glucocorticoid (corticosteroid) levels, normally induced by pain and inflammation, but also by mental stress, as illustrated by a study of a Japanese macaque mother whose carrying of her dead infant lowered her glucocorticoid levels, suggesting that the common primate practice of dead infant-carrying may serve as a strategy to mitigate stress from infant loss.[41]

These chemically-induced behavioural changes, essentially, and for us all, form our basic reactions to death. Although it remains the case that funereal, ritual, or sociocultural aspects are not apparent in the practice of other animals in any way that approaches the symbolism of those enacted by numerous hominins, the actions and interactions displayed by so many animals around death can certainly be complex and emotional.

However, the type of advanced cognitive functions that transcend the fundamental chemical response, and that are thought to pre-empt the symbolism and rituals of funerals, may relate to a distinction that can be drawn between 'grieving' and 'mourning'. In this, grief, of the kind widely observed in the animal kingdom, may be an expression of a short-term passive process; while acts of mourning remain part of an active, long-term process — 'a process that involves a profound transformation of our assumptions about self in the world, a search for meaning in the loss, and the creation of and interaction with an inner representation of the deceased'.[42] Whether only humans create mourning from grief, may, ultimately, be unknowable.

Notes to Chapter 9

1. P. M. Küsters, 'Das Grab der Afrikaner', *Anthropos*, 14/15 (1919/20), 639–728, and 16/17 (1921), 183–229, 913–59 (p. 956), cited in Lewis R. Binford, 'Mortuary Practices: Their Study and Their Potential', *Memoirs of the Society for American Archaeology*, 25 (1971), 6–29 (p. 13). Ian Morris also draws attention to this quotation in *Death-ritual and Social Structure in Classical Antiquity* (Cambridge: Cambridge University Press, 1992), p. 31.
2. Paige Madison, 'Who First Buried the Dead?', *Sapiens*, 16 February 2018 <https://www.sapiens.org/culture/hominin-burial/> [accessed 10 November 2020].
3. Ian Tattersall, 'The Minimalist Program and the Origin of Language: A View from Paleoanthropology', *Frontiers in Psychology*, 10 (2019) <https://www.frontiersin.org/articles/10.3389/fpsyg.2019.00677/full> [accessed 11 August 2021].
4. Binford, 'Mortuary Practices'.
5. Joanna R. Sofaer, *The Body as Material Culture: A Theoretical Osteoarchaeology* (Cambridge:

Cambridge University Press, 2006), p. 12, with reference to Mike Parker Pearson, *The Archaeology of Death and Burial* (Stroud: Sutton, 1999).

6. Morris, *Death-ritual and Social Structure in Classical Antiquity*, p. 1.
7. Bernard Vandermeersch and Ofer Bar-Yosef, 'The Paleolithic Burials at Qafzeh Cave, Israel', *PALEO*, 30–31 (2019), 256–75 (p. 264).
8. Avraham Ronen, 'The Oldest Burials and their Significance', in *African Genesis: Perspectives on Hominin Evolution*, ed. by Sally C. Reynolds and Andrew Gallagher (Cambridge: Cambridge University Press, 2012), pp. 554–70.
9. Joanna R. Sofaer, 'The Body as an Archaeological Resource', in *The Body as Material Culture*, pp. 12–30.
10. H. J. Rose, 'Celestial and Terrestrial Orientation of the Dead', *The Journal of the Royal Anthropological Institute of Great Britain and Ireland*, 52 (1922), 127–40 (p. 129), cited in Binford, 'Mortuary Practices', p. 13.
11. John M. Tyler, *The New Stone Age of Northern Europe* (New York: Charles Scribner's Sons, 1921), pp. 125–26, cited in Binford, 'Mortuary Practices', p. 13.
12. M. J. Horowitz and others, 'Diagnostic Criteria for Complicated Grief Disorder', *American Journal of Psychiatry*, 154 (1997), 904–10.
13. Amanda Bennett, 'When Death Doesn't Mean Goodbye', *National Geographic*, March 2016 <https://www.nationalgeographic.com/magazine/2016/04/death-dying-grief-funeral-ceremony-corpse/> [accessed 10 November 2020].
14. Dimitri Tsintjilonis, 'Death and the Sacrifice of Signs: "Measuring" the Dead in Tana Toraja', *Oceania*, 71 (2000), 1–17.
15. Mary Midgley, *Beast and Man: The Roots of Human Nature*, rev. edn (London: Routledge Classics, 2002), p. 114.
16. Francesco d'Errico and Chris B. Stringer, 'Evolution, Revolution or Saltation Scenario for the Emergence of Modern Cultures?', *Philosophical Transactions of the Royal Society B*, 366 (2011), 1060–69 (p. 1060) <https://royalsocietypublishing.org/doi/10.1098/rstb.2010.0340> [accessed 11 August 2021].
17. 'Ritual', in *A Dictionary of Sociology*, ed. by John Scott, 4th edn (Oxford: Oxford University Press, 2014), p. 651.
18. Wesley A. Niewoehner, 'Behavioral Inferences from the Skhul/Qafzeh Early Modern Human Hand Remains', *Proceedings of the National Academy of Sciences*, 98 (2001), 2979–84.
19. Bernard Vandermeersch, 'The Excavation of Qafzeh: Its Contribution to Knowledge of the Mousterian in the Levant', *Bulletin du Centre de recherche français à Jérusalem*, 10 (2002), 65–70 (p. 67).
20. Emma Pomeroy and others, 'New Neanderthal Remains associated with the "Flower Burial" at Shanidar Cave', *Antiquity*, 94 (2020), 11–26.
21. Ella Been and others, 'The First Neanderthal Remains from an Open-air Middle Palaeolithic Site in the Levant', *Sci Rep*, 7.2958 (2017), 1–8.
22. William Rendu and others, 'Evidence Supporting an Intentional Neandertal Burial at La Chapelle-aux-Saints', *Proceedings of the National Academy of Sciences*, 111 (2014), 81–86.
23. D. L. Hoffmann and others, 'U-Th Dating of Carbonate Crusts reveals Neandertal Origin of Iberian Cave Art', *Science*, 359 (2018), 912–15.
24. Pomeroy and others, 'New Neanderthal Remains associated with the "Flower Burial" at Shanidar Cave'.
25. Jeffrey D. Sommer, 'The Shanidar IV "Flower Burial": A Re-evaluation of Neanderthal Burial Ritual', *Cambridge Archaeological Journal*, 9 (1999), 127–29.
26. Emily Tilby, email to the author, 27 October 2020.
27. Paul Pettitt, 'The Neanderthal Dead: Exploring Mortuary Variability in Middle Palaeolithic Eurasia', *Before Farming*, 4.1 (2002), 1–26 (p. 18).
28. John Hawks and others, 'New Fossil Remains of *Homo naledi* from the Lesedi Chamber, South Africa', *eLife*, 6 (2017) <https://elifesciences.org/articles/24232> [accessed 11 August 2021].
29. Lee R. Berger and others, '*Homo naledi*, a New Species of the Genus *Homo* from the Dinaledi Chamber, South Africa', *eLife*, 4 (2015) <https://elifesciences.org/articles/09560> [accessed 11 August 2021].

30. Debra R. Bolter and others, 'Immature Remains and the First Partial Skeleton of a Juvenile *Homo naledi*, a Late Middle Pleistocene Hominin from South Africa', *PLoS ONE*, 15 (2020) <https://journals.plos.org/plosone/article?id=10.1371/journal.pone.0230440> [accessed 11 August 2021].
31. Simon Neubauer, Jean-Jacques Hublin, and Philipp Gunz, 'The Evolution of Modern Human Brain Shape', *Science Advances*, 4.1 (2018) <https://advances.sciencemag.org/content/4/1/eaao5961.short> [accessed 11 August 2021].
32. Eiluned Pearce, Chris Stringer, and R. I. M. Dunbar, 'New Insights into Differences in Brain Organization between Neanderthals and Anatomically Modern Humans', *Proceedings of the Royal Society B*, 280 (2013) <https://royalsocietypublishing.org/doi/full/10.1098/rspb.2013.0168> [accessed 11 August 2021].
33. Ralph L. Holloway and others, 'Endocast Morphology of *Homo naledi* from the Dinaledi Chamber, South Africa', *Proceedings of the National Academy of Sciences of the USA*, 115 (2018) <https://www.pnas.org/content/115/22/5738> [accessed 11 August 2021].
34. Rudyard Kipling, 'The Elephant's Child', in *Just So Stories* (London: Collector's Library, 2004), pp. 45–57 (pp. 50–51).
35. Jane Goodall, *Through a Window: My Thirty Years with the Chimpanzees of Gombe* (Boston, MA: Houghton-Mifflin, 1990), pp. 196–97.
36. Lucy Rutherford and Lindsay E. Murray, 'Personality and Behavioral Changes in Asian Elephants (*Elephas maximus*) Following the Death of Herd Members', *Integrative Zoology*, 16.2 (2021), 170–88 (p. 170).
37. Edward O. Wilson, *The Insect Societies* (Cambridge, MA: Belknap Press of Harvard University Press, 1971); Wilson and Hölldobler, 'Eusociality'.
38. Anderson, Biro, and Pettitt, 'Evolutionary Thanatology'.
39. James R. Anderson, 'Responses to Death and Dying: Primates and Other Mammals', *Primates*, 61 (2020), 1–7.
40. Ibid., p. 2.
41. Rafaela S. C. Takeshita and others, 'Changes in Social Behavior and Fecal Glucocorticoids in a Japanese Macaque (*Macaca fuscata*) Carrying her Dead Infant', *Primates*, 61 (2020), 5–40.
42. Marrone, 'Grieving and Mourning', p. 320.

INTERMEZZO NO. 3

❖

Selected Poems

Elena Buia Rutt

translated from the Italian by Andrew Rutt

For Miriam and Thomas

I will not see you grow old.

I will not be there to support you
when your legs
tremble
from exhaustion
or the fear of dying.

But even if I were there,
you would not ask anything of me
I, who battle now
to tame the wind
which lashes against your backs
on your way to school.

So I ask myself
what will remain
of this wild love
of this love with claws
plunged deeply
until its last breath
into the word
children.

The Goldfish

We all do things.
And at the close of the day
we seal
the page
with the word end.

I however spend my time
under the table
collecting the pen tops
dropped
by my children.

And again
and again.

But this afternoon
we will bury the goldfish
amidst the rosemary
on the balcony.

Me and you
together
for the first time
— hand in hand —
in the pregnant womb
of death.

The Balloon

Grandma, I telephone you
and you reply
feeble
as I have never heard you,
so much so
I tie you to my wrist
— as if you were a balloon —
with the earthly things of life
with the children's cough
with the money that is never there.

And you docile
let yourself be held
for a last race
a last smile
while the string starts
to pull —
because the destiny
of every balloon
is to hover so high
in the sky
until it can no longer be seen,
but only regretted
and then admired
for the lightness
for the freedom
with which it soars to eternity.

Water and Flour

I knew I would not find you,
and yet I came to search
where a white part of your body
still belongs to the world
and to me.

Your leap happened elsewhere
— at home, during the night, unexpectedly —
but now,
walking around this countryside cemetery
I would like to reach out
as in a movie
beyond the liquid wall in front of me
and pierce through
to see what you are doing
and if you can see me
now
— and then —
forever.

Perhaps I would realize
that you have changed somehow
and only goodness is left in you,
and I who received it
would recall how
truth
sat
on Sunday
at your kitchen table
where kids and grownups
together kneaded
water and flour into dough.

The Dream

Last night I dreamt
that my mother
was dying

and I, lying close
to her polished stone body
looking up high, told her:
'Go, go gentle, and do not worry about us.
Dad will manage to
pick up the kids from school
by himself
and I will learn
how to use the freezer
to store food.

But you must not be afraid now,
it seems that it is only dark at the beginning
you will then meet a bright light
that will welcome you
without blinding you.

Yet, every so often, in the evenings
if you see that I can't manage
to hem my trousers
guide my hand
so that I can
still
feel
the curt yet devoted care
of your love for me.'

The Dead Frog

You sing a lullaby
to a dead frog
at the edge of a pond
of a city park:
you want to comfort it.

And in this sweet stuttering,
of a child
your piety intuits
what for centuries
the wise men
baffled,
have tossed and turned,
racking their brains...
and twisted
like snakes
round a stick.

While you are singing,
absorbed
in the certainty of a
life that
does not die.

PART IV

Breaking the Silence

CHAPTER 10

A Grief Narrated: The Contemporary Grief Memoir

Simona Corso

> 19 [September 1917]
> Have never understood how it is possible for almost everyone who writes to objectify his sufferings in the very midst of undergoing them; thus I, for example, in the midst of my unhappiness, in all likelihood with my head still smarting from unhappiness, sit down and write to someone: I am unhappy. [...] And it is not a lie, and it does not still my pain; it is simply a merciful surplus of strength at a moment when suffering has raked me to the bottom of my being and plainly exhausted all my strength. But then what kind of surplus is it?
>
> FRANZ KAFKA, *Diaries*[1]

The title of my chapter draws on the title of the famous mourning diary that C. S. Lewis composed in 1961 for his wife Joy Davidman, who died of cancer at the age of forty-five. The book, entitled *A Grief Observed*, was published under the pseudonym N. W. Clerk; when, two years later, after the death of C. S. Lewis, the book was republished under his own name, Joy's name remained hidden under a capitalized 'H' (Helen), that, although her real name, neither she nor Lewis had been in the habit of using. Such screens reveal the reserve with which a famous writer like C. S. Lewis felt he must face the public exposure of his grief and evoke the silence that engulfed the discourse of mourning in those days. It is a silence that has been narrated by historians, anthropologists, and sociologists, and the very fact that many have undertaken the task of narrating it reveals that it is finally breaking down.

In this chapter, I will look back at the history of that silence, or rather at some stages of it, and at the gradual, often contradictory and not always successful, attempts at breaking it. I will then explore a 'new' literary genre that has been enjoying great editorial success in the last ten years: the grief memoir. I argue that the contemporary grief memoir, composed by writers, journalists, and intellectuals, points to a new phase in the long history of our confrontation with death. It can be interpreted as an attempt to bring back into daily conversation and into the life of ordinary people the theorization about death that literature has always performed, in the form of a testimony. Focusing in particular on *Levels of Life* by Julian Barnes

(2013), *Grief is a Thing with Feathers* by Max Porter (2015), and *Patrimony: A True Story* by Philip Roth (1991), I will explore the reasons for the grief memoir's success and its therapeutic force for many readers: the way in which these works can perform, also for the benefit of readers, what Freud called, with dazzling intuition, the *work* of mourning.

Breaking the Silence

Let me take a step back and return to Lewis's diary. In *A Grief Observed*, the British author remarks:

> I cannot talk to the children about her. The moment I try, there appears on their faces neither grief, nor love, nor fear, nor pity, but the most fatal of all non-conductors, embarrassment. They look as if I were committing an indecency.[2]

With the passing of time, Lewis came to understand that the children's embarrassment was shared by many others: it appeared to be the dominant sentiment among those he met, even months after Joy's death: 'It isn't only the boys either. An odd by-product of my loss is that I'm aware of being an embarrassment to everyone I meet. [...] Perhaps the bereaved ought to be isolated in special settlements like lepers'.[3]

A few years after the first publication of *A Grief Observed*, the British anthropologist Geoffrey Gorer completed his revolutionary study of mourning rituals and contemporary attitudes towards death in British society, entitled *Death, Grief, and Mourning in Contemporary Britain* (1965), a book which built on his earlier, groundbreaking essay 'The Pornography of Death' (1955). Gorer writes:

> Death and mourning are treated today with much the same prudery as sexual impulses were a century ago. [...] The gratitude with which a number of my informants thanked me for talking to them without embarrassment about their grief must, I think, be similar to the gratitude felt a couple of generations earlier by people when their sexual secrets could finally be discussed without prudery or condemnation.[4]

Many of Gorer's assumptions recur in Philippe Ariès's monumental study *L'Homme devant la mort* (1977), in which the French historian identifies two fundamental cultural shifts in twentieth-century post-industrial society: first, an increasing medicalization of death, which comes to be seen as a private matter that can be delegated to professionals (doctors, nurses, funeral home managers); second, the emergence of a new death taboo, a desire to exclude the topic from daily conversation, which tragically culminates in a 'rejection and elimination of mourning' — 'the second great milestone,' in Ariès's words, 'in the contemporary history of death'.[5]

Ariès's position has been embraced by some of the most influential commentators of contemporary Western society. Jean Baudrillard, for example, adopts the central hypothesis of *L'Homme devant la mort* when he claims in *L'Échange symbolique et la mort* (1976) that:

> At the very core of the 'rationality' of our culture, however, is an exclusion that precedes every other, more radical than the exclusion of madmen, children or inferior races, an exclusion preceding all these and serving as their model: the exclusion of the dead and of death.[6]

More recently, Zygmunt Bauman has argued that secular industrialized societies do not provide us with a language in which to address the dying: 'We may offer the dying only the language of survival; but this is precisely the one language which cannot grasp the condition from which they [unlike us] can hide no more'.[7]

In 1983, in *La Mort et l'Occident de 1300 à nos jours*, French historian Michel Vovelle noticed that the debate on death, during the twentieth century, was mined by an underlying schizophrenia, which, Vovelle held, belonged to the century itself.[8] The century during which life expectancy incessantly rose, due to progress in the medical field, was also the epoch of extraordinarily violent wars, genocides, and new apocalyptic anxieties (the atomic bomb, cancer). These contradictions determined a schizophrenic attitude in our perception of death: from the mid-century onward, according to Vovelle, the silence about death in daily life and conversation went hand in hand with a growing spectacularization of death in cinema, popular literature, and comic strips, but also with an uninterrupted reflection on death in philosophy and high literature. While cinema and television thrust death in our faces, the growing medicalization and commercialization of death took the dead away from us. As soon as a person stopped breathing, and often even before then, they disappeared from our view: stolen from our embrace, they were delivered into the care of doctors, nurses, and, finally, funeral managers. Vovelle observed that the two phenomena — the hypertrophy of death on the one hand, the repression of death on the other — only apparently contradicted each other. One attitude compensated for the other: there were places where one could speak and places where one should keep silent. He writes: 'These whispers and cries [of literature, philosophy, cinema] are the inevitable complement of the collective silence'. Up to the point when 'that silence becomes intolerable, the tongues become freer and death is rediscovered: something that has been happening,' Vovelle concluded, 'in the last fifteen years or so'.[9]

New scenarios are now emerging. Indeed, the recent proliferation of medical, scientific, sociological, and psychological works on mourning suggests that the death taboo may be slowly vanishing. If we consider, for instance, the secondary literature consulted by Sandra Gilbert for her remarkable study *Death's Door: Modern Dying and the Ways We Grieve*, we note that the scholarly field, today, is more vibrant than ever.[10] The embarrassed silence criticized by Gorer, it appears, is rapidly becoming a thing of the past. After all, more than fifty years have gone by since the first publication of his study.

Writers are once again interested in mourning. And yet, C. S. Lewis's considerations about the embarrassment that surrounds the mourner still ring true, especially for those who have recently lost a loved one. In her introduction to *Death's Door*, Gilbert explains that her project was initially prompted by an urgent psychological need, following the death of her beloved husband:

> I think I felt driven to *claim* my grief and — almost defiantly — to *name* its particulars because I found myself confronting the shock of bereavement at a historical moment when death was in some sense unspeakable and grief — or anyway the expression of grief — was at best an embarrassment, at worst a social solecism or scandal.[11]

The need to 'claim one's grief and name its particulars' is so strong and widespread that we might be tempted to consider it an emotion that spans and transcends periods and cultures. In *The Vehement Passions*, a vertiginous study of human passions in Western thought, Philip Fisher argues that mourning is perhaps the only human passion which no culture has ever managed to tame completely. While we may conceive of a culture based on the deliberate constraint (or, on the contrary, the deliberate display) of anger, fear, or erotic desire, it is more difficult to imagine a culture capable of controlling and transforming the characteristics of mourning. 'Unlike the case of fear or anger,' Fisher writes, 'we do not usually imagine reducing or applying therapeutic control to ordinary mourning or grief. In fact, we regard as inhuman someone incapable of feeling and expressing loss, distress, and grief'.[12] 'Applying therapeutic control to grief': this expression is used by Fisher as a *reductio ad absurdum*, and yet it captures an important trend in contemporary society, which relates directly to Ariès's account of the death taboo and the prohibition of mourning. The recent proliferation of specialized texts on mourning goes hand in hand, it seems, with a widespread conception of mourning as a pathology in need of a cure. The exclusion of death from everyday conversation, which Ariès and Vovelle, among others, see as one of the prime characteristics of contemporary Western society, has caused a general prohibition of mourning. Yet, at the same time — and perhaps the contrast is only apparent — it has also brought about a medicalization of grief.

In this confusing situation, mourners today feel more disoriented than ever. Haunted, on the one hand, by the imperative of pleasure of the dominant ideology, but oppressed, on the other, by the ever-increasing medicalization of grief, mourners feel themselves marked by the stigma of Job. In the words of C. S. Lewis, 'To some I'm worse than an embarrassment. I am a death's head'.[13] The mourner, Lewis suggests, is embarrassing because they have looked beyond death's door, perhaps even crossed its threshold for a brief moment. But they are also embarrassing in the way ill people are, even when they are not contagious, because their presence propagates suffering. In today's society, increasingly shaped by secularism, common rites of mourning seem to have vanished.[14] The person who grieves often finds themself isolated and alone, suffering from shame and hypochondria. As Gilbert puts it:

> To what's surely a traditional, essentially moral and cross-cultural question — am I doing the right things to honour the memory of the dead? — twentieth-century Western society has added another distinctively clinical anxiety: Am I *recovering* from the *illness* of grief at the proper rate?[15]

'All *judicious* societies, however, have prescribed and codified the externalization of mourning. Uneasiness of ours insofar as it denies mourning,' writes Roland Barthes in *Journal de deuil* [*Mourning Diary*], a posthumously published diary in which he narrates the continuous, chaotic, excruciating pain caused by his mother's death.[16] The traditional mourning rituals mentioned by Barthes — wearing black clothes for years, withdrawing from society for months, regular visits to the graveyard — are conventional ways of articulating pain in public, which used to help (and in many parts of the world still help) the survivors to carry on. In contemporary society, these rituals have apparently vanished, perhaps as the result of an intentional, collective decision, as has been suggested by sociologist David Moller. The absence of 'communal rituals for grieving,' writes Moller, 'is reflective of a society that seeks to disengage pain from the fabric of every-day social activity'.[17] But is such a project sustainable? Could we really conceive of a society that prohibits mourning, permanently? The answer seems self-evident: even if we aspire to contain the suffering of mourners, in our efforts to medicalize, 'cure', or silence them; even if we meet their pain with embarrassed silence, deny them any public attention or the right to speak; even if we impose a social etiquette of self-control, their profound suffering will always find new channels through which to flow.

The Grief Memoir: A New Genre?

The grief memoir is one of these channels: not the only one, but perhaps one of the most interesting. The genre of the grief memoir, with the slightly different variant of the mourning diary, often written by well-known novelists or journalists, has registered a great editorial success in the last ten years. The genre is of course not new — it goes back at least as far as the Latin tradition of *consolationes* (see Cicero's *De consolatione*, written on the occasion of the death of his daughter Tullia, or Seneca's well-known *Consolationes*), which were often collections of letters, essays, and short poems, written in an intimate, sometimes autobiographical language, with the aim of alleviating not only the author's pain, but also the suffering of others, who had similarly lost a beloved person. There exists no period in literature without such works: from Milton's *Lycidas* (a pastoral elegy written for his drowned friend Edward King) and Shelley's *Adonais* (composed for John Keats), to Thomas Hardy's *Poems* for his late first wife. Twentieth-century American confessional poetry, too, is full of extraordinary poems written to commemorate the death of loved ones — from Sylvia Plath to Thom Gunn and Sharon Olds. And yet, the great popularity of grief memoirs, in recent years, perhaps marks a new trend.[18]

This is suggested by the numerous grief memoirs that have been published to great acclaim over the span of little more than a decade: Roland Barthes's *Journal de deuil* (composed between 1977 and 1979, but posthumously published in 2009), dedicated to the memory of his mother; *Say Her Name* (2011) by American writer Francisco Goldman, a love story between the author and the aspiring novelist Aura Estrada, ended abruptly by her death, at the age of 29, on a Mexican beach; *A Widow's Story: A Memoir* (2011) by American novelist Joyce Carol Oates; *Fai bei sogni* [Sweet Dreams] (2012) by Italian journalist and writer Massimo Gramellini, which describes a long period of mourning that followed the death of his mother, thirty years earlier; Julian Barnes's *Levels of Life* (2013), dedicated to his beloved wife Pat who died of cancer thirty-seven days after having been diagnosed; *H is for Hawk* (2014) by Helen Macdonald, which narrates the story of the year she spent training a goshawk soon after the death of her father, and how the bird helped her through the grieving process; *Vous n'aurez pas ma haine* [You Will Not Have My Hate] (2016) by French journalist Antoine Leiris, a personal memory dedicated to his wife Hélène who was killed in Paris in November 2015 during the terrorist attacks at the Bataclan centre; *Grief is the Thing with Feathers* (2016) by Max Porter, in which the author elaborates, thirty years later, the death of his own father, as he revealed in several interviews; *Mon frère* [My Brother] by Daniel Pennac (2018); not to mention *Patrimony: A True Story* (1991) by Philip Roth, the great forerunner in this genre.

All these books have been international bestsellers for months; they have been awarded literary prizes, and have given life to virtual communities of 'grieving readers', who have expressed their compassion in millions of messages. What is the attraction of these works for so many readers? I wish to suggest, quite simply, that by interweaving trauma into storytelling, grief memoirs provide us with an opportunity to converse about death and grief, something which many readers feel is otherwise absent from their lives.

Literature, of course, has always dealt with experiences of death and loss. While theorizing that contemporary Western society (during the past fifty years or so) has been afflicted by the taboo of death and mourning, Ariès acknowledged that literature had never stopped talking about it. In a vein similar to that of Vovelle, Ariès writes: 'The chasm between the discussion of death in books, which is still prolific, and actual death, which is shameful and not to be talked about, is one of the strange but significant signs of our times'.[19] We may ask ourselves whether the grief memoir continues the work that literature has always performed or whether it achieves something new. In a way, the grief memoir embodies literature's vocation in its purest form. In *Seminar VII* Jacques Lacan writes that all art explores the mystery of reality, or, in his famous words, organizes the void of the Thing.[20] Like literature, the grief memoir organizes the terror of death and grief. Unlike fictional accounts of mourning, however, autobiographical literature on mourning is always rooted in the writer's experience. The reader knows it beforehand; this is their 'pact' with the author. Although the distinction between autobiographical and fictional writing is notoriously slippery and difficult to assess, grief memoirs — even the most elaborate ones from a literary point of view — often display their autobiographical inspiration. Sometimes the autobiographical experience is reworked in forms that make it unrecognizable for the reader — unless the author chooses to give their readers a clue. In *Grief is the Thing with Feathers* (to which I will return), for instance, Max Porter narrates the story of an experience of mourning (a young man and his two little boys grieving for the sudden death of the wife/mother) that fictionalizes his own mourning experience as a boy. As he explained in an interview with Sarah Crown, the novel stems from the trauma of his father's death, many years prior, when he was six.[21]

Grief memoirs thus establish a close relation between writer and reader. Through them, the reader experiences the consolation of an intimate, embodied voice, which we can associate with an actual name and a real, familiar story of suffering. This voice, which speaks to us from the pages of a book, is like a hand that reaches out, a caring presence that promises to repair a broken dialogue. It is this dialogue which mourners crave and need, however strong the temptation might be to seclude themselves in 'special settlements', like lepers, as Lewis despondently suggested. The appeal of the grief memoir, however, from the reader's perspective, does not only lie in the intense communality that readers and author experience in sharing the trauma of loss. Formal, aesthetic organization also plays an important role. In fact, the therapeutic value of the grief memoir, I claim, is greatest where its form succeeds, aesthetically. This should not come to us as a surprise. Art, as Lacan reminds us, is not only a cognitive tool, but also the protective shield that enables us to pursue our existential inquiry unharmed.

Levels of Life: Soaring and Crashing

At a basic level, reparation — for the author and indirectly for the reader — comes from the act of writing itself.[22] In *Journal de deuil* Roland Barthes eloquently describes the healing power of writing:

> Always (painfully) surprised to be able — finally — to live with my suffering, which means that it is literally endurable. But — no doubt — this is because I can, more or less [...] utter it, put it into words. My culture, my taste for writing gives me this apotropaic or integrative power: I integrate, by language.[23]

Writing breaks the inarticulate flux of pain, which is unbearable in its incessancy, and announces its elaboration. It eases the suffering and reorients the mourner's energy towards an act that, as many writers acknowledge, is salutary in itself. For the narrator of Marcel Proust's novel *A la recherche du temps perdu* [*In Search of Lost Time*], writing is 'a healthy and necessary function, the fulfilment of which makes [the writer] happy, just as exercise, sweating and baths do men of a more physical bent'.[24] For Italo Svevo's Zeno, it 'serve[s] a hygienic purpose' and is something which he imposes upon himself every evening before taking his physic.[25]

The creative effort of articulating grief, and thereby containing it, is not limited to a choice of words, but also concerns narrative structure itself. As Blake Morrison remarks in his review of *Levels of Life*, it took Julian Barnes five years to write about his wife's death, not because he was lost for words, but because he lacked a form.[26] In writing his memoir, Barnes finally achieved that form, however elusive and enigmatic. The story of the writer's grief, narrated in an anguished first person, is anticipated by two other stories that are narrated in the third person: one recounts the vicissitudes of the first daring balloonists at the turn of the nineteenth century, the other reconstructs a passionate love story between two of them. The first story focuses on Nadar (the pseudonym of Félix Tournachon), a visionary French photographer with a passion for aerostatic travels. The second story narrates the brief but ardent love affair between the actress Sarah Bernhardt and Colonel Fred Burnaby. Commenting on their relationship, Barnes notes:

> We live on the flat, on the level, and yet — and so — we aspire. Groundlings, we can sometimes reach as far as the gods. Some soar with art, others with

> religion; most with love. But when we soar, we can also crash. [...] Every love story is a potential grief story. If not first, then later. If not for one, then for the other. Sometimes for both. So why do we constantly aspire to love? Because love is the meeting point of truth and magic. Truth, as in photography; magic, as in ballooning.[27]

Fred Burnaby does, in fact, crash dramatically. For some months his love for Sarah burns with an intensity and spontaneity that neither of them, used to leading professional lives behind masks, suspected they possessed. One day, however, Fred asks Sarah to marry him, and she flinches: the flight has come to an end. Many years later, the narrator observes, 'it still cut him' (p. 63).

Having explored the heights of audacity and passion, Barnes turns to probe the depths of loss. The last section of his book takes the form of an intimate essay: a mourning diary for the death of his wife. 'We were together for thirty years. I was thirty-two when we met, sixty-two when she died' (p. 68). We observe Barnes during the last days of Pat's life, his gloomy rides from the hospital to their house, his empty days after her death, while the dialogue with friends, even life-long ones, suddenly becomes difficult and tiresome. We are offered piercing reflections on mourning, and its tormenting questions:

> What is 'success' in mourning? Does it lie in remembering or in forgetting? [...] The ability to hold the lost love powerfully in mind, remembering without distorting? The ability to continue living as she would have wanted you to (though this is a tricky area, where the sorrowful can easily give themselves a free pass)? And afterwards? What happens to the heart — what does it need, and seek? (p. 116)

Barnes explains the common thread that links the three parts of his book in the following terms: 'You put together two things that have not been put together before, and the world is changed' (p. 3). The two things could be balloons and photography, or a man and a woman who love each other, whose match changes their perspective on the world, or rather the world itself, the way the first aerial photography changed our perspective and maybe our vision for ever. This elaborate structure, rather than making the autobiographical story of grief less poignant, adds to its intensity. The reader soon discovers the thread linking the three sections, and maybe also the message they carry: flight is the best thing that can happen to us, even though flying contains the risk of crashing. In Barnes's terse style, in his limpid reasoning, in the enthralling stories he narrates, in the lucid desolation of the book's last section, the reader finds a consolation similar to the solace that Barnes, during the first months of his grief, discovered in opera, a genre that he claims never to have loved or understood. Barnes discovers that opera — an art that delivers 'the characters as swiftly as possible to the point where they can sing of their deepest emotions' (p. 92) — has a mysteriously curative power. This consolation derives, at least in part, from aesthetic pleasure. In the gloomiest days of his grief, when nothing interests him any longer, Barnes attends a performance of Gluck's *Orfeo e Euridice* and is moved: 'the miraculous trickery of art happened again,' he comments (p. 93).

Max Porter: Words with Feathers

The miraculous trickery of art occurs also in Max Porter's *Grief is the Thing with Feathers*, which narrates grief through the most classical of literary devices: a prose verging on poetry, a generous use of inter-textuality (scattered references to Ted Hughes, Emily Dickinson, Sylvia Plath), a triptych structure with three voices (Dad, Boys, Crow), and an elegant use of fairytale. This sophisticated and carefully crafted literary structure does not make the narrator's grief appear preposterous. On the contrary, as the story unravels urgently the narrative voices ring true, and even the Crow sounds humane.

A young mother suddenly dies, leaving behind her husband and two boys. The young widower — a Ted Hughes scholar who is working on a book entitled *Ted Hughes' Crow on the Couch: A Wild Analysis* — feels like 'an accidental remnant' in a family flat that has been transformed into 'a physical encyclopedia of no-longer hers, which shocks and shocks'.[28] While Dad's life is plunged into a state of paralysis, camouflaged by automatic gestures, a gigantic black crow knocks at the door. The Crow — trickster, healer, baby-sitter, doctor, ghost — tells Dad and Boys that he will stay as long as they need him. With his primitive and bestial wisdom, his brusque ways, sometimes funny, sometimes cruel, Crow rekindles life in the three wretched beings that he has taken in his care.

Crow forces the family to articulate their pain, wresting narrative and meaning from raw sorrow. He encourages the boys to create a model of Mother and announces that the best one ('Not the most realistic, but the best, the truest', p. 29) will take life. The boys get to work with furious determination. One of them draws a portrait of Mother on thirty-seven taped-together sheets of A4 paper, using the full rainbow of crayons; the other assembles all the objects that remind him of Mother — toys, rubbers, books, buttons, cutlery — and, manically leaping up, creates a majestic mosaic. 'Which one of these fake mums has won us a real one?' ask the boys, in trepidation (p. 30). Crow starts crying and looks at them, disarmed. With Dad, Crow is equally severe. But thanks to his graceless, therapeutic methods, Dad resumes working:

> Today I got back to work.
> I managed half an hour and then
> doodled. I drew a picture of the funeral. Everybody had crow faces, except for the boys. (p. 11)

Crow is the promise of a rebirth that comes from below. In a period of immense pain, he offers the only kind of solidarity that a filthy animal, feeding off garbage, can provide. Crow is also, perhaps, a metaphor for the dark, hard, psychological work of mourning. After the initial scenes of despair, the narrative slowly opens itself to more hopeful experiences: memories, the games of the children, walks in the park. A few years after Mother's death, the book on Ted Hughes is published. Against all odds, Dad was able to write it. One day Dad returns home, with a happy smile on his face and a folded copy of the *TLS*, which contains a positive review of his book. He finds the boys laughing and throwing balls of wet toilet paper at each other. He makes dinner, puts them to bed and only then realizes that Crow has left.

As Crow puts it, Dad is not 'done grieving' but 'done being hopeless. | Grieving is something you're still doing, and something you don't need a crow for' (p. 103). Dad admits that his grief is changing. And Crow explains:

> [Grief] is everything. It is the fabric of selfhood,
> and beautifully chaotic. It shares mathematical
> characteristics with many natural forms. (p. 103)

(He then enumerates some examples of these many natural forms: feathers, turds, waves, honeycomb, string, intestines...).

With the help of fairytales, of interweaving voices, and of a crow that appears to have stepped straight out of our worst childhood nightmares, Porter handles mighty themes with levity: death, grief, conjugal and paternal love, creativity, terror, the urge to live. In one of his monologues, Crow compares Dad, Boys, and himself to a triptych. On the left Dad, 'the empty church', in the middle himself, 'the nails in the hands' — death, desperation... and on the right?

> But don't stop looking. The triptych is about ways
> of never stopping. It is culture. On the right we have
> the boys [...] four little legs and four little arms
> [...] tiny little hopeful faces. And
> sense is suddenly made of the previous panels. (pp. 47–48)

Like in the art of the triptych, culture provides a way to keep looking, of wresting meaning from what appears senseless. In Porter's book 'a kind of magic takes place — through metaphor, through make-believe, through words,' as Kirsty Gunn writes in her review for the *Guardian*.[29] The book contains many cruel fairytales: probably the most appropriate narrative form available to the two boys, through which they can narrate their grief. These fairytales, where dreams and nightmares abound and where the narrative, as Kafka puts it, takes its feet off the ground of experience, manage to capture the boys' pain, and even, maybe, to soften its impact.[30]

Patrimony: On Remembering and Retelling

On the cover of a recent edition of Philip Roth's *Patrimony: A True Story*, we read, among other statements, the following observation, which is taken from a review in the *Sunday Times*: 'A true story, yes, but told with all the powerful authority and cunning narrative order of a major writer'.[31] *Patrimony* tells the story of the last year and a half of the life of Herman Roth, the writer's father, from the day when he is diagnosed with a brain tumour to his funeral, with a coda dwelling on the first few weeks after his death. Explorations of personal memory broaden the scope of Roth's narrative and offer a wider picture. The narrative of Herman's illness also evokes the narrator's family history and the history of the Jewish community in Newark. Roth gives voice to the experiences and thoughts of a first generation of American-born children: educated, sophisticated, and at ease with their language and their world. This success is owed to the efforts of their uneducated and resilient parents. The young men and women became doctors, lawyers, and writers, thanks to their parents' heroic sacrifices, but their achievements opened a profound gap between the two generations.

Like any story of illness and death, Roth's memoir also addresses the big questions of life. As Adam Phillips puts it, 'Herman Roth's question "Why should a man die?", stripped of its portentousness because he was clearly a man who didn't need to be grand, becomes a good question, again'.[32] *Patrimony* explores the meaning of a human life and our relationship with the body, with suffering, with death; in particular, with the death of those who brought us into the world. It investigates the love of a son for his father and the magnetic power of paternal authority, even in the most irreconcilable conflicts. It analyses a son's psychological need for a *patrimony*, while at the same time questioning the true value and nature of this patrimony. Finally, it probes the inexplicable and, to some extent, inappropriate relief that a suffering person can find in writing.

Patrimony has been described as a great novel, with all the ingredients of Roth's mastery. Few other novelists write about the American family with comparable tenderness and irony. Herman Roth — with his fierce vitality, impatience, and boundless capacity for love and care, but also with his prejudices and ancestral ignorance — is one of Roth's most irresistible characters. And yet, this novel presents itself as a true story. Its autobiographical inspiration gives the narrative a sense of urgency, just as its formal elegance makes Roth's personal experience more poignant. The reader experiences aesthetic pleasure and the magical healing power that stems from a great writer's grief memoir. Roth turns his attention to the incandescent theme of mourning, and reveals, for the benefit of his readers, what is well known to those who have lost a loved person: grief does not begin at the moment of death, but with the diagnosis of a terminal illness.

The author also explores the thaumaturgical power of memory: 'You mustn't forget anything', his father tells him (p. 124). During his inexorable decline, the old man keeps himself alive by spasmodically remembering. 'To be alive, to him,' writes his son, 'is to be made of memory — to him if a man's not made of memory, he's made of nothing' (p. 124). Even during the darkest moments of despair, Herman Roth knows, deep-down, that he is only one member of a community: 'a clan whose trials he knew and accepted' (p. 71). In order to relate his brain tumour to this larger history of suffering, Herman forces himself to recall all 'the illnesses, the operations, the fevers, the transfusions, the recoveries, the comas, the vigils, the deaths, the burials' (p. 70) of his many relatives and friends. Since his life has brought joy as well as pain, Herman also recollects the many happy experiences that made his life worth living: the births, the marriages, the promotions, the achievements of his children and of his grandchildren, of his brothers and cousins... Herman tells stories of his family life to whomever he meets — his personal *Deuteronomy*, as his son puts it, his sacred history, which he can deliver in more or less abridged form, as circumstances require. Roth realizes that his father's warning 'to always remember' is a powerful antidote against one of the direst aspects of grief: the agonizing fear of oblivion. As his father's illness progresses, the writer's sense of time becomes distorted; recollection, however, helps him mend the broken frame of time. At every turn, memories soothe his pain and help him reassemble the shattered pieces of his life and recover its design. While rubbing his father's back in the bath tub, the narrator, who has now turned into his father's father, stares at his penis:

> I looked at it intently [...] reminding myself to fix it in my memory for when he was dead. It might prevent him from becoming ethereally attenuated as the years went by. 'I must remember accurately', I told myself, 'remember everything accurately so that when he is gone I can re-create the father who created me'. (p. 177)

At the end of the book, the narrator reveals a dream that he had at the time of the first diagnostic examinations. He dreamed of a group of children waiting on the pier of Port Newark fifty years before, and of a battle-grey boat, a warship stripped of its armaments and disabled, floating without a pilot towards the shore. It is not clear whether the boat is coming or leaving and whether the children are waiting to embark to be evacuated or, on the contrary, have just disembarked and been safely put down on the pier. In the dream, five-year-old Philip waits for his father to disembark, but all of a sudden 'that dead-silent picture, that portrait of the aftermath of a disaster' becomes too frightening and eerie, and fifty-five-year-old Roth wakes up and realizes that 'it wasn't that my father was aboard the ship but that my father was the ship. And to be evacuated was physiologically just that: to be expelled, to be ejected, to be born' (p. 236). Reflecting on this dream a year later, just after his father's death, Roth comments:

> The defunct warship drifting blindly into shore ... this is not a picture of my father [...] that my wide-awake mind, with its resistance to plaintive metaphor and poeticized analogy, was ever likely to have licensed. Rather, it was sleep that, in its wisdom, kindly delivered up to me this childishly simple vision so rich with truth and crystallized my own pain so aptly in the figure of a small, fatherless evacuee on the Newark docks. (p. 237)

We can interpret this dream, 'so rich with truth' and crystallizing 'my own pain so aptly', as a *mise en abyme* of the grief memoir itself. As in this dream, in the grief memoir the narrator splits into two voices: the suffering boy and the grown-up man who observes him, or the mourning son and the novelist who writes about him. The latter seeks to interpret the former. This particular writer does not find it easy to interpret and narrate his other self, also because he feels a certain resistance 'to plaintive metaphor and poeticized analogy'. Nevertheless, the narration takes shape and, with the wisdom that belongs to dreams, it delivers some unexpected visions. In the same way, the act of narrating one's pain may appear unexpected: 'This book,' writes Roth, 'which in keeping with the unseemliness of my profession, I had been writing all the while he was ill and dying' (p. 237).

Conclusion

I would like to return to the question with which I started: what kind of consolation can an artistically accomplished grief memoir offer? First, there is the consolation that comes from identifying with a real experience of suffering. The grief memoir offers a mirror in which our grief can be reflected, and reminds us that, however tragically individualized, our mourning is also something that deeply unites us. Our personal experiences, like those of Herman or Philip Roth, are part of a larger history of suffering that transcends and defines us. Moreover, by allowing us to contemplate a story of grief from a safe distance, the author of a grief memoir engages us in a most lacerating psychological process, while saving us, at the same time, from the pain of living through it directly. If it were only that, however, there would be little difference between a grief memoir and a self-help manual.

Blake Morrison opens his review of Barnes's *Levels of Life*, to which I referred earlier, by quoting an illuminating passage from *Old School* (2003) by Tobias Wolff. In this novel, a pretentious young teacher called Ramsey asks Robert Frost whether form really matters: is not spontaneous, even disorderly writing a better way to reflect the traumas of modern-day experience? Frost replies:

> I lost my nearest friend in the one they called the Great War. So did Achilles lose his friend in war, and Homer did no injustice to his grief by writing about it in dactylic hexameters [...]. Such grief can *only* be told in form. Maybe it only really exists in form. Form is everything. Without it you've got nothing but a stubbed-toe cry — sincere, maybe, for what that's worth, but with no depth or carry. No echo. You may have a grievance but you do not have grief.[33]

The consolation that readers derive from 'good' grief memoirs is of course part of the consolation that any work of good literature can offer. The idea that literature may offer solace, and even a cure, is age-old, and it has recently been revitalized in literary studies.[34] In her discussion of the uses of literature, Rita Felski gives prominence to 'recognition', or to what may be called an 'existential' reading of texts. One of the joys, and mysteries, of literature, according to Felski, consists in 'the flash of connection' that is unexpectedly experienced by the reader, while turning the pages.[35] All discussions of literature, as Felski puts it, cannot leave aside the question of 'why we are drawn to such texts in the first place'.[36] 'Bibliotherapy' and, by extension, art therapy have recently enjoyed a great revival: best-selling books such as *The Novel Cure: An A-Z of Literary Remedies* or *Art as Therapy* proclaim this idea clearly in their titles.[37] The poet Don Paterson, in his preface to the *Picador Book of Funeral Poems*, writes, 'In our deepest grief we turn instinctively to poetry — to comfort and solace us, or to reflect our grief, give it proper public expression, or help us feel less alone in our experience of it'.[38]

Artistically accomplished grief memoirs do something similar: they deliver a vision that is rich with truth and crystallize pain by giving it social expression; they articulate a human experience that is often particularly resistant to words. Readers of *Patrimony* may find solace in the Rothian sentence: now solemn, now racy, semantically accurate, syntactically dense, ironic, and deeply resonant with the changing pace of human minds and hearts. Or they may find comfort in the candour and courage with which a great writer has decided to expose himself. Most likely, they will find consolation in both. Similarly, readers of *Levels of Life* and of *Grief is the Thing with Feathers* may feel comforted by Barnes's terse prose and Porter's visionary imagination, or they may experience the solace that comes with identifying with the suffering of others. Probably, the former consolation will enhance the latter.

This is the most important solace that grief memoirs can offer and it probably explains their unprecedented editorial success: they narrate and contemplate grief from the perspective of someone who has not only survived the loss of a loved one but has been able to extract words, images, visions, stories, dreams, or fairytales from one of the most brutal of human experiences.

Notes to Chapter 10

1. *The Diaries of Franz Kafka, 1910–23*, ed. by Max Brod (London: Minerva, 1992), p. 384.
2. C. S. Lewis, *A Grief Observed* [1961] (New York: Harper One, 1989), p. 21.
3. Ibid., pp. 22–23.
4. Geoffrey Gorer, *Death, Grief, and Mourning in Contemporary Britain* (London: Cresset Press, 1965), p. 111.
5. Ariès, *The Hour of Our Death*, p. 575.
6. Jean Baudrillard, *Symbolic Exchange and Death*, trans. by Iain Hamilton Grant (London: SAGE, 2017), pp. 469–70.
7. Zygmunt Bauman, *Mortality, Immortality and Other Life Strategies* (Stanford, CA: Stanford University Press, 1992), p. 130.
8. Michel Vovelle, *La mort et l'Occident de 1300 à nos jours* (Paris: Gallimard, 1983).
9. Ibid., p. 739. All English translations my own unless stated otherwise.
10. Sandra M. Gilbert, *Death's Door: Modern Dying and the Ways We Grieve* (New York & London: Norton, 2006).
11. Ibid., p. xix.
12. Philip Fisher, *The Vehement Passions* (Princeton, NJ: Princeton University Press, 2002), p. 202.
13. Lewis, *A Grief Observed*, p. 23.
14. All considerations on death engage with religious discourse. Vovelle, among others, connects the death taboo with the decline of religious thought in contemporary society. See *La mort et l'Occident de 1300 à nos jours*, p. 726 and ff.
15. Gilbert, *Death's Door*, p. 257.
16. Roland Barthes, *Mourning Diary: October 26, 1977-September 15, 1979*, ed. by Nathalie Léger and trans. by Richard Howard (New York: Hill and Wang, 2010), p. 162 (24 June 1978).
17. David Wendell Moller, *Confronting Death: Values, Institutions, and Human Mortality* (Oxford: Oxford University Press, 1996), p. 134, quoted in Gilbert, *Death's Door*, p. 259.
18. Both as a formal mode and as a mood, elegy functions as a background to the grief memoir, although the latter appears mostly in narrative form and is therefore indebted to the conventions of other genres as well, from the novel to the journal. On the elegy, with reference to the English tradition, see the seminal study by Peter Sacks, *The English Elegy: Studies in the Genre from Spenser to Yeats* (Baltimore, MD: Johns Hopkins University Press, 1985); Dennis Kay, *Melodious Tears: The English Funeral Elegy from Spenser to Milton* (Oxford: Clarendon Press, 1990); Jahan Ramazani, *Poetry of Mourning: The Modern Elegy from Hardy to Heaney* (Chicago: University of Chicago Press, 1994). In the more recent *Elegy* (New York: Routledge, 2007), David Kennedy explores the diffusion of elegy beyond poetry into contemporary writing, but does not address the grief memoir.
19. Philippe Ariès, 'The Reversal of Death: Changes in Attitudes Toward Death in Western Societies', *American Quarterly*, 26.5 (1974), 536–60 (p. 537).

20. Jacques Lacan, *The Ethics of Psychoanalysis 1959–1960: The Seminar of Jacques Lacan: Book VII*, ed. by Jacques-Alain Miller and trans. by Dennis Porter (London: Routledge, 1992), pp. 129–30.
21. Sarah Crown, '"The experience of the boys in the novel is based on my dad dying when I was six", Max Porter interviewed by Sarah Crown', *Guardian*, 12 September 2015 <https://www.theguardian.com/books/2015/sep/12/max-porter-books-interview-grief-is-a-thing-with-feathers> [accessed 2 November 2020]. Although not a grief memoir in the strictest sense, then, we can legitimately include Porter's novel in the genre, since he invites us to do so.
22. On the reparative power of writing, also but not only in psychoanalytical terms, see Stefano Ferrari, *Scrittura come riparazione: saggio su letteratura e psicoanalisi* (Rome & Bari: Laterza, 2012), especially Chapter 4.
23. Barthes, *Mourning Diary*, p. 182 (1 August 1978).
24. Proust, *In Search of Lost Time*, VI (*Finding Time Again*), 211.
25. Italo Svevo, 'The Old Old Man', in *Further Confessions of Zeno*, trans. by Ben Johnson and P. N. Furbank (Berkeley & Los Angeles: University of California Press, 1969), pp. 11–23 (p. 16). These quotations are also cited by Ferrari, *Scrittura come riparazione*, pp. 11 and 112.
26. Blake Morrison, '*Levels of Life* by Julian Barnes — review', *Guardian*, 10 April 2013 <https://www.theguardian.com/books/2013/apr/10/levels-life-julian-barnes-review> [accessed 31 October 2020].
27. Barnes, *Levels of Life*, pp. 36–37 (hereafter references given in the main text).
28. Max Porter, *Grief is the Thing with Feathers* (London: Faber & Faber, 2015), p. 20 (hereafter references in the main text).
29. Kirsty Gunn, '*Grief is the Thing with Feathers* by Max Porter Review — Words Take Flight', *Guardian*, 12 September 2015 <https://www.theguardian.com/books/2015/sep/18/grief-is-the-thing-with-feathers-by-max-porter-review-ted-hughes> [accessed 2 November 2020].
30. See Kafka, *Diaries*, p. 80.
31. Philip Roth, *Patrimony: A True Story* (London: Vintage, 1999) (hereafter references in the main text).
32. Adam Phillips, 'How to be your Father's Mother', *London Review of Books*, 13.17 (12 September 1991) <https://www.lrb.co.uk/the-paper/v13/n17/adam-phillips/how-to-be-your-father-s-mother> [accessed 1 November 2020] (repr. 'Philip Roth's Patrimony', in Adam Phillips, *On Flirtation* (London: Faber & Faber, 1994), pp. 167–74 (p. 170)).
33. Tobias Wolff, *Old School* (London: Bloomsbury, 2004), pp. 52–53. Cited in Morrison, '*Levels of Life* by Julian Barnes — Review'.
34. On this topic, see Jürgen Pieters, 'Fragments of a Consolatory Discourse: Literature and the Fiction of Comfort', *Barthes Studies*, 1 (2015), 123–47 <http://sites.cardiff.ac.uk/barthes/files/2015/11/PIETERS-Fragments-of-a-Consolatory-Discourse.pdf> [accessed 31 October 2020], and Pieters, *Literature and Consolation*.
35. Felski, *Uses of Literature*, p. 23. In Chapter 4 in this volume, Jennifer Rushworth offers a compelling analysis of how Felski's notion of reading as recognition resonates with Barthes's practice of criticism.
36. Felski, *Uses of Literature*, p. 1.
37. *The Novel Cure: An A-Z of Literary Remedies*, ed. by Ella Berthoud and Susan Elderkin (Edinburgh & London: Canongate, 2015); Alain de Botton and John Armstrong, *Art as Therapy* (London & New York: Phaidon, 2013).
38. Paterson, 'Introduction', in *The Picador Book of Funeral Poems*, p. xiii. I am indebted to Jürgen Pieters for calling my attention to this beautiful collection of poems.

CHAPTER 11

Visualizing Mourning: The Legacy of Roland Barthes's *La Chambre claire*

Adina Stroia

It is necessary to keep loss as loss.
— Jacques Derrida[1]

Photography and death have cultivated an intimate relationship within the framework of French theory, a statement which is by now academic cliché, but which has nonetheless kept its critical and historical validity. It would therefore prove impossible to discuss photography within a contemporary French context — and of course, beyond — without referencing Roland Barthes's seminal, as well as final work, *La Chambre claire: note sur la photographie* (1980), published in English translation as *Camera Lucida: Reflections on Photography.*[2] Barthes's volume inaugurated a new mode of thinking about photography by reframing its commemorative meanings through an understanding focused on its thanatological potential. The author developed the intrinsic relationship between photography and death by moving away from an external perspective to an internal one, declaring photography itself, together with the act of having one's photograph taken, as 'une micro-expérience de la mort (de la parenthèse)' [a micro-version of death (of parenthesis)].[3] Often referred to as 'the most quoted book in the photographic canon', and more controversially as 'the least scholarly of the central texts of visual studies', *La Chambre claire* has also established itself as a referential work on mourning written as it was within the context of a *Trauerarbeit.*[4] Barthes started writing what would become a seminal text on photography whilst grieving for his mother, Henriette, with whom he had lived for most of his life and until the end of her days. The inseparable entanglement between the photographic framework of the text and his deceased mother is recorded in the author's posthumously published text *Journal de deuil* [Mourning Diary], wherein he referred to his work in progress as the 'livre *Photo-Mam*' [the *Photo-Maman* book] in an entry dated 9 June 1978.[5] As Eugenie Brinkema notes in *The Forms of the Affects*, the loss of his mother 'informs the text, however, in the ways in which we might say light in-forms the image: it impresses itself, it bends the text to its force'.[6]

La Chambre claire is infamously built around the forceful void created by maternal loss and moreover materially signals this absence by constructing the text around a photograph of the mother that Barthes withholds from the reader. The loss of his mother prompted a search for an image of her former self, one that would do her justice — 'mon chagrin voulait une image juste' [my grief wanted an accurate image] — and that would be truthful, allowing him to discover 'la vérité du visage que j'avais aimé' [the truth of the face I had loved].[7] So began the unearthing of old photographs which only stopped when Barthes found one of his mother as a five-year-old, the now infamously absent 'Photographie du Jardin d'Hiver' [Winter Garden Photograph]: 'J'observai la petite fille et je retrouvai enfin ma mère. La clarté de son visage, la pose naïve de ses mains, la place qu'elle avait occupée docilement sans se montrer ni se cacher, son expression enfin' [I studied the little girl and at last rediscovered my mother. The distinctness of her face, the naïve attitude of her hands, the place she had docilely taken without either showing or hiding herself, and finally her expression].[8]

Barthes went on to explain its exclusion from the volume:

> Je ne puis montrer la Photo du Jardin d'Hiver. Elle n'existe que pour moi. Pour vous, elle ne serait rien d'autre qu'une photo indifférente, l'une des milles manifestations du 'quelconque'; elle ne peut en rien constituer l'objet visible d'une science; elle ne peut fonder une objectivité, au sens positif du terme; tout au plus intéresserait-elle votre *studium*: époque, vêtements, photogénie; mais en elle, pour vous aucune blessure.
>
> [I cannot reproduce the Winter Garden Photograph. It exists only for me. For you, it would be nothing but an indifferent picture, one of the thousand manifestations of the 'ordinary'; it cannot in any way constitute the visible object of a science; it cannot establish an objectivity, in the positive sense of the term; at most it would interest your *studium*: period, clothes, photogeny; but in it, for you, no wound.][9]

So present is this absent photograph in the reader's mind through ekphrastic evocation that I almost scrambled to find it for inclusion in this chapter. The absence of the photograph deepens its centrality and it is perhaps the photograph its readers remember best though Barthes provides us with in-depth analyses of twenty-three other black-and-white photographs. The absent but ekphrastically present photograph of his mother finds a counterpoint in a photograph included in the volume and yet never discussed within the body of the text.

The first photograph in the volume and which acts as a frontispiece to *La Chambre claire* is a colour Polaroid, simply entitled *Polaroïd* by Daniel Boudinet (1979), part of a portfolio, *Fragments d'un labyrinthe / OPUS IV* (1979).[10] The photograph depicts a detail of a bedroom with the bed facing the slightly parted curtains through which a sliver of light infiltrates, all bathed in a cerulean blue with a secondary chromatic green tone. The presence of this photographic frontispiece has overall been rather neglected in discussions of the book even by the most eagled-eyed Barthes scholars. It is also worth mentioning that the seemingly extraneous quality of this photograph led the editors of the English-language edition of *La Chambre claire* to omit it entirely. Indeed, as Geoffrey Batchen points out, 'any translated edition of *La Chambre claire* that does not include the Boudinet image should be regarded as fatally flawed'.[11] The 'ex-centric' quality of this photograph does not necessarily point to an insufficiently thorough reading of Barthes's *La Chambre claire* as a photo-text, but points instead to a hyper-focused reading of the very body of the text which, I suggest, defies the author's theoretical dexterity and open modes of reading developed in earlier texts such as *S/Z* (1970) or later works such as *Le Neutre* [The Neutral] (2002), together with his fondness for *parenthèse* [parenthesis].

It is neither my wish nor purpose here to open the door to ridiculous interpretations of what may or may not lie beyond the curtain or to discuss the significance of the colour blue, though the coldness of the colour together with the expression 'to be blue' and its French counterpart 'avoir le blues', are in line with the themes of death and mourning. However, I do believe that Boudinet's *Polaroïd* and its present/absent status gestures towards a different kind of disappearing act within the photographic realm. Barthes wrote *La Chambre claire* at a time when photography as we knew it was undergoing a shift from analogue photography and its temporally extended processes to the almost instantaneous Polaroid, presaging the move into digital photography. The Polaroid thus becomes the 'image fantôme', the ghost image, to borrow a term from Hervé Guibert, seen but not remembered (and never discussed in the text itself), the counterpoint to the absent Jardin d'Hiver photograph which leaves such a mark on readers of *La Chambre claire*.[12] In her analysis, Diana Knight takes a further critical step and interlinks these two photographs in a mirroring gesture:

> Boudinet's dawn Polaroid is certainly an integral part of Barthes's symbolic narrative of refinding his mother in the literal *chambre claire* of the glass conservatory. Just before he relates the discovery of the Winter Garden photo, Barthes refers to the brightness (*clarté*) of his mother's eyes as something that stands out in all her photos: 'For the moment it was simply a physical luminosity, the photographic trace of a colour, the blue-green of her pupils'. This, he says, is the mediating light that will lead him at last to the essence of her face, a blue-green luminosity which is also that of the Boudinet Polaroid.[13]

I am resistant to Knight's attempt to introduce the photograph in the very narrative of the text through a chromatic and, I would argue, forced analogy. Brinkema echoes my resistance to Knight's insistence to read the photograph as other than supplement, by stating that:

> Criticism that lets the image function as an avatar for the maternal falls for the lure, in the sense of enticement and trap, of all images, putting this image to work for a narrative in criticism, reading it as though it were placed in the text instead of above, around, or before it.[14]

I propose however that the Polaroid does bear on the narrative text but it does so at a structural, formal level. The textual disposition present in *La Chambre claire* embraces the photographic snapshot logic of a Polaroid rather than of the narrative photographs it analyses in depth. The volume's forty-eight chapters run the gamut and the text's unusual disposition, with bibliographical references arranged alongside the wide-margined texts, is reminiscent of an exhibition catalogue with its taglines or even an exhibition itself with the objects' titles positioned alongside them. The textual disposition, the spatialization — in the sense of both leaving *and* making space — express the affective rhythms of mourning. *La Chambre claire* is a hybrid text, and even 'unstable', as James Elkins argues: 'on one page it lectures, and then suddenly it becomes a rhapsody or a soliloquy; at one point it is lucid, and then instantly nearly incomprehensible; in another place it is gentle and calm, then almost demented with sadness'.[15] The photographic logic subtending the text has borne some considerable weight on subsequent texts dealing with the experience of loss within the French literary sphere over the last few decades.

The present chapter, as the title clearly announces, discusses the further legacy of Barthes's *La Chambre claire* at a visual and textual level in the realm of texts of mourning. While Barthes's *Journal de deuil* would also invite analysis in the context of loss, in this chapter I limit the propagating influence of his work on texts of mourning to *La Chambre claire*, given that the *Journal* was posthumously published in 2009 when the *récit de mort* had already drawn its generic contours. I thus suggest that following *La Chambre claire*, French-language death texts or *récits de mort* are imbued with a photographic logic which extends into the aesthetics of the text. This is signalled in the text through two types of visualization: through ekphrastic invocation and through textual disposition (manifested through fragmentation and often hybridity). While the absence of photographs is affectively determined in Barthes and in other works dealing with loss, as the *récit de mort* proliferates as a genre, this photographic present absence has taken on an aesthetic dimension. Secondly, whereas photographs of the dead are in a state of 'missing', the state of the mourner can be visualized through textual disposition, the fragmentation, and the resulting visual blanks which are evocative of the loss that has taken place. The starkness and the economy of words imprint in the readers' minds much in the manner of photographs.

I will focus my analysis on texts by the contemporary French author Camille Laurens, the brief *récit Philippe* (1995) and *Cet absent-là: figures de Rémi Vinet* (2004), the latter a photo-text published in collaboration with photographer Rémi Vinet.[16] Both texts deal with the perinatal death of the author's son, Philippe, due to medical negligence, a mere two hours after his birth in 1994. I have selected Laurens not solely for her direct engagement with Barthes's theory but also due to the spectral echoes of space, for Laurens lived across the street from Barthes, a proximity which further cemented her fondness for his critical work. Furthermore, her death text *Philippe* was published in 1995, at the start of this mourning 'boom' in France and stands out as an accomplished literary text. I will end this chapter by gesturing towards the aesthetic dimensions of the *récit de mort* by looking briefly at the aptly entitled *Deuil* [Mourning] (2018) by the writer and poet Dominique Fourcade, which strikes me as one of the most salient examples of the 'affectation' of mourning texts.[17] Following a strange and perhaps perverse thanatological umbilical chord, *Deuil* mourns the death of Paul Otchakovsky Laurens, who was the publisher who ushered Camille Laurens's *Philippe* into the world.[18] But first, a few generic considerations.

The *récit de mort*

If Romantic poetry is characterized by its death-inspired elegies and the Victorian epoch is famous for its elaborate and intense expressions of mourning, the contemporary era appears to be less equipped with the ritualized means to represent grief. Within the distinct realm of contemporary French writing, authors are countering this lack and are seeking to break through the walls of silence surrounding death. The term *récit de mort* has become the nomenclature par excellence when discussing texts which recount the experience of loss through death within the French context. The designation has been gaining widespread currency and was first used in an academic context by Gill Rye.[19] Despite scholarly usage, the terminology was first introduced by the writer Jacques Drillon in his *récit* entitled *Face à face*, which charts the decay and subsequent death of his stepson.[20] As the term has entered academic vocabulary and can no longer be contained within the initially suggested parameters, I propose an expanded definition. I thus refer to the *récit de mort* as an account in which the events recounted are of a non-fictional nature, written by an author who entertained a close relationship with the deceased — whether kin or not — and who recounts the direct effects of the death narrated on their identity and life-narrative. The term *récit* positions the texts outside a purely fictional sphere while offering the possibility to situate themselves at the juncture with autofiction/autobiographical form. This definition is not meant to be exhaustive and will undoubtedly be subject to revision as the genre proliferates. Alexandre Gefen observes this expansion, remarking that 'en quelques décennies, le *récit de deuil* est devenu un sous-genre majeur de la production littéraire contemporaine' [over a few decades, the *récit de deuil* has become a major sub-genre of contemporary literary production].[21] A discussion imposes itself at this point. Although motivated by private affects, the genre's proliferating presence in the French literary landscape invites discussion of its aesthetic forms and narrative structure which go beyond the psychoanalytical algorithm. As Angela Woods remarks:

> Genre, with its three dimensions of formal organisation, rhetorical structure and thematic content, is a universal feature of all textuality and a careful examination of how it enables and constrains the production of certain kinds of narratives in an array of medical and broader cultural contexts is [...] overdue.[22]

Bearing in mind generic considerations, the next section interrogates whether we can perhaps think of the fragment as a new form of elegy and reflects on the kind of reading the fragmented form invites.

Fragmentation as Photographic Logic

Accounts of mourning often exist on a looping temporal continuum that stretches out over a bereaved author's *œuvre*, and are characterized by repetition, variation, and fragmentation. The formal breaking-away from linearity brings us closer to a self governed by affect and its rhythms through 'broken', snapshot-like writing. The psychic landscape of the bereaved person is often replicated in textual form through fragmentation, manifested in the spatialized textual arrangement — the textual canvas is punctured by gaps and blanks — as well as through a meta-narrative layer which exposes the processes of negotiation and the ensuing difficulties and hesitations inherent in the expression of loss. Immediacy imprints on the textual object, fraying it and exposing its seams, thus letting the reader navigate the affective rhythms of the narrative. This can be observed in Laurens's *Philippe*, a text synchronous with the process of mourning. The author explains how the scriptural act imposed itself swiftly after the death of her child:

> Je me souviens, j'étais encore à la clinique quand j'ai commencé à écrire sur de petits bouts de papier. J'écrivais sur ce que je trouvais et je notais des bribes, des morceaux de phrase, des mots. Philippe s'est écrit sur ce mode-là. [...] le livre s'était écrit par bribes. Je suis revenue à l'écriture puisque c'était vital pour moi, mais ce n'était pas du tout d'un point de vue éditorial, ni même littéraire. Ce n'est que plus tard que j'ai parlé à mon éditeur de l'époque, P.O.L. J'ai parlé de ces notes et il m'a demandé si je ne voulais pas les publier. Je les lui ai montrées et à ce moment-là je les ai mises en forme et j'ai fait les quatre parties qui composent Philippe.[23]
>
> [I remember that I was still at the clinic when I started writing on bits of paper. On whatever I could find, I would write down snippets, parts of phrases, words. *Philippe* was written so. The book was written in snippets. I came back to writing as it was vital for me to do so, but I did not do it thinking of it as a publication or as a literary piece. It was not until later when I mentioned it to my then editor, P.O.L. I told him about these notes I had written and he asked me if I did not want to have them published. I showed them to him and it was at that point that I gave them a form and divided *Philippe* into four parts.]

Philippe remains characterized by a pervasive sense of urgency, rendered through its tone and fragmented, hybrid form which is kept in the published version. Laurens powerfully places together excerpts from the medical reports filed in the hospital and from the medical expertise conducted in the wake of the tragic event which evaluate her situation and the doctor's conduct, alongside quotations from dictionaries and specialized books. Thus, a formally linear narrative whereby the reader is guided through the events by one narrative voice is replaced by snapshots of her experience. The fragmented text thus invites a reading that is at the same time visual and (non)-narrative. Patrick Crowley and Shirley Jordan propose that 'these authors have us advance through their texts not in a linear fashion but by looping, spiralling and, in the case of Laurens, by thinking about experience, memory and affect through the idea of concentric circles'.[24]

Seventy-two pages long in the first edition, the brevity of the text together with its formal characteristics evoke the impossibility of narrative and of a life disrupted by loss. *Philippe* is a *texte d'absence*, captured discursively by Laurens who underlines in the text the void left in the wake of her loss, as well as structurally through the blanks which puncture the text at a visual level. The blanks capture the unrepresentable character of loss and the subsequent impossibility of its expression, for words only graze the surface of such a profound loss. As I have already remarked, fragmentation is a typical feature of death narratives in contemporary French literature, signalling at once the broken life narrative and the absence which is at the heart of the texts, echoed visually through the blanks of the page where the *non-dit*, the unsaid, also resides. The spaces inserted within the sparse writing evoke a deep feeling of loneliness and despondency, marking the lack of development of a life-narrative with the child who was gone too soon. As Rye remarks, 'in this way, the narrative conveys something of the pain of loss, although it cannot actually express that pain [and] the reader can only attempt to interpret it through the gaps and silences of the text'.[25] The empty interstices of the texts are a visual echo of the blanks that neither life nor narrative will fill. Through the structure of the text, however, Laurens reveals the essential truth that resides at its core: that a parent, without a child, is a fragmented being. The absence of the lost Other is furthermore marked in the text by photographic absence through the ekphrastic invocation of a visual artefact that remains hidden from view.

Photography: The Presence of Absence

It is through the intimate relationship that Roland Barthes has cultivated between death and photography that his theory of photography finds particular resonance with Laurens's engagement with the visual within her work. Barthesian echoes are present in Laurens's text. In *Cet absent-là*, Laurens makes clear her adherence to a Barthesian reading of the photograph's function:

> La photographie est le meilleur support de la mort, son meilleur supporter. Toute photo fait une ovation à la mort, et même elle la provoque, elle la donne: on vise, on appuie, ça tue. C'est la 'mort plate' dont parle Barthes, qui, 'sous l'alibi dénégateur de l'éperdument vivant', transforme un sujet en *spectre*.[26]
>
> [Photography is the best medium for death, its best supporter. All photos give an ovation to death, they even provoke it, bestow it upon us: we aim, we press a button, it kills. It's the 'flat death' that Barthes talks about, which 'with the denying alibi of the distractedly alive' transforms a subject into a *spectre*.]

Bound together within the space of a book, text and image run parallel to each other throughout *Cet absent-là*, as the text does not explicitly and sustainedly engage with the photographs. The visual and the textual are divorced from a 'show and tell' perspective and now exist under the sign of interrogation. In texts where photographs are included, the readers often ask themselves 'what is it that I am being shown?' and 'what is this photograph's relationship to the text?'. Photographs are evoked, their subject invoked through descriptions of photographs and, even when photography is present, its meaning is undermined in the text by various means. The photographs are not always mentioned in the text or may even belong to a different temporal era than that to which the accompanying text refers. A textual/visual incompatibility becomes a feature of the text, with an effect of 'friction' being generated, to borrow Catherine Poisson's term.[27]

In *Philippe* and *Cet absent-là*, as well as in subsequent works, Laurens points out that the only images she owns of her son are Polaroids of a forensic nature. They were taken by the medical staff and trace Philippe's quick demise:

> J'ai des photographies de Philippe. Elles ont été prises par le pédiatre de l'hôpital, comme il est d'usage, je crois, pour les enfants mort-nés, afin que les mères gardent la preuve qu'ils ont vécu et n'étaient pas des monstres ou des fantômes. C'est le seul cas où, dans la photographie, la vie est métaphorique. Cela rend l'image horrible, écrit Barthes, 'parce qu'elle certifie, si l'on peut dire, que le cadavre est vivant: c'est l'image vivante d'une chose morte'.[28]
>
> [I own photographs of Philippe. They were taken by the hospital's paediatrician, as I believe is customary when it comes to babies born dead so that the mothers keep the proof that they had lived and that they were neither monsters nor ghosts. It's the only time when, in photography, life is metaphorical. This renders the image horrible, writes Barthes, 'because it certifies, one could say, that the corpse is living: it's the living image of a dead thing'.]

Therefore, an analysis of the photographs mentioned by Laurens is further complicated by the fact that the child was in fact on the cusp of death and shortly after dead:

> J'ai tâtonné un peu à l'aveuglette, puis j'ai ramené ce qui, par le format me semblait être un Classique Larousse, et qui en fait était *Philippe*, ce petit livre écrit par moi sur notre fils Philippe, sur sa mort, c'était l'exemplaire de Julien, qu'il avait dû cacher là pour éviter qu'Alice ne le trouve, et d'où sont tombées pêle-mêle sur le carrelage les photographies de Philippe prises par le pédiatre de l'hôpital — lui mourant, lui mort.[29]
>
> [I felt around the bookshelf a bit blindly and I took out what seemed to be a Classique Larousse and which was in fact *Philippe*, this small book I had written about our son Philippe, on his death. It was Julien's copy, which he had probably hidden to avoid Alice finding it. Out fell in a jumble on the floor the photos taken by the hospital's paediatrician — of him dying, of him dead.]

The photographs of Philippe are not only part of the act of remembrance, but capture the moment of death itself, taking Barthes's reading of photography as a 'micro-expérience de la mort' [micro-version of death] beyond the metaphorical.[30] Laurens could clearly never have included reproductions of the Polaroids taken of Philippe within the sheaves of her text. Due to their highly private nature, these are not artefacts that one would wish to introduce into the public sphere and, unlike Barthes's volume, Laurens's works are not specifically about photography. Even when Laurens does show pictures of her dead child to people from her close circle, people shy away as if they have been shown something obscene. The only pictures that Laurens has of Philippe are determinedly outside tradition. If photographs of newborns are oftentimes integral to their recognition as a new member of the family, the forensic nature of the Polaroids cancels out that effect. Tragically outside the realm of the 'cute', the photographs are of Philippe's body at the morgue.

For Laurens, the emotional charge that Barthes invests in the *punctum* is in stark contrast to the *studium* characterizing the forensic style of the photographs of her dying child. Like Barthes's photograph of his mother, the only images Laurens has of her son present an essential truth that is only accessible through the lens of personal attachment: 'il faut de l'amour pour saisir un visage, l'amour est ce qui rend visible' [we need love to be able to see a face, love is what renders it visible].[31] Laurens thus adapts the Barthesian paradigm and suggests that love is the condition which reveals the piercing detail of the *punctum*. However, Laurens's personal Polaroids position the experience of the *punctum* in reverse: as opposed to a grown son looking at the photograph of his mother as a child, it is the mother who is looking at the image of her infant child. The Polaroids depicting Philippe are thus themselves presences of an absence, the full significance of which can only be captured by those who closely witnessed the death event.

The absent visual artefacts mentioned in *Philippe* are instead narrated, giving rise to a hybridity which transforms and translates the image into a 'prose picture' where, as Marianne Hirsch explains, 'the estrangement of the image/text division is overcome, and a sutured, synthetic form, a verbal icon [...] arises in its place', in what W. J. T Mitchell describes as an 'imagetext'.[32] Occupying a textual space instead of a visual one, the image of Philippe is thus woven into the text through an ekphrastic turn in subsequent texts, such as in *Cet absent-là*:

> Les photos que j'ai de Philippe sont des Polaroïd. Sur deux d'entre eux, il est relié par des fils et des électrodes, sur les deux autres il n'est relié à rien. Il y a donc dans cette figuration du temps un instant *t* où il meurt.[33]
>
> [The photographs of Philippe I have are Polaroids. In two of them, he is connected to wires and electrodes, in the other two he is not connected to anything. There is thus in this figuration of time a precise instant when he dies].

The visual artefacts are summoned through the textual fabric, resulting in an emanation of the spectral that ensures the continued underlying presence of the referent.

Another image problematizes the absence/presence duality characteristic of photography, this time a 'present' one. Immediately following Laurens's first mention of her son, the reader is confronted with a *figure* of a newborn child.[34] The *figure* is focused on the baby's face, with wide open eyes, his head held lovingly by two hands, presumably those of his mother. The figure of the child invariably evokes the dead Philippe in an act of symbolic reappropriation. Philippe is thus part of the text, invoked by the conflation of text and photography in an ekphrastic turn. According to Shirley Jordan, there is 'an intimate, implied album underlying this one, available only through ekphrasis but evoked by this phototext's core image, Vinet's *figure* of a newborn baby'.[35] The *figure* inhabits the *entre-deux* of presence and absence, for whilst we are aware that this is not in fact Philippe, we cannot overcome the sense of haunting presence and the absence subtending it. Much in the manner of the Jardin d'Hiver photograph, it is this photograph which remains imprinted in the mind's eye of the reader and repeatedly gets recalled as a photograph of Philippe, even if the narrative truth immediately contradicts it. *Cet absent-là*, published a decade after *Philippe*, thus fulfils a memorial function by poignantly bringing to the fore the figure of the child and reaffirming the vital and enduring quality of the author's loss.

The *récit de mort* as Genre: From Affect to Affectation

As these texts proliferate, the repetition of the same narrative devices does beg the question: at what point is it intentional? Has death writing reached the point of formal saturation? I argue that the *récit de mort* reaches an extreme form with Dominique Fourcade's *Deuil* (2018), published following the sudden death in a car crash of his editor Paul Otchakovsky Laurens, head of P.O.L., the acronymically named publishing house. Fourcade makes crude use of the formal devices established by the affective rhythms of grief, chief among them fragmentation (syntactically and as textual disposition), hybridity, and meta-narrative. Throughout the text, and in particular in the first half, Fourcade makes several references to form, instilling the text with a grating self-awareness which positions the text several degrees away from authenticity. As the author meta-textually indicates, *Deuil* was conceptualized as an elegy, or at least as an elegiac gesture: 'je n'écris pas l'élégie seul | l'élégie ne s'écrit pas seule [I am not writing the elegy alone | the elegy is not writing itself].[36] The textual disposition is indicative of the fragmented nature of the text, with large blanks interspersed throughout. This is not to say that grief and the reconfiguration of the world that loss precipitates do not bring about a sense of a fragmented perception and an inability to create a narrative discourse that smooths out the crevices of our daily lives. However, the repetition of such rhythms at a formal level in grief account after grief account may well dilute their effects on the readers. As Jordan so astutely asks, 'but when is repetition legitimized in art forms and when is it reprehensible?'[37] It is my belief that Fourcade offers us an example of 'reprehensible' repetition through imitation:

> présent, dans l'ignominie de t'aimer
> dans l'interdit de ne pas t'écire, nouvelle donne
> défonce toute forme[38]
>
> [present, in the ignominy of loving you,
> in the prohibition of not writing you, the new order of things
> destroys any form]

Fourcade employs different tactics to signal that the death of his editor has brought about a disintegration of form and language, among them the lack of capitalization of words at the beginning of sentences throughout the text. Punctuation is often omitted, in particular full stops at the end of prose-like passages, as if the author could not quite make up his mind and wished to opt for an open, poetic form instead, at least at the level of textual disposition.

Hybridity is achieved through markers of erudition, with the author inserting poems by famous poets of death: Emily Dickinson's 'There's a Certain Slant of Light' and Rainer Maria Rilke's 'Sonnet to Orpheus I, IX'. The memorial function is visible as the book ends with a final dedication akin to an inscription on a tombstone. The genesis of the book and its end are inscribed with precision (whereas customarily it would follow a month-year model, here it is a day-month-year model, indicating that it was written in little over two months: '3 JANVIER–23 MARS 2018' [3 January–23 March 2018].[39] Fourcade repeatedly points to the immediacy of the writing act following his editor's death: 'un livre on l'écrit. Je ne veux pas savoir qui. Ça s'écrit. Ça vous écrit. Ça suffit comme ça' [one writes a book. I don't want to know who. It writes itself. It writes you. This suffices].[40] This requirement imposed by the present is displayed in all its seemingly visceral form: 'présent je t'aime je te vomis' [present I love you I vomit you].[41]

Deuil does not strike the reader as an accomplished book, nor should a *récit de mort* aspire to such an accolade. Published in a critical void, with hardly any reviews, *Deuil* fails both as an affecting book and as a generic attempt. Were it not for the real-life events which brought about the genesis of *Deuil*, the reader might feel as if they were reading a parody of a *récit de mort*. The style can only be referred to as what the French would call *cherché*, cultivated, as if the book were assembled following instructions, piece by piece. Fourcade's text fails to convince either as an aesthetic and literary artefact or as a recording of his own narrative as a mourner. In the guise of a conclusion, I wish to raise two questions to bear in mind as the genre of the *récit de mort* evolves and with it, our critical engagement. Where and how do we move from affect to affectation? What are the ethical implications of analysing affect-driven forms as aesthetic forms?

Notes to Chapter 11

1. Jacques Derrida, *Copy, Archive, Signature: A Conversation on Photography*, ed. by Gerhard Richter and trans. by Jeff Fort (Stanford, CA: Stanford University Press, 2010), p. 19.
2. Roland Barthes, *La Chambre claire: note sur la photographie* (Paris: Gallimard, 1980); *Camera Lucida: Reflections on Photography*, trans. by Richard Howard (London: Vintage, 1993).
3. Barthes, *La Chambre claire*, p. 21; *Camera Lucida*, p. 14.
4. Geoffrey Batchen, 'Palinode: An Introduction to *Photography Degree Zero*', in *Photography Degree Zero: Reflections on Roland Barthes's 'Camera Lucida'*, ed. by Geoffrey Batchen (Cambridge, MA: MIT Press, 2009), pp. 3–30 (p. 3); James Elkins, 'Camera Dolorosa', *History of Photography*, 31 (2007), 22–30 (p. 26).
5. Barthes, *Journal de deuil*, p. 148; *Mourning Diary*, ed. by Léger and trans. by Howard (2011), p. 136.
6. Eugenie Brinkema, *The Forms of the Affects* (Durham, NC: Duke University Press, 2014), p. 85.
7. Barthes, *La Chambre claire*, p. 106; *Camera Lucida*, p. 70.
8. Ibid., p. 107; p. 69.
9. Barthes, *La Chambre claire*, p. 115; *Camera Lucida*, p. 73. This paragraph best captures in a distilled form the new tools for an understanding of photography that Barthes had forged and explained earlier in the volume: the *studium* and the *punctum*. The *studium* is of an intellectual and objective nature, and is aligned with the photographic gaze, defined as 'une sorte d'investissement général, empressé, certes mais sans acuité particulière' [a kind of general enthusiastic commitment, of course, but without special acuity] which is revealing of the photographer's intention and can only be situated on the side of 'to like' and 'not to love' (Barthes, *La Chambre claire*, pp. 48, 50; *Camera Lucida*, pp. 26, 27). On the side of the spectator and in opposition to the *studium* which is 'en définitive toujours codé' [ultimately always coded], we find the fulguration of the *punctum*, the thing 'qui fait tilt en moi' [that sets me off], the detail 'qui part de la scène, comme une flèche, et vient me percer' [shoots out of it like an arrow, and pierces me], and which unlike the *studium* is not static and fixed a priori, but is subject to change (Barthes, *La Chambre claire*, pp. 81, 49; *Camera Lucida*, pp. 26, 19).
10. Boudinet is also responsible for making Barthes 'present' in the visual collective consciousness as the photographer behind one of the most circulated photo-portraits of Barthes, entitled 'Le Gaucher' which features a trench-coat-wearing Barthes, lighting a cigarette, eyes closed in concentration.
11. Batchen, 'Palinode', p. 17.

12. Hervé Guibert, *L'Image fantôme* (Paris: Minuit, 1981); *Ghost Image*, trans. by Robert Bononno (Chicago: University of Chicago Press, 2014).
13. Diana Knight, 'Roland Barthes, or The Woman without a Shadow', in *Writing the Image after Roland Barthes*, ed. by Jean-Michel Rabaté (Philadelphia: University of Pennsylvania Press, 1997), pp. 132–43 (p. 138), citing here from Barthes, *Camera Lucida*, p. 66.
14. Brinkema, *The Forms of the Affect*, p. 88.
15. James Elkins, *What Photography Is* (New York: Routledge, 2011), p. 10.
16. Camille Laurens, *Philippe* (Paris: P.O.L., 1995), and *Cet absent-là: figures de Rémi Vinet* (Paris: Léo Scheer, 2004). The intrinsic tension between absence and expression is prefigured by the sub-title of the latter volume: Vinet's special technique involved the capturing of models' faces — usually close friends and family — which he would then re-photograph as projected images. Vinet's technique thus stages the absence of the subject within the very act of representation.
17. Dominique Fourcade, *Deuil* (Paris: P.O.L., 2018).
18. Despite the shared surname, the two are unrelated (and 'Camille Laurens' being in any case a pen name).
19. Gill Rye, 'Family Tragedies in Recent French Literature', in *Affaires de famille: The Family in Contemporary French Culture and Theory*, ed. by Marie Claire Barnet and Edward Welch (Amsterdam: Rodopi, 2007), pp. 267–81.
20. Jacques Drillon, *Face à face* (Paris: Gallimard, 2003).
21. Alexandre Gefen, 'Philippe Forest et les injonctions paradoxales du *récit de deuil*', in *Philippe Forest: une vie à écrire: actes du colloque international*, ed. by Aurélie Foglia and others (Paris: Gallimard, 2018), pp. 26–38 (p. 26). All translations from the French are mine, unless otherwise stated.
22. Angela Woods, 'The Limits of Narrative: Provocations for the Medical Humanities', *Medical Humanities*, 37 (2011), 73–78 (p. 74).
23. Cited in Adina Stroia, 'Camille Laurens: l'écriture depuis soi', *Dalhousie French Studies*, 112 (2018), 27–35 (p. 28).
24. Patrick Crowley and Shirley Jordan, 'Introduction', in *What Forms Can Do: The Work of Form in 20th- and 21st-century French Literature and Thought*, ed. by Patrick Crowley and Shirley Jordan (Liverpool: Liverpool University Press, 2020), pp. 1–20 (p. 10).
25. Gill Rye, *Narratives of Mothering: Women's Writing in Contemporary France* (Newark: University of Delaware Press, 2009), p. 45.
26. Laurens, *Cet absent-là*, p. 35 (my emphasis).
27. Catherine Poisson, 'Frictions: mot et image chez Marie NDiaye et Camille Laurens', *Contemporary French and Francophone Studies*, 11.4 (2007), 489–96.
28. Laurens, *Cet absent-là*, p. 43.
29. Camille Laurens, *L'Amour, roman* (Paris: P.O.L., 2003), p. 25.
30. Barthes, *La Chambre claire*, p. 21; *Camera Lucida*, p. 14.
31. Laurens, *Philippe*, p. 15.
32. Marianne Hirsch, *Family Frames: Photography, Narrative and Postmemory* (Cambridge, MA: Harvard University Press, 1997), p. 3; W. J. T. Mitchell, *Picture Theory: Essays on Verbal and Visual Representation* (Chicago: University of Chicago Press, 1994), p. 192.
33. Laurens, *Cet absent-là*, p. 92.
34. See ibid., p. 41.
35. Shirley Jordan, 'Chronicles of Intimacy: Photography in Autobiographical Projects', in *Textual and Visual Selves: Photography, Film, and Comic Art in French Autobiography*, ed. by Natalie Edwards, Amy L. Hubbell, and Ann Miller (Lincoln: University of Nebraska Press, 2011), pp. 51–77 (p. 59).
36. Fourcade, *Deuil*, p. 35.
37. Shirley Jordan, 'The Time of Our Lives: Repetition, Variation and Representation in French Women's Life Writing', in *What Forms Can Do*, ed. by Crowley and Jordan, pp. 113–30 (p. 116).
38. Fourcade, *Deuil*, p. 13.
39. Ibid., p. 61.
40. Ibid., p. 55.
41. Ibid. p. 12.

CHAPTER 12

❖

Ecological Mourning: From Elegy to Expanded Grief

Florian Mussgnug

Una apis, nulla apis. [A single bee is not a bee.]
Latin proverb

The rub now is that we have to learn to die
not as individuals, but as a civilization.
— Roy Scranton[1]

Grief is communal. In the absence of a single, shared cultural tradition, contemporary practices of mourning have taken on numerous and different forms, from time-honoured rituals to eclectic 'personal rites'.[2] Notwithstanding this diversity, all expressions of grief are bound up with the communal needs of the living. Every loss is unique but no experience of mourning is altogether solitary. We, the heterogeneous, more-than-human, mortal denizens of this living, symbiotic planet, live, grieve, and die in the company of others, share our time and vulnerability with them, and exist in need of their care. In this important sense, even the most private experience of grief belongs to others. It is well known that the death of a loved one holds the power to set us apart from the familiar and predictable flow of everyday life. It isolates us and makes us experience time as slow, sluggish, or unbearably fraught with emotion. But mourning also connects us, not only with the dying and the dead, whose memories and stories we treasure and share, but also with the living, whose presence we crave, even when we cannot bear their company. As Lisa Baraitser explains, practices of care are frequently bound up with suspended time, existential dilemmas, and with the 'inescapable troubles of interdependent existences'. Care emerges here in response to a 'basic nameless dread, that [...] requires containment by another'.[3] This makes care structurally similar to grief, which is likewise shaped by its relation to what, following philosophers Emmanuel Levinas and Simon Critchley, we shall describe as an 'infinite demand'. Responsibility towards the other, according to this tradition of thought, is non-reciprocal, asymmetrical, and non-chosen. It does not arise out of a social contract, but exists *before* individual freedom. For Levinas, it originates from the shared vulnerability of humans and non-humans, which imposes ethics as the first and most important principle of philosophy, above and beyond the quest for knowledge.[4] Consequently, the meaning of care cannot be reduced to either benevolence, consideration, or respect. For Critchley, it rather needs to be understood as 'the obsessive experience of a responsibility that persecutes me with its sheer weight'.[5] Similarly, many encounters with grief place an excessive demand on the mourner. They mark a burden that exceeds what is socially acceptable and test the limits of reasonable accommodation. Each individual death, as Jacques Derrida reminds us, is the loss of a world, a personal apocalypse: 'the emotion of mourning that we all know and recognize, even if it hits us each time in a new and singular way, like the end of the world'.[6] In this sense, no consolatory gesture can ever be adequate. The time of mourning and the duty of care are similarly interminable. Baraitser writes:

> We could say that care without ending is neither the time of memory, which is the time that remains, nor the time of working through, which is the time of acceptance, but the interminable time of living on with the knowledge that one's time will end.[7]

In this manner, mourning and care foster a strength that finds its power to act through the acknowledgement of its weakness. As any bereaved person will confirm, grief and care are closely related. Mourning strikes us with near-intolerable ferocity, but it also heightens our awareness of social relations. Loss alerts us to the importance of kinship and love. In mourning, we suffer the absence of ties that have been tragically severed by death, but we also test the strength of the bonds that remain, and which may guide us in our struggle for survival and meaning. Death belies the permanence of social attachment, but mourning affirms the capacity of the living to begin again. In the words of historian Thomas Laqueur, 'the living need the dead far more than the dead need the living. [...] the dead make social worlds'.[8] All mourning rituals, then, are experiences of community-building, which connect our past, present, and future.

As this book goes to press, more than 300 million people worldwide have contracted the new coronavirus, and the number of global deaths has exceeded 5.5 million. Our collective encounter with COVID-19 has inspired new practices of care, fresh modes of wakefulness, and a heightened attention to the quotidian. It has also revealed troubling hierarchies of power and exposed stark social inequalities. As Rosi Braidotti suggests, the cultural and political experience of the unfolding health crisis 'can make us more intelligent about what we are ceasing to be and who we are capable of becoming'.[9] On a more tragic note, COVID-19 has normalized mass death, to a degree that was unfamiliar in the prosperous global North for more than sixty years. According to a frequently stated opinion, modern consumer society, since the middle of the twentieth century, has been shaped by a desire to evict death. Philosopher Jean Baudrillard has described the foundations of contemporary society as a death-taboo that resembles the one suffered by sex in the nineteenth century: an 'exclusion that precedes every other' and that functions as 'the very core of the rationality of our culture'.[10] In a similar vein, historian Philippe Ariès notoriously argued that in industrialized, urbanized, and technologically advanced societies 'everything in town goes on as if nobody died any more'.[11] More recently, sociologist Zygmunt Bauman proclaimed the 'banalization' of grief in an age of mass media, and contended that death, endlessly reflected in popular entertainment, has 'come to be viewed as considerably less than absolute; as revocable and reversible, just one more banal event among so many others'.[12] David Kennedy takes a similar approach in his recent work on twenty-first-century elegy. According to the British poet and literary critic, present-day attitudes towards death leave little room for the work of mourning, and have moved away from the idea of reading and writing as a prolonged, transformative encounter with grief. Instead, contemporary elegy, for Kennedy, offers a stark choice between melancholia and resilience: it either depicts loss as an open wound that remains 'forever fresh and raw' or assumes that pain can and must be resisted, 'over-written by the language of incomprehension [...] and by the language of reaction'.[13] As a result, the dead, who are no longer elegized and thereby inscribed in a new and different relationship with the living, continue to haunt us. Contemporary elegy, in Kennedy's words, does 'not refuse consolation so much as try to avoid doing anything that might set the work of mourning in motion'.[14] In this manner, writing becomes a space where the dead's uncanny presence is perpetually reanimated, but never resolved.

Against these assumptions, the experience of the COVID-19 pandemic has been a powerful reminder of the omnipresence of death, but also of the inexhaustible, generative force of human and more-than-human communities, and of the strength of social ties. In every part of the world, people have responded to hardship and to the prospect of mass death with purposefulness, immediacy, and surprising creativity.[15] Sadly, these expressions of care have failed, in many cases, to prevent or slow down the global spread of the virus, which, in the words of human geographer Andreas Malm, 'propagated through the world like a pulse through a grid'.[16] Nevertheless, they must not be ignored. Despite the ongoing devastation wrought by COVID-19, vulnerability needs to be understood not only as a catastrophe but also as an opportunity for re-thinking the importance of social and ethical bonds that engage the relational power of mourning and care. Braidotti writes:

> It would be obscene and unethical to theorize about the epidemiological catastrophe that is unfolding under our very eyes. This is not a time for grandiose theorizing but for collective mourning, affective resistance, and regeneration. We need to mourn the dead, humans and non-humans and not build theories on their dead bodies — that would be a shameless abuse of intellectual power. But over and above all else, we also need to develop different ways of caring, a more transversal, relational ethics that encompasses the non-humans.[17]

The COVID-19 crisis has brought us face to face with death, and has inspired new forms of mourning and care. Attention to non-human vulnerability is an integral part of this experience. As Malm remarks, the coronavirus pandemic and the climate emergency are inextricable. They appear, at a superficial level, like two different scenarios of loss but 'are, on closer inspection, exactly one and the same'.[18] The new coronavirus has emerged from human interactions with non-human animals, whose habitats were ravaged by pollution, deforestation, animal trade, and urban sprawl. COVID-19 then spread through networks of globalized trade and transportation that have long threatened the survival of many non-human species. Indeed, the threat from zoonotic pathogens, just like the risk of environmental collapse, is a direct result of what Malm calls 'ecologically unequal and pathological exchange'.[19] While human communities continue to battle with COVID-19, carbon dioxide emissions have tipped the planet's biological and geochemical systems towards progressive devastation, and are triggering a series of overlapping environmental crises. This marks an existential threat to numerous species and may put human survival at risk. Extinction rates have grown disproportionately in recent decades, as a result of habitat destruction, pollution, invasive species, human population growth, and overharvesting, and evolutionary biologists have warned that a mass extinction of species — only the sixth to occur in the 3.5 billion years of life on Earth — is taking place in our present, as a result of human activities.[20] The destruction of habitats and non-human species will trigger cataclysms that are impossible to predict, as a result of the fatal interconnectedness of ecological and economic systems: what Jean-Luc Nancy has described as 'the spread or proliferation of repercussions from every kind of disaster'.[21] It is hardly surprising, then, that analyses of global risk describe species extinction as one of the greatest and most urgent existential threats to human survival.[22]

Mass extinction places an unprecedented urgency on practices of individual and collective mourning. Ethnographer Deborah Bird Rose has found powerful words to describe this new relationship with the dead. 'There are two big contexts of death,' she writes:

> The first is the fact that death resides within life. With the exception of some bacteria, life involves death both for individuals and, in much longer time frames, for most species. Death, as a corollary to life, happens to all of us complex creatures.[23]

Acknowledgement, however, does not fully prepare us for what Rose calls 'double death' or the 'wreckage that results from the justification of suffering in the name of progress'.[24] In this second sense, death is *not* a fact of life, but rather marks the boundaries of ethical meaning. It conveys what literary critic David Farrier has called 'a profound rupture with ethical time represented by [a] catastrophic scale of loss [that] is difficult to comprehend'.[25] Mass extinction provokes such a rupture.

Transfixed by the human tragedy of the COVID-19 pandemic, many people under lockdown have paid growing attention to the chronic emergency of unfolding environmental disaster. In Braidotti's words:

> If it is undeniable that the 'capitalocene' — the greed of consumers' society — is responsible for the abuse of animal life that produced the infections of the bats and generated COVID-19, it is equally true that neoliberal governance has laid the foundations for the spread of the contagion by exacerbating socio-economic power differences.[26]

It can be expected, then, that future cultural and political responses to COVID-19 will become tied up with debates about the political and social consequences of modernization and globalization. Individual and collective mourning for the victims of the coronavirus will resonate with environmental grief and with worries over mass extinction. Already, in recent years, theorists and advocates of human climate justice have evoked extinction to highlight the multiple threats faced by vulnerable *human* communities and to criticize the inequities and injustices that have resulted from colonialism and from the growth of the world-capitalist economy.[27] Similarly, the chronic health emergency of recent months, with its intense experience of suffering and political volatility, will command further attention to the more-than-human world. Like the climate crisis, COVID-19 will come to be understood not only as a trigger for urgent political action: both emergencies also call for a radical re-orientation of ethical and aesthetic values. In the second part of my chapter, I will test some of these claims by turning my attention to the honeybee.

∞

More than 20,000 known species of bees currently live on every continent except Antarctica. Many of them are indispensable to the ecosystems they inhabit. As biologist Mark Winston points out, a world without bee pollination 'would be almost impossible to contemplate and likely one in which we would never have evolved in the first place'.[28] Bees make their homes just about anywhere and have shaped our planet long before humans, just as thoroughly as they have colonized every cultural landscape since the beginnings of human history. The value of bees is incalculable. Their ecological importance, by contrast, is clearly apparent if we consider the number of flowering plants that require or benefit from bee pollination — at least 65 per cent of the more than 350,000 known species of *magnoliophyta* — and the rich palette of animal species that depend on these plants, as providers of food and shelter, and because they stabilize soil, prevent erosion, and maintain Earth's life-supporting atmosphere. This diverse assemblage of animals includes ourselves, of course. Born into a world formed by bees, *Homo sapiens* has been intimately entangled with their/our apian companions since the very beginning.[29] The beekeeper, a much more recent genus than *apis*, has evolved in close contact with the hive, first as a hunter, who raided wild nests, and later as an apiculturist. People of all ages have been fascinated by the honeybee's sophisticated social behaviour, 'almost as if the purpose of bees on earth were to teach man the ways of enlightened self-interest and how to behave fairly and reasonably'.[30] Like many companion species, bees and humans share a common history and a drawn-out intimacy that long predates modern notions of (human) individuality or subjectivity. They 'infect each other all the time'.[31] Indeed, one theory suggests that human evolution was advanced by the consumption of honey, which provided the critical energy for an enlarged brain.[32] If this hypothesis is correct, then the broad cognitive capacities of *Homo sapiens*, often evoked as a reason for species privilege, are in fact the result of their/our entanglement with bees: a product of the collisions, frictions, confluences, and intimacies between species, or, in the words of Stacy Alaimo, of 'the literal contact zone between human corporeality and more-than-human nature'.[33]

Nonhuman ways of being, like human ones, are shaped by historical forces. In her influential work on the syncopated and juxtaposed temporalities of biological and economic growth, anthropologist Anna Lowenhaupt Tsing describes human narratives of linear progress as an impediment to multispecies worldmaking. According to Tsing:

> Progress is a forward march, drawing other kinds of time into its rhythms. Without that driving beat, we might notice other temporal patterns. Each living thing remakes the world through seasonal pulses of growth, lifetime production patterns, and geographies of expansion.[34]

This means, for Tsing, that critical thinking about (human) political power and about the impact of transnational chains of economic, cultural, and political connectedness needs to venture across species lines and must encompass an ever-wider range of non-human stories. On the other hand, it also entails that reflection on more-than-human communities and intersections must attend to the knowledge practices and imaginative frameworks of political and economic globalization, and to its global cartographies. In this context, it is worth pointing out that some bee species, in particular, have benefitted from humanity's global spread, extending their range and adapting their habits to anthropogenic conditions. Cultural history overwhelmingly features just one such species: *apis mellifera*, the western honeybee. Admired by human thinkers of all ages for its colonial behaviour, ingrained sociality, and the rich culinary rewards of its hive, this species originated in southern Asia and expanded from there to Africa and Europe. As Claire Preston explains, the honeybee 'has been more carefully observed, more celebrated, more storied and mythologized' than most other animals.[35] Bees feature in Mesolithic cave paintings, and a bee hunt is described in one of the oldest known texts in any Indo-European language, the *Rigveda*. Hesiod describes artificial hives as early as 750 BCE, and Aristophanes's *The Wasps*, written in the fifth century BCE, pokes fun at the greed of honey thieves and honey merchants. From Ancient Mesopotamia to the Abbasid Caliphate, honey has always been traded in large quantities in western Asia.[36] In Ancient Greece, bees were associated with the underworld and the souls of the dead. The Heavenly Jerusalem of the Christian Bible contains fountains of honey, and the Qu'ran promises rivers of it in paradise. On the other hand, apian symbolism appears largely confined to the Mediterranean and continental Europe. Ancient Chinese literature contains few mentions of beekeeping, and the honeybee only reached South America in the 1530s. It was first imported to North American by the Dutch in the seventeenth century, when it became known to native Americans as 'the white man's fly'.[37]

Human admiration for the honeybee is often stated in anthropocentric terms. For Winston, 'we, and honeybees, represent two pinnacles of sociality among the earth's creatures, and we can learn much about ourselves by observing them'.[38] The bee signifies human qualities, but its complex cultural meaning points beyond the limits of bounded individualism. From the earliest Greek poetry to the latest debates about environmental standards, *apis mellifera* has long stood for health and collective wellbeing and for the importance of sustainability and care. According to

Preston, bees are popular representations of both public *and* private human virtues: 'on the one hand, publicly oriented, part of a complex, highly evolved hierarchical commonwealth, and on the other, private, modest, secret, retiring, unindividuated, seeking no more than to be an anonymous and identical cog in a wonderful natural machine'.[39] Their inherently relational forms of social organization have been celebrated, from Virgil's *Georgics* to Maurice Maeterlinck's *The Life of the Bee*. Winston praises honeybees as models for a good human life, and describes the complex symbiotic relation between humans and bees as an unwritten pact between species:

> What is unique about our relationship with honeybees is not only how much we depend on their services but also the fact that their health and survival depend on how well we manage the environment on which they rely. If we had a formal contract with honeybees, its executive summary might read something like this: We, the bees, will provide you with honey and other products of the hive, as well as pollination services. In return you, the humans, will maintain an environment in which we can thrive, free of toxic pesticides and rich in diverse flowering plants.[40]

Sadly, this 'pact' has been increasingly ignored or deliberately broken by humans. In an age of rapid environmental degradation, honeybees are dying all over the globe, at an astonishing rate. Colony Collapse Disorder (CCD), as the phenomenon became known, was first observed in spring 2006, when numerous North American beekeepers found that the animals in their colonies had mysteriously vanished. Since then, great efforts have gone into studying the reasons for CCD, but the disaster has not abated. Scientists have dismissed the hypothesis of a single cause, such as a new disease or novel pesticide. Instead, it is now widely assumed that CCD is the catastrophic result of multiple factors, including pests, exposure to anthropogenic environmental stresses, and the long-term effects of low-level toxicants.[41] Every year, global losses run into many millions of colonies, with severe economic implications for beekeeping and crop production. The United Nations estimates that of one hundred crops grown for human consumption, seventy-one are pollinated by bees, constituting approximately ninety per cent of global yield.[42] More than ever, the time-honoured bond between humans and honeybees appears vital to the survival of both species. In Preston's words, 'the bee gravely insists by example that we look beyond ourselves'.[43]

∞

As ecocritic Ursula K. Heise has explained in her ground-breaking study, *Extinction: The Cultural Meanings of Endangered Species* (2016), discourses about endangered species are shaped by a tendency to treat non-human animals as screens for the projection of human interests and meanings. Growing awareness of mass extinction has inspired a profusion of literary and filmic narratives, documentaries, popular-scientific books, and travel writings, but many of these texts offer a limited understanding of what is lost. Human compassion, as Heise points out, has generally focused on large, vaguely anthropomorphic mammals — 'flagship species' or 'charismatic megafauna' — that are also recurrent as cultural figurations of human communities and qualities. In the context of climate politics, such exclusive attention to the human relationship with nature may prevent a more consistent engagement with unfamiliar scales and complex and intrinsically diverse ecosystems: 'biological crisis typically becomes a proxy for cultural concerns'.[44]

How can we find a language that speaks to human anxiety and grief without losing sight of multispecies relations of care? As ecocritic Timothy Clark points out, the climate crisis demands new forms of linguistic and conceptual inventiveness that can alert readers to unfamiliar and counterintuitive scales. Much environmental damage is brought about by individual human actions that are not ecologically significant in themselves. This relation between individual observable causes and vast global effects marks a stark challenge to familiar anthropocentric narratives: 'Issues such as global warming or ocean acidification, so overwhelming in scale, can threaten to dwarf any individual or state action, even as both phenomena cannot immediately be seen, localised, or in many cases, even acknowledged'.[45] Consequently, the success of concerted responses to the climate crisis depends on our ability to express and relate different scales and points of view, beyond what is revealed by immediate human perception. Discourses of ecological mourning, I suggest, must similarly strive for multiscalar complexity. Like the best environmental writing, they can explore the relational qualities of grief and care and help us imagine death, not as an ominous apocalypse-to-come or as a spectacular theatre of the uncanny (Kennedy), but as the plight of ecological, earthbound beings. Haraway writes: 'Grief is a path to understanding entangled shared living and dying; human beings must grieve with, because we are in and of this fabric of undoing'.[46]

Much environmental writing, according to Heise, deploys:

> The genre conventions of elegy and tragedy in such a way that the endangerment of a particular species comes to function as a synecdoche for the broader environmentalist idea of nature's decline as well as for the stories that communities and societies tell about their own modernization.[47]

But does elegy — with its rich and nuanced attention to individual loss — offer a sufficient guide to ethical and artistic practice on a warming and vulnerable planet? Twentieth-century elegists, from Wallace Stevens and Robert Lowell to Sylvia Plath, rejected traditional religious ideas of death as meaningful closure and explored loss as a disruption and deferral of meaning.[48] Death, according to this tradition, marks a loss of control, and a crisis of public language. Symbolic representations of death fail to capture the real experience of death, which is located outside of the sphere of the semiotic. Kenneth Burke, for example, suggests that 'death' is placed beyond the register of images that the living body can know; it can only be read as a signifier with an incessantly receding, ungraspable signified, pointing back self-reflexively to other signifiers.[49] Similarly, Simon Critchley remarks that 'representations of death are misrepresentations or rather representations of an absence'.[50]

Theorists and advocates of ecological mourning, by contrast, understand grief and care as relational processes. In an influential account of his work with endangered bird species, anthropologist and environmental thinker Thom van Dooren explains how the expanded temporality of species extinction runs counter to established ideas of death as a singular, unspeakable moment of catastrophic rupture:

> I have become acutely aware that extinction is never a sharp, singular event — something that begins, rapidly takes place, and then is over and done with. Rather, the edge of extinction is more often a 'dull' one: a slow unravelling of intimately entangled ways of life that begins long before the death of the last individual and continues to ripple forward long afterward, drawing in living beings in a range of different ways.[51]

Analogously, Ursula Heise has suggested that environmental storytelling must resist the tendency of poetic elegy to signal 'distinctions between who or what is worthy of our collective moral consideration, and who or what is not'.[52] The story of the honeybee is relevant here, since it does not appear to fit the cultural conventions of anthropocentric mourning. According to environmental philosopher Freya Mathews, elegy, with its emphasis on individual loss, fails to articulate the ecological, economic, and cultural importance of our long-standing bond with *apis mellifera*:

> Affirming the moral value of individual bees or bee colonies or bees as a species doesn't quite seem to get to grips with the peculiar horror we feel at the current unexplained — but clearly anthropogenic — disappearance of honeybees. It's not the same kind of horror — the moral outrage — we feel when we hear of atrocities and genocides inflicted on people. Nor is it even quite the same moral anguish we feel when we hear of vast losses of dolphins and seals, penguins and albatrosses incurred as 'by-catch' in the fishing industry, for instance, or the destruction and endangerment of orang-utans as South East Asian forests are converted to crops for bio-fuels. What we feel, in the case of marine animals and orang-utans, is indeed moral outrage as we witness creatures with as much right to live and blossom as ourselves being crushed in the relentless human drive to turn every last quantum of biological resource on this planet to our own use. Confronting the mass disappearance of honeybees, however, in parts of Europe, South America, Asia and particularly the USA, incurs a slightly different register of despair.[53]

Since the publication of Mathews's essay in 2011, such 'different registers of despair' have commanded growing political and cultural attention, as CCD has come to be viewed by many as a particularly visible sign of the climate crisis. Launched in January 2019, the cryptic marketing campaign for New York journalist David Wallace-Wells's new book spelt a simple, but daunting message: 'The Uninhabitable Earth... Coming Soon'.[54] With only a small mention of the author's name in the margins, Wallace-Wells's publishers left the immediate context of their apocalyptic warning unexplained. The campaign's wider meaning, however, was clearly spelt out by the recurrent image of a dead honeybee: not any lifeless animal, but a member of the particular non-human species whose decline, since the turn of the millennium, has been most frequently associated with the complex and inextricable relationship between society and nature. Curled on itself and resting on its side, the small insect marks not only the visual centre point of Penguin's publicity campaign, but also a locus of particular vulnerability. It lies at the symbolic heart of a tangled pattern of intersecting and mutually reinforcing calamities that are no longer perceived as singular, catastrophic events, but rather experienced as the immanent condition of our planetary present and near future.

CCD also finds abundant expression in twenty-first-century literature. 'Bees are becoming more human,' muses cultural geographer Jake Kosek, 'in that human sentiments become part of the bee and humans come to know the world in part through the bee'.[55] At the same time, human stories are becoming more apian. Bees occupy a place of honour in several recent works of autobiographical writing. Wildlife gardener and nature writer Kate Bradbury, for example, uses the figure of the bee as a trope of ecological mourning in the following emotional and nostalgic description of her tiny garden in suburban Brighton:

> It's where wool carder bees chase butterflies, house sparrows hang out with collared doves, red and blue damselflies catch flies while great fat bumblebees spill pollen and petals as they buzz from bloom to bloom. [...] Where plants grow, flower and die — some of them to rise again and others to set seed before returning to the earth. Where compost is made, where birth, death, and everything in between happens in a wild, unfathomable mess of struggle and pain and luck and fate. Where my heart beats.[56]

Similarly, authors of speculative fiction have explored the mobilizing power of ecological mourning, and the significance of the honeybee, as a symbol of looming environmental collapse. Maja Lunde's international bestseller, *The History of Bees* (2015), for example, narrates the history, present crisis, and uncertain future of beekeeping in three closely related stories that are set, respectively, in nineteenth-century England, the contemporary United States, and an imaginary future China, where bees have disappeared and humans must painstakingly pollinate their fruit trees by hand.[57] Similarly, James Bradley's melodramatic, intergenerational novel *Clade* (2017) evokes the disturbing effects of successive and incrementally apocalyptic environmental futures. In each chapter, protagonist Adam Leith and his descendants over four generations are described, as they seek to come to terms with aggressive modernization, environmental collapse, and survival in an impoverished, toxic world that is also a world without honeybees.[58] The work of Finnish science-fiction novelist Johanna Sinisalo, in particular, stands out as a compelling example of multiscalar ecological mourning. In her award-winning novel, *The Blood of Angels* (2011), Sinisalo stages a highly symbolic conflict between four successive generations, in the setting of a once-idyllic rural community that has been transformed by progressive industrialization into 'a dull, grey, noisy world', smelling of 'blood and exhaust'.[59] Sinisalo's commitment to realism — her attempt to give precise and vivid expression to unfolding processes of environmental degradation in her home country — is balanced by a bold homage to three different, and seemingly incompatible, non-mimetic literary genres: magical realism, tragedy, and dystopian science fiction.[60] The events of *The Blood of Angels* take place in a catastrophic near future, sometime in the 2030s, when CCD has destroyed all honeybee colonies in North America, but not, as yet, in northern Europe. Against this background, Sinisalo's family story unfolds with the tremendous and fatal coherence of a Greek tragedy. Each character is highly symbolic. Pupa, the taciturn beekeeper, stands for the wisdom of the old, quiet grace, and companionship with the non-human world. Ari, his overconfident son, has made a fortune from intensive animal farming and from a slaughterhouse that has replaced the old family farm. Next in line is the novel's melancholy first-person narrator, Orvo, who feels no love for his father, Ari, or for a world that seems tainted by pollution and death. Instead of joining the family business, he decides to become a funeral director and divides his time between care for the dead and the 'basic beauty and lovableness' of a dozen beehives: 'just a hobby. About four hundred kilograms of honey a year. Not enough to pay a minimum wage'.[61] Finally, there is Orvo's son Eero: a brilliant and charismatic animal rights activist, and the leader of a small non-violent group who call themselves the Animalist Revolutionary Army (a fictionalized version of the Animal Liberation Front). Each man's political convictions conspire to shape the novel's darkly consequential ending. Eero persuades his friends to organize a protest in the slaughterhouse that is owned by his grandfather, Ari employs a private security guard who shoots and kills Eero, and it falls upon Orvo, the hobbyist beekeeper, to prepare the funeral for his only son. In a desperate effort to convey his feelings to the other members of ARA, Orvo posts the following message on his son's website:

> We think we have the blood of angels in us. In action how like an angel. The paragon of animals. But if any species has the blood of angels, the bees do. The wisdom of bees is the wisdom of the super-organism.[62]

∞

We are living in the future. As Malm explains, the global warming that is felt today is the result of human actions *in the past*, whose devastating consequences are becoming deeper, clearer, and more frequent over time. Similarly, our own, growing political awareness of climate change, in the present, is necessarily directed *towards the future*, when the catastrophic impact of our own actions will be more acutely felt, but when the chances for organized, collective resistance will have dwindled. Faced with this temporal discordance, Malm concludes that political climate activism is best served by *diachronic* conceptual maps:

> There is no synchronicity in climate change. Now more than ever, we inhabit the diachronic, the discordant, the inchoate. [...] History has sprung alive, through a nature that has done likewise. We are only in the very early stages, but already our daily life, our psychic experience, our cultural responses, even our politics show signs of being sucked back by planetary forces into the hole of time, the present dissolving into past and future alike.[63]

What forms of mourning does this state of diachronic confusion bring about, and which cultural practices does it exclude? Political discussions about the climate crisis, *pace* Malm, have mostly focused on just one temporal vector: the negative long-term effects of present-day human behaviour on future humans. Climate activists and authors of climate fiction have sketched countless versions of dystopian or apocalyptic futures. Against this trend, it is important to remember that environmental catastrophe is already happening all around us. As philosopher and literary scholar Timothy Morton points out, imaginative engagement with future catastrophe can easily become a distraction or a form of escapism: ‘a way for us to try to install ourselves at a fictional point in time before global warming happened. We are trying to anticipate something inside which we already find ourselves’.[64] In this chapter, I have suggested that ecological mourning enables us to face our difficult and troublesome present without losing sight of diachronic entanglement. Ecological mourning can take us beyond solitary grief and help us engage with mass death, not as an unspeakable apocalypse-to-come but as a maker of the fundamental unpredictability of post-holocenic societies and ecologies. In a time of environmental catastrophe and of global pandemic disease, when so many people face terminal illness or the death of their human and non-human loved ones, this makes ecological mourning particularly relevant.

Notes to Chapter 12

1. Roy Scranton, *Learning to Die in the Anthropocene: Reflections on the End of a Civilization* (San Francisco: City Lights Books, 2015), p. 21.
2. Jonathan Dollimore, *Death, Desire and Loss in Western Culture* (Harmondsworth: Penguin, 1998), p. xxviii.
3. Lisa Baraitser, *Enduring Time* (London: Bloomsbury, 2017), p. 15.
4. Levinas, *Autrement qu'être ou au-delà de l'essence*, p. 31.
5. See Critchley, *Infinitely Demanding*, pp. 60–61.
6. Derrida, *The Work of Mourning*, ed. and trans. by Brault and Naas, p. 158.
7. Baraitser, *Enduring Time*, p. 184.
8. Laqueur, *The Work of the Dead*, p. 1.
9. Rosi Braidotti, ‘“We” Are in *This* Together, But We Are Not One and the Same’, *Bioethical Inquiry*, 25 August 2020 <https://doi.org/10.1007/s11673-020-10017-8> [accessed 3 December 2020].
10. Baudrillard, *L'Échange symbolique et la mort*; *Symbolic Exchange and Death*, trans. by Iain Hamilton Grant (London: Sage, 1993), p. 126.
11. Philippe Ariès, *L'Homme devant la mort* (Paris: Seuil, 1977); *The Hour of Our Death*, trans. by Helen Weaver (New York: Alfred Knopf, 1981), p. 560.
12. Zygmunt Bauman, *Liquid Fear* (Cambridge: Polity Press, 2006), p. 49. For further discussion of this idea, see Florian Mussgnug, ‘Apocalyptic Narcissism and the Difficulty of Mourning’, *Between*, 5.10 (2015) <doi:10.13125/2039-6597/2214> [accessed 3 December 2020].
13. Kennedy, *Elegy*, p. 139.
14. Ibid., p. 145.
15. See Rebecca Solnit, ‘The Way We Get Through This is Together’, *Guardian*, 14 May 2020 <https://www.theguardian.com/world/2020/may/14/mutual-aid-coronavirus-pandemic-rebecca-solnit> [accessed 3 December 2020].
16. Malm, *Corona, Climate, Chronic Emergency*, p. 2.
17. Braidotti, ‘We Are in *This* Together’.
18. Malm, *Corona, Climate, Chronic Emergency*, p. 4.
19. Ibid., p. 50.
20. See E. O. Wilson, *The Future of Life* (New York: Knopf, 2004); Elizabeth Kolbert, *The Sixth Extinction: An Unnatural History* (New York: Henry Holt, 2014).
21. Jean-Luc Nancy, *After Fukushima: The Equivalence of Catastrophes*, trans. by Charlotte Mandell (New York: Fordham University Press, 2015), p. 3.
22. See, for example, the *Global Risks Report*, which is published annually by the World Economic

Forum <https://reports.weforum.org/global-risks-report-2020/survey-results/the-global-risks-interconnections-map-2020/> [accessed 20 November 2020].
23. Deborah Bird Rose, *Wild Dog Dreaming: Love and Extinction* (Charlottesville: University of Virginia Press, 2011), pp. 81–82.
24. Ibid., p. 89.
25. David Farrier, *Anthropocene Poetics: Deep Time, Sacrifice Zones, and Extinction* (Minneapolis: University of Minnesota Press, 2019), p. 91.
26. Braidotti, 'We Are in *This* Together'.
27. See, for example, Claire Colebrook, *Death of the PostHuman: Essays on Extinction, vol. 1* (Ann Arbor: Open Humanities Press/University of Michigan Press, 2014); and *Sex After Life: Essays on Extinction, vol. 2* (Ann Arbor: Open Humanities Press/University of Michigan Press, 2014); Ashley Dawson, *Extinction: A Radical History* (New York: OR Books, 2016); *Anthropocene or Capitalocene? Nature, History and the Crisis of Capitalism*, ed. by Jason W. Moore (Oakland, CA: PM Press, 2016); Kathryn Yusoff, *A Billion Black Anthropocenes or None* (Minneapolis: University of Minnesota Press, 2018).
28. Mark L. Winston, *Bee Time: Lessons from the Hive* (Cambridge, MA: Harvard University Press, 2014), p. 7.
29. Pronouns are tricky. According to Timothy Morton, 'there is no pronoun entirely suitable to describe ecological beings' (*Humankind: Solidarity with Nonhuman People* (London: Verso, 2017), p. 3).
30. Claire Preston, *Bee* (London: Reaktion Books, 2006), p. 9.
31. Haraway, *Staying with the Trouble*, p. 29.
32. Alyssa N. Crittenden, 'The Importance of Honey Consumption in Human Evolution', *Food and Foodways*, 19.4 (2011), 257–73.
33. Stacy Alaimo, *Bodily Natures: Science, Environment, and the Material Self* (Bloomington: Indiana University Press, 2010), p. 2.
34. Anna Lowenhaupt Tsing, *The Mushroom at the End of the World: On the Possibility of Life in Capitalist Ruins* (Princeton, NJ: Princeton University Press, 2015), p. 21.
35. Preston, *Bee*, p. 8.
36. Eva Crane, *The World History of Beekeeping and Honey Hunting* (New York: Routledge, 1999), p. 491.
37. Preston, *Bee*, p. 11.
38. Winston, *Bee Time*, p. 229.
39. Preston, *Bee*, pp. 163–64.
40. Winston, *Bee Time*, p. 9.
41. See Thor Hanson, *Buzz: The Nature and Necessity of Bees* (New York: Basic Books, 2018), Chapter 9.
42. United Nations Environment Programme, 'Global Honey Bee Colony Disorders and Other Threats to Insect Pollinators', quoted in Farrier, *Anthropocene Poetics*, p. 99.
43. Preston, *Bee*, p. 166.
44. Ursula K. Heise, *Imagining Extinction: The Cultural Meaning of Endangered Species* (Chicago: University of Chicago Press, 2016), p. 49.
45. Timothy Clark, *The Value of Ecocriticism* (Cambridge: Cambridge University Press, 2019), p. 38.
46. Haraway, *Staying with the Trouble*, p. 39.
47. Heise, *Imagining Extinction*, p. 32.
48. See Ramazani, *Poetry of Mourning*; Helen Vendler, *Last Looks, Last Books: Stevens, Plath, Lowell, Bishop* (Princeton, NJ: Princeton University Press, 2010).
49. Kenneth Burke, 'Thanatopsis for Critics: A Brief Thesaurus of Deaths and Dyings', *Essays in Criticism*, 2.4 (1952), 369–75 (p. 372).
50. Simon Critchley, *Very Little... Almost Nothing: Death, Philosophy, Literature* (London: Routledge, 1997), p. 26.
51. Thom van Dooren, *Flight Ways: Life and Loss at the Edge of Extinction* (New York: Columbia University Press, 2014), p. 12.
52. Heise, *Imagining Extinction*, p. 34.

53. Freya Mathews, 'Planet Beehive', in *Unloved Others: Death of the Disregarded in the Time of Extinctions*, ed. by Deborah Bird Rose and Thomas van Doornen (= *Australian Humanities Review*, 50 (2011)) <http://australianhumanitiesreview.org/2011/05/01/issue-50-may-2011/> [accessed 3 December 2020].
54. David Wallace-Wells, *The Uninhabitable Earth: A Story of the Future* (London: Penguin, 2019), pp. 26–27. For information about the publicity campaign, see <https://www.wamc.org/post/uninhabitable-earth-life-after-warming-david-wallace-wells> [accessed 3 December 2020].
55. Jake Kosek, 'Ecologies of Empire: On the Uses of the Honeybee', *Cultural Anthropology*, 25.4 (2010), 650–78 (p. 663).
56. Kate Bradbury, *The Bumblebee Flies Anyway: A Memoir of Love, Loss and Muddy Hands* (London: Bloomsbury, 2018), p. 9. Other examples of the genre include Helen Jukes, *A Honeybee Heart Has Five Openings: A Year of Keeping Bees* (New York: Pantheon Books, 2020); Andrew Coté, *Honey and Venom: Confessions of an Urban Beekeeper* (New York: Ballantine Books, 2020).
57. Maja Lunde, *Bienes historie* (Olso: Aschehoug, 2015); *The History of Bees*, trans. by Diane Oatley (London: Simon & Schuster, 2015).
58. James Bradley, *Clade* (London: Titan Books, 2017). Concerns about toxicity and the survival of bees are also central to the plot of Mireille Juchau, *The World Without Us* (London: Bloomsbury, 2015).
59. Johanna Sinisalo, *Enkelten verta* (Helsinki: Teos, 2011); *The Blood of Angels*, trans. by Lola Rogers (London: Peter Owen, 2014), p. 189. According to Hanna Samola, Sinisalo's attention to typically 'Finish milieus and references to the culture and history of Finland' needs to be understood as a deliberate provocation against the hegemony of global Anglophone cli-fi. See Hanna Samola, 'From Gilead to Eusistocratia: The Dialogue between Margaret Atwood's Dystopian Novel *The Handmaid's Tale* and Johanna Sinisalo's *The Core of the Sun*', in *New Perspectives on Dystopian Fiction in Literature and Other Media*, ed. by Saija Isomaa, Jyrki Korpua, and Jouni Teittinen (Newcastle upon Tyne: Cambridge Scholars Publishing, 2020), pp. 45–64 (p. 47).
60. Sinisalo's fascination with different genres has been explored by Hanna Riikka Roine and Hanna Samola, who compare her work to the North American and British 'New Weird'. See Hanna Riikka Roine and Hanna Samola, 'Johanna Sinisalo and the New Weird: Genres and Myths', in *Lingua Cosmica: Science Fiction from around the World*, ed. by Dale Knickerbocker (Champaign: University of Illinois Press, 2018), pp. 183–200.
61. Sinisalo, *The Blood of Angels*, pp. 36, 29.
62. Ibid., pp. 213–14.
63. Andreas Malm, *The Progress of the Storm: Nature and Society in a Warming World* (London: Verso, 2018), p. 11.
64. Timothy Morton, *Being Ecological* (Cambridge, MA: MIT Press, 2018), p. xxiii.

EPILOGUE

❖

'Grief — A Work in Progress'

Zoe Papadopoulou

(Performed at the Southbank Centre, 5 March 2017)

Forty-seven-year-old female presents with swelling to the right side of her neck, fatigue, and nausea. She has a history of bowel cancer; the GP thought it was a cyst.

'Hi, I am the consultant Dr. How are you?'

'Not great.'

'Who are you?'

'Her partner.'

'Have a seat. Malignant. Cancer. High grade small cell neuroendocrine cancer. Unknown Primary. Advanced.

Aggressive. Metastatic. Terminal. Chemotherapy.

Palliative. Any questions?'

'How long?'

'Two years. Maybe.'

'Thank you.'

'Goodbye.'

'Goodbye.'

Soaking. So this is how my introduction to anticipatory grief happened, in wet trousers, soaking in the urine I can't hold on to. Overtaken by fear, my nervous system can't tell if I should fight or flight. My limbic system rushes that much energy to my heart, muscles, and lungs that it shuts down the more trivial areas. I guess, keeping urine in my bladder is not as important as fighting or flighting. I stand up and form a fist, but then I look at you, distraught but calm.

I go to bed (30 minutes before you).

I cry (silently, for 15 minutes).

I wake up (30 minutes before you).

I make sure you are asleep.

I go to the bathroom.

I close the door.

I cry (silently, for 15 minutes).

I come back to bed.

Side rooms are allocated to patients based on their clinical need. For example, they may have an infection or they may need more frequent visitors which could be disruptive to the rest of the ward. The consultant oncologist, the four junior doctors, the consultant radiologist, the palliative care nurse, the two physiotherapists, the palliative consultant, the chaplain, the priest, the specialist nurse, the ward sister, the ward housekeeper, and the on-duty nurses are all frequent visitors.

The heavily pregnant nurse brings some banana loaf, I get distracted and forget how much I hate small talk. I ask if she knows the sex of her unborn child. 'A girl, we are going to call her Sophia'. 'Greek for wisdom,' I say and she seems delighted with her choice but still can't decide on a middle name. 'You see, it has to be a type of pasta. Are you religious?' she asks. 'Well, if I was I'm not anymore,' I reply. 'My husband and I are pastafarians hence the choice of pasta.' Pastafarians. I'm not sure if this is Canadian humour or if she's trying to cheer me up. 'It's about promoting a light-hearted view of religion, so what types of pasta do you like the sound of?' she asks.

Get up
call the nurse
ask for morphine
get up
call the nurse
ask for morphine
get up
call the nurse
ask for morphine
get up
call the nurse
ask for morphine
get up
nurse
morphine
up
nurse
morphine
nurse
morphine
nurse
morphine
nurse
morphine
nurse
morphine
morphine
morphine
morphine
morphine
morphine
morphine

morphine
morphine
morphine
morphine
morphine
morphine
morphine
morphine
morphine
morphine
morphine
morphine
morphine
morphine
morphine
morphine
morphine
morphine
morphine
morphine
morphine
morphine
morphine
morphine
morphine
morphine
morphine
morphine
morphine
morphine
morphine
morphine
morphine
morphine
morphine
morphine
morphine
morphine
morphine
morphine
morphine
morphine
morphine
morphine
morphine
morphine
morphine
morphine
morphine
morphine
morphine

morphine
morphine
morphine
morphine
morphine
morphine
morphine
morphine
morphine
morphine
morphine
morphine
morphine
morphine
morphine
morphine
morphine
morphine
morphine
morphine
morphine
I'm taken to the storage room, by a junior doctor.
There must be something stronger. Midazolam. But now
I have to decide for you. She needs my consent.
It's like anaesthetic; no, she won't wake up again.
You have two hours. Two hours to become the accomplice. She never says palliative sedation.

Day 1 (after palliative sedation). Palliative nurse 8am:
'She seems peaceful.'

Day 2 (after palliative sedation). Palliative nurse 8am:
'Sometimes it helps to tell them it's ok to go.'

Day 3 (after palliative sedation). Palliative nurse 8am:
'She has the heart of an ox.'

Day 4 (after palliative sedation). Palliative nurse 8am:
'I really didn't expect to see you this morning.'

Day 5 (after palliative sedation). Palliative nurse 8am:
'Do you think she's waiting for someone else to come?'

Day 6 (after palliative sedation).

THE END is not what I imagined. I expect myself to collapse as my oxytocin, dopamine, and serotonin levels crash to a twenty-year low.

I lean forward and look at the floor, left foot, right foot, flat, rigid, still on my feet.

But next to me another version of myself, the one worthy of my Greek heritage, on my knees, wailing, weeping, beating my chest.

This is what my brain thinks I should be doing, but adrenaline and cortisol are keeping me upright. This time I don't want to fight or flight.

'We'll leave you alone, take as much time as you need.'

The nurse leaves the side room. I stare at you with a single thought on repeat.

'Is this it? Is this it? Is this it? Is this it?'

The nurse comes back to tell me the porter is on his way to collect you. I don't want to see them take you, I know where you'll be going. I've seen it in the movies. I go for a cigarette instead. I come back to find your bed has gone, my camp bed is unmade, folded and sits in the middle of the room. I guess this means I have to go now. I want to stay here, one last night. It's 2am. THIS IS IT.

I am now sitting in a fucking bereavement group comparing my grief to that of others. At least her husband lived until he was sixty-eight, that's twenty years longer. But then, a latecomer walks in.

'My husband died when I was pregnant.'

I decide to pursue more elaborate ways to add weight to my grief. I record my blood pressure, sleeping patterns, new aches and pains – some real some imaginary – time spent thinking about you or what clinical psychologists call yearning. I even keep an hourly record of the number of steps I take through my iPhone: not that many, because I never go out. I spend my time waiting for the stress-induced cardiomyopathy also known as broken heart syndrome. I envy the couples who die within days of each other, the poeticism of death. Maybe it's all those Nick Cave songs I play on repeat.

Cry
stop crying
feel better
forget to cry
feel bad
cry
stop crying
feel better
forget to cry

```
feel bad
cry
stop crying
feel better
forget to cry
feel bad
cry
stop crying
feel better
forget to cry
feel bad
cry
stop crying
feel better
forget to cry
feel bad
cry
```

The performance 'Grief — A Work in Progress' was inspired by a personal encounter with grief, when my partner died from neuroendocrine cancer. From the moment a loved one is given a terminal diagnosis, through their death and beyond, we suffer a barrage of physical, cognitive, and psychological grief reactions.

When we experience loss, the nervous system goes into a stress mode known as 'fight or flight'. Higher levels of the peptide hormone and neurotransmitter corticotropin produce anxiety-like symptoms, which in turn increase our heart rate and blood pressure. This leads to over-stimulation of our central nervous system. Sleeping and eating are disturbed as well as our digestion, which can lead to gastrointestinal symptoms, and changes in our metabolism, circulation, and respiration. We feel fatigued, experience unusual aches and pains, struggle to concentrate. Grief also makes the blood 'stickier', and more likely to clot. Basal body temperature drops, the immune system is compromised, and the heart can become misshapen, making us susceptible to infection and even cardiac arrest.

'Grief — A Work in Progress' took place at the Southbank Centre in London as part of the 'Belief and Beyond Belief' festival in March of 2017. It was performed by a group of participants who had been attending workshops I developed as part of a Wellcome Trust-funded project of the same name, exploring physiological and narrative responses to death. Showcasing written and spoken word compositions developed with the participants during the course of the workshops, the performance incorporated experimental choral and soundscape elements highlighting the physiological dimensions of the grieving process. It was structured around chronological narratives — of terminal diagnosis, death, and aftermath — recollections captured in the course of the workshops. The excerpt reproduced here is from my personal contribution to the performance.

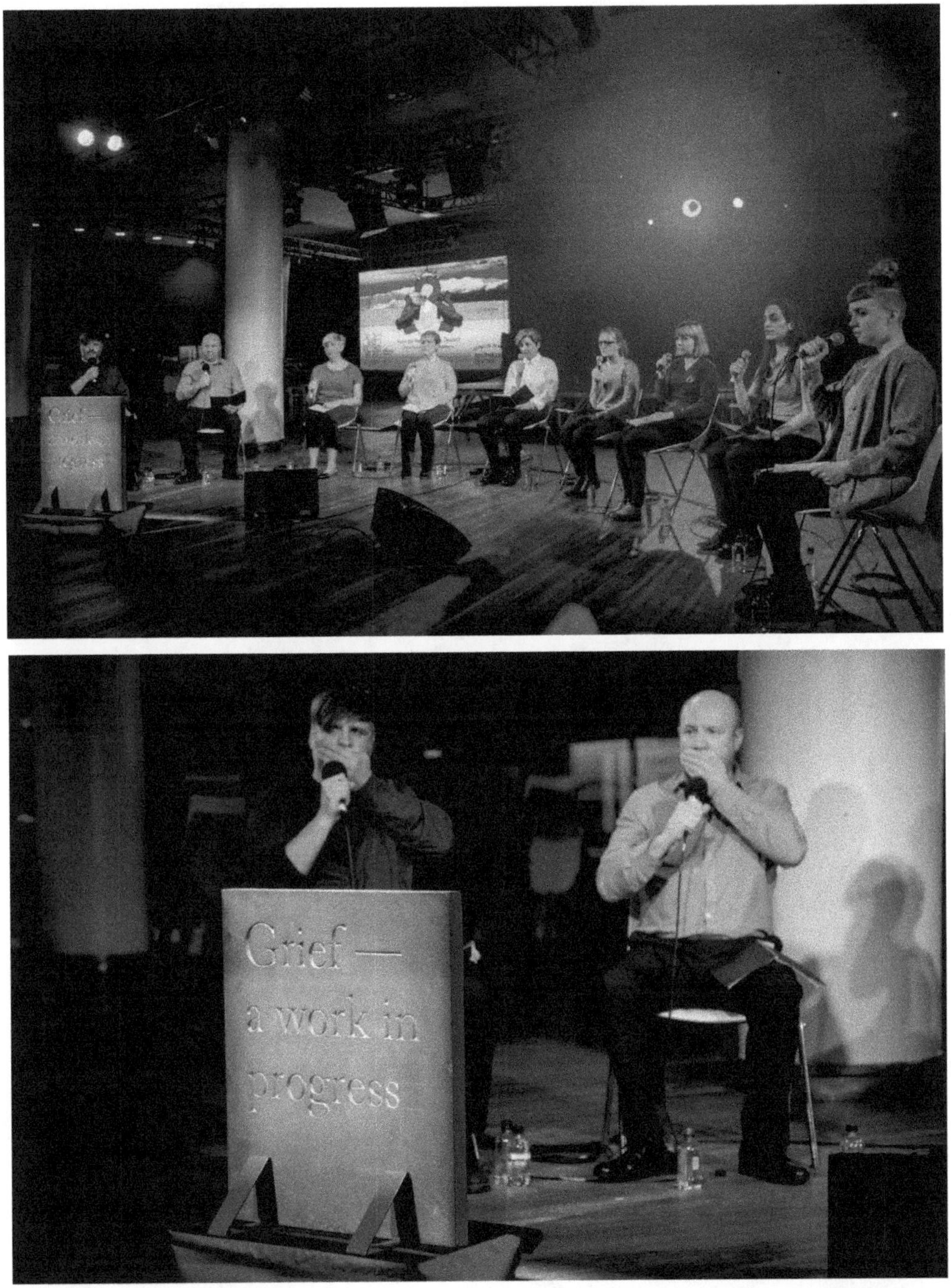

FIG. 13.1–2. Photographs from the event 'Grief — A Work in Progress' held at the Southbank Centre on 5 March 2017. Photography by Nina Pope.

The 'Grief — A Work in Progress' workshops are still taking place today, exploring loss in its myriad forms, including the individual and collective grief we are currently experiencing in the face of climate change, the undoing of democracy, and the COVID-19 pandemic. A converted 1973 Fiat ambulance, repurposed as a mobile workshopping space, or 'Griefmobile', has begun taking the workshops on the road to participants around the UK and beyond. The van, the workshops, and a recently launched 'I Remember' online archive, are together developing new spaces for the confrontation, documentation, curation, and dissemination of our collective chronicles of grief.

For more information about the project, workshops, and the online archive, G-WIP, see <www.griefaworkinprogress.net> [accessed 24 August 2021].

WORKS CITED

Abraham, Nicolas, and Maria Torok, 'Introjection-Incorporation: Mourning or Melancholia', in *Psychoanalysis in France*, ed. by Serge Lebovici and Daniel Widlöcher (New York: International Universities Press, 1980), pp. 3–16

Adler, Anthony, 'Deconfabulation: Agamben's Italian Categories and the Impossibility of Experience', *Diacritics*, 43.3 (2015), 68–94

Agamben, Giorgio, *Categorie italiane: studi di poetica* (Venice: Marsilio, 1996)

—— *The End of the Poem: Studies in Poetics*, trans. by Daniel Heller-Roazen (Stanford, CA: Stanford University Press, 1999)

—— *La follia di Hölderlin: cronaca di una vita abitante (1806–1843)* (Turin: Einaudi, 2021)

—— *Stanze: la parola e il fantasma nella cultura occidentale* (Turin: Einaudi, 1977)

—— *Stanzas: Word and Phantasm in Western Culture*, trans. by Ronald L. Martinez (Minneapolis: University of Minnesota Press, 1993)

Alaimo, Stacy, *Bodily Natures: Science, Environment, and the Material Self* (Bloomington: Indiana University Press, 2010)

Anderson, James R., 'Responses to Death and Dying: Primates and Other Mammals', *Primates*, 61 (2020), 1–7

Anderson, James R., Dora Biro, and Paul Pettitt, 'Evolutionary Thanatology', *Philosophical Transactions of the Royal Society B*, 373 (2018) <https://royalsocietypublishing.org/doi/full/10.1098/rstb.2017.0262>

Arendt, Hannah, *The Human Condition* (Chicago: University of Chicago Press, 1998)

Ariès, Philippe, *L'Homme devant la mort* (Paris: Seuil, 1977)

—— *The Hour of Our Death*, trans. by Helen Weaver, 2nd edn (New York: Alfred Knopf, 2004)

—— 'The Reversal of Death: Changes in Attitudes Toward Death in Western Societies', *American Quarterly*, 26.5 (1974), 536–60

Ascoli, Albert Russell, *Dante and the Making of a Modern Author* (Cambridge: Cambridge University Press, 2008)

Auerbach, Erich, '*Passio* as Passion', in *Time, History, and Literature: Selected Essays of Erich Auerbach*, ed. by James I. Porter and trans. by Jane O. Newman (Princeton, NJ: Princeton University Press, 2014), pp. 165–87

Badmington, Neil, *The Afterlives of Roland Barthes* (London: Bloomsbury Academic, 2016)

Bakka, Egil, 'The Alfred Jewel and Sight', *Antiquaries Journal*, 46 (1966), 277–82

Bakker, D. M., 'Huygens' Op de dood van Sterre: analyse van interpretaties van de eerste regel', in *Opstellen door vrienden en vakgenoten aangeboden aan Dr. C. H. A. Kruyskamp*, ed. by H. Heestermans ('s-Gravenhage: Nijhoff, 1977), pp. 15–24

Baldwin, Thomas, *Roland Barthes: The Proust Variations* (Liverpool: Liverpool University Press, 2019)

Baraitser, Lisa, *Enduring Time* (London: Bloomsbury, 2017)

Barański, Zygmunt G., 'Dottrina degli affetti e teologia: la rappresentazione della beatitudine nel *Paradiso*', in *Dante poeta cristiano e la cultura religiosa medievale: in ricordo di Anna Maria Chiavacci Leonardi*, ed. by Giuseppe Ledda (Ravenna: Centro dantesco dei Frati minori conventuali, 2018), pp. 259–312

BARAŃSKI, ZYGMUNT G., and THEODORE J. CACHEY JR, eds, *Petrarch and Dante: Anti-Dantism, Metaphysics, Tradition* (Notre Dame, IN: University of Notre Dame Press, 2009)
BARDAZZI, ADELE, FRANCESCO GIUSTI, and EMANUELA TANDELLO, eds, *A Gaping Wound: Mourning in Italian Poetry* (Oxford: Legenda, forthcoming)
BARNES, JULIAN, *Levels of Life* (London: Jonathan Cape, 2013)
BAROLINI, TEODOLINDA, 'The Case of the Lost Original Ending of Dante's *Vita nuova*: More Notes Towards a Critical Philology', *Medioevo letterario d'Italia*, 11 (2014), 37–43
——*Dante and the Origins of Italian Literary Culture* (New York: Fordham University Press, 2006)
——*Dante's Poets: Textuality and Truth in the 'Comedy'* (Princeton, NJ: Princeton University Press, 1984)
BAROLINI, TEODOLINDA, and H. WAYNE STOREY, eds, *Dante for the New Millennium* (New York: Fordham University Press, 2003)
BARTHES, ROLAND, *Album: inédits, correspondances et varia*, ed. by Éric Marty (Paris: Seuil, 2015)
——*Album: Unpublished Correspondence and Texts*, trans. by Jody Gladding (New York: Columbia University Press, 2018)
——*La Chambre claire: note sur la photographie* (Paris: Gallimard, 1980)
——*Camera Lucida: Reflections on Photography*, trans. by Richard Howard (London: Vintage, 1993)
——*Journal de deuil: 26 octobre 1977–15 septembre 1979*, ed. by Nathalie Léger (Paris: Seuil/Imec, 2009)
——*Mourning Diary: October 26, 1977–September 15, 1979*, ed. by Nathalie Léger and trans. by Richard Howard (New York: Hill & Wang, 2010; London: Notting Hill Editions, 2011)
——'"Longtemps, je me suis couché de bonne heure"', in *Œuvres complètes*, ed. by Éric Marty, new edn, 5 vols (Paris: Seuil, 2002), v, 459–70
——'*Longtemps, je me suis couché de bonne heure*', in *The Rustle of Language*, trans. by Richard Howard (Berkeley & Los Angeles: University of California Press, 1989), pp. 277–90
——*Marcel Proust: mélanges*, ed. by Bernard Comment (Paris: Seuil, 2020)
——*Œuvres complètes*, ed. by Éric Marty, 3 vols (Paris: Seuil, 1993–95)
——*La Préparation du roman I et II: notes de cours et de séminaires au Collège de France 1978–1979 et 1979–1980*, ed. by Nathalie Léger (Paris: Seuil/IMEC, 2003)
——*The Preparation of the Novel: Lecture Courses and Seminars at the Collège de France (1978–1979 and 1979–1980)*, ed. by Nathalie Léger and trans. by Kate Briggs (New York: Columbia University Press, 2011)
BARTOLONI, PAOLO, 'Dante Alighieri', in *Agamben's Philosophical Lineage*, ed. by Adam Kotsko and Carlo Salzani (Edinburgh: Edinburgh University Press, 2017), pp. 125–30
BATCHELOR, KATHRYN, *Translation and Paratexts* (Abingdon: Routledge, 2018)
BATCHEN, GEOFFREY, 'Palinode: An Introduction to *Photography Degree Zero*', in *Photography Degree Zero: Reflections on Roland Barthes's 'Camera Lucida'*, ed. by Geoffrey Batchen (Cambridge, MA: MIT Press, 2009), pp. 3–30
BATTAGLIA, SALVATORE, 'Linguaggio reale e figurato nella *Divina Commedia*', in *Atti del Congresso nazionale di studi danteschi (Caserta, 21–25 maggio 1961): Dante nel secolo dell'unità italiana* (Florence: Olschki, 1962), pp. 21–44
BAUDELAIRE, CHARLES, *Œuvres complètes*, ed. by Claude Pichois, 2 vols (Paris: Gallimard, 1975–76)
BAUDRILLARD, JEAN, *L'Échange symbolique et la mort* (Paris: Gallimard, 1976)
——*Symbolic Exchange and Death*, trans. by Iain Hamilton Grant (London: Sage, 1993; 2017)
BAUMAN, ZYGMUNT, *Liquid Fear* (Cambridge: Polity Press, 2006)
——*Mortality, Immortality and Other Life Strategies* (Stanford, CA: Stanford University Press, 1992)

Been, Ella, and others, 'The First Neanderthal Remains from an Open-air Middle Palaeolithic Site in the Levant', *Sci Rep*, 7.2958 (2017), 1–8

Bennett, Amanda, 'When Death Doesn't Mean Goodbye', *National Geographic* (March 2016) <https://www.nationalgeographic.com/magazine/2016/04/death-dying-grief-funeral-ceremony-corpse>

Benvenuto da Imola, *Comentum super Dantis Aldigherij Comœdiam*, ed. by Jacobo Filippo Lacaita, 5 vols (Florence: G. Barbera, 1887)

Berger, Lee R., and others, '*Homo naledi*, a New Species of the Genus *Homo* from the Dinaledi Chamber, South Africa', *eLife*, 4 (2015) <https://elifesciences.org/articles/09560>

Bersani, Leo, *The Freudian Body: Psychoanalysis and Art* (New York: Columbia University Press, 1986)

Berthoud, Ella, and Susan Elderkin, eds, *The Novel Cure: An A-Z of Literary Remedies* (Edinburgh & London: Canongate, 2015)

Bettarini, Rosanna, *Lacrime e inchiostro nel 'Canzoniere' di Petrarca* (Bologna: CLUEB, 1998)

Bianca, Concetta, 'Nascita del mito dell'umanista nei compianti in morte del Petrarca', *Quaderni Petrarcheschi*, 9–10 (1992–93), 293–313

Binford, Lewis R., 'Mortuary Practices: Their Study and Their Potential', *Memoirs of the Society for American Archaeology*, 25 (1971), 6–29

Blanco, Maria-Jose, and Ricarda Vidal, eds, *The Power of Death: Contemporary Reflections on Death in Western Society* (New York: Berghahn, 2014)

Blom, Frans R. E., and A. Leerintveld, '"Vrouwen-schoon met Mannelicke reden geluckigh verselt": de *perfect match* met Susanna van Baerle', in *Vrouwen rondom Huygens*, ed. by E. Kloek, F. Blom, and A. Leerintveld (Hilversum: Verloren, 2010), pp. 97–114

Blumenberg, Hans, *Beschreibung des Menschen* (Frankfurt: Suhrkamp, 2006)

Bolter, Debra R., and others, 'Immature Remains and the First Partial Skeleton of a Juvenile *Homo naledi*, a Late Middle Pleistocene Hominin from South Africa', *PLoS ONE*, 15 (2020) <https://journals.plos.org/plosone/article?id=10.1371/journal.pone.0230440>

Bone, Gavin, *Anglo-Saxon Poetry: An Essay with Specimen Translations in Verse* (Oxford: Clarendon Press, 1943)

Botton, Alain de, and John Armstrong, *Art as Therapy* (London & New York: Phaidon, 2013)

Bourne-Taylor, Carole, and Sara-Louise Cooper, eds, *Variations on the Ethics of Mourning in Modern Literature in French* (Oxford: Peter Lang, 2021)

Bowe, David, 'Rubrics and Red Dresses: Ordering the *Vita nova*', *LaRivista*, 8.1 (2020), 5–29

Bozhchenko, Olga A., 'Faktory formirovaniia istoricheskoi pamiati' [The Factors Forming Historical Memory], *Voprosy kul'turologii* [Issues of Cultural Study], 9 (2012), 57–62

Bradbury, Kate, *The Bumblebee Flies Anyway: A Memoir of Love, Loss and Muddy Hands* (London: Bloomsbury, 2018)

Bradley, James, *Clade* (London: Titan Books, 2017)

Braidotti, Rosi, '"We" Are in *This* Together, But We Are Not One and the Same', *Bioethical Inquiry*, 25 August 2020 <https://doi.org/10.1007/s11673–020–10017–8>

Brinkema, Eugenie, *The Forms of the Affects* (Durham, NC: Duke University Press, 2014)

Brovia, Romana, 'In morte di Francesco Petrarca: consolatorie, commemorazioni, epitaffi. Primo regesto dei manoscritti', *Petrarchesca*, 8 (2020), 63–80

Brown, Malcolm Hamrick, ed., *A Shostakovich Casebook* (Bloomington: Indiana University Press, 2004)

Burke, Kenneth, 'Thanatopsis for Critics: A Brief Thesaurus of Deaths and Dyings', *Essays in Criticism*, 2.4 (1952), 369–75

BUTLER, JUDITH, *Antigone's Claim: Kinship between Life and Death* (New York: Columbia University Press, 2000)
CAMILLETTI, FABIO, *The Portrait of Beatrice: Dante, D. G. Rossetti, and the Imaginary Lady* (Notre Dame, IN: University of Notre Dame Press, 2019)
CANO, CHRISTINE M., *Proust's Deadline* (Urbana: University of Illinois Press, 2006)
CARLSON, KRISTINA, *Mr Darwin's Gardener*, trans. by Emily Jeremiah and Fleur Jeremiah (London: Peirene, 2013)
CARRAI, STEFANO, *Dante elegiaco: una chiave di lettura per la 'Vita nova'* (Florence: Olschki, 2006)
CARSON, ANNE, '*The Designated Mourner* by Wally Shawn, Final Production, NYC, June 2013', *London Review of Books*, 35.21 (7 November 2013), p. 12
—— *Float* (London: Jonathan Cape, 2016)
—— *Grief Lessons: Four Plays by Euripides* (New York: NYRB Classics, 2006)
CECIL, HUGH, and MIRABEL CECIL, *In Search of Rex Whistler: His Life and His Work* (London: Frances Lincoln, 2012)
CESTARO, GARY P., *Dante and the Grammar of the Nursing Body* (Notre Dame, IN: University of Notre Dame Press, 2003)
CHAGANTI, SEETA, *The Medieval Poetics of the Reliquary: Enshrinement, Inscription, Performance* (New York: Palgrave Macmillan, 2008)
CHIAPPELLI, FREDI, 'Non satis triste principium', *Modern Language Notes*, 100.1 (1985), 70–81
CHIECCHI, GIUSEPPE, *La parola del dolore: primi studi sulla letteratura consolatoria tra medioevo e umanesimo* (Rome & Padua: Antenore, 2005)
CICERO, *De senectute; De amicitia; De divinatione*, trans. by William Amistead Falconer (Cambridge, MA: Harvard University Press, 1923)
CLARK, TIMOTHY, *The Value of Ecocriticism* (Cambridge: Cambridge University Press, 2019)
CLOUGH, PATRIZIA, ED., WITH JEAN HALLEY, *The Affective Turn: Theorizing the Social* (Durham, NC: Duke University Press, 2007)
COLEBROOK, CLAIRE, *Death of the PostHuman: Essays on Extinction, vol. 1* (Ann Arbor: Open Humanities Press/University of Michigan Press, 2014)
—— *Sex After Life: Essays on Extinction, vol. 2* (Ann Arbor: Open Humanities Press/ University of Michigan Press, 2014)
CONTINI, GIANFRANCO, *Un'idea di Dante* (Turin: Einaudi, 1970)
——, ed., *Poeti del Duecento*, 2 vols (Milan: Ricciardi, 1960)
COTÉ, ANDREW, *Honey and Venom: Confessions of an Urban Beekeeper* (New York: Ballantine Books, 2020)
CRANE, EVA, *The World History of Beekeeping and Honey Hunting* (New York: Routledge, 1999)
CRITCHLEY, SIMON, *Infinitely Demanding: Ethics of Commitment, Politics of Resistance* (London: Verso, 2007)
—— *Very Little... Almost Nothing: Death, Philosophy, Literature* (London: Routledge, 1997)
CRITTENDEN, ALYSSA N., 'The Importance of Honey Consumption in Human Evolution', *Food and Foodways*, 19.4 (2011), 257–73
CROWLEY, PATRICK, and SHIRLEY JORDAN, 'Introduction', in *What Forms Can Do: The Work of Form in 20th- and 21st-century French Literature and Thought*, ed. by Patrick Crowley and Shirley Jordan (Liverpool: Liverpool University Press, 2020), pp. 1–20
CROWN, SARAH, 'Max Porter interviewed by Sarah Crown', *Guardian*, 12 September 2015 <https://www.theguardian.com/books/2015/sep/12/max-porter-books-interview-grief-is-a-thing-with-feathers>
CULLER, JONATHAN, *Barthes: A Very Short Introduction* (Oxford: Oxford University Press, 2002)

DANTE ALIGHIERI, *Convivio: A Dual Language Critical Edition*, ed. and trans. by Andrew Frisardi (Cambridge: Cambridge University Press, 2018)
——*Dante's 'Vita Nuova'*, ed. and trans. by Mark L. Musa (Bloomington: Indiana University Press, 1973); also available at <https://dante.princeton.edu/pdp/vnuova.html>
——*Dante's Lyric Poetry*, ed. and trans. by Kenelm Foster and Patrick Boyde, 2 vols (Oxford: Clarendon, 1967)
——*La Divina Commedia*, ed. by Anna Maria Chiavacci Leonardi, 3 vols (Milan: Mondadori, 1991–94)
——*La Divine Comédie*, trans. by Alexandre Masseron (Paris: Albin Michel, 1947)
——*La Divine Comédie: traduction nouvelle par A. Brizeux; La Vie nouvelle, traduite par M. E.-J. Delécluze* (Paris: Charpentier, 1841)
——*The Divine Comedy*, trans. by Robin Kirkpatrick, 3 vols (London: Penguin, 2006–07)
——*Œuvres complètes*, trans. by André Pézard (Paris: Gallimard, 1965)
——*Vita nova*, ed. by Guglielmo Gorni (Turin: Einaudi, 1996)
——*Vita nuova; Rime*, ed. by Donato Pirovano and Marco Grimaldi (Rome: Salerno, 2015)
Dartmouth Dante Project <https://dante.dartmouth.edu/>
D'AVRAY, DAVID, *Medieval Marriage Sermons: Mass Communication in a Culture without Print* (Oxford: Oxford University Press, 2001)
DAVIS, COLIN, and HANNA MERETOJA, eds, *The Routledge Companion to Literature and Trauma* (Abingdon: Routledge, 2020)
DAWSON, ASHLEY, *Extinction: A Radical History* (New York: OR Books, 2016)
DELCORNO, CARLO, 'Medieval Preaching in Italy (1200–1500)', in *The Sermon*, ed. by Beverly Mayne Kienzle (Turnhout: Brepols, 2000), pp. 449–560
D'ERRICO, FRANCESCO, and CHRIS B. STRINGER, 'Evolution, Revolution or Saltation Scenario for the Emergence of Modern Cultures?', *Philosophical Transactions of the Royal Society B*, 366 (2011) <https://royalsocietypublishing.org/doi/10.1098/rstb.2010.0340>
DERRIDA, JACQUES, *Aporias*, trans. by Thomas Dutoit (Stanford, CA: Stanford University Press, 1993)
——*Chaque fois unique, la fin du monde* (Paris: Galilée, 2003)
——*The Work of Mourning*, ed. and trans. by Pascale-Anne Brault and Michael Naas (Chicago: University of Chicago Press, 2001)
——*Copy, Archive, Signature: A Conversation on Photography*, ed. by Gerhard Richter and trans. by Jeff Fort (Stanford, CA: Stanford University Press, 2010)
——*Learning to Live Finally: The Last Interview. An Interview with Jean Birnbaum*, trans. by Pascale-Anne Brault and Michael Naas (New York: Palgrave Macmillan, 2007)
——*Memoires for Paul de Man*, trans. by Cecile Lindsay, Jonathan D. Culler, and Eduardo Cadava (New York: Columbia University Press, 1986)
——*Of Hospitality*, trans. by Rachel Bowlby (Stanford, CA: Stanford University Press, 2000)
DESCARTES, RENÉ, *The Passions of the Soul*, trans. by Stephen Voss (Indianapolis, IN, & Cambridge: Hackett, 1989)
DESCHARNES, ROBERT, *Dalí* (New York: Harry N. Abrams, 2003)
DIAZ, JOSÉ-LUIS, and MATHILDE LABBÉ, eds, *Les XIXes siècles de Roland Barthes* (Brussels: Impressions Nouvelles, 2019)
DOLLIMORE, JONATHAN, *Death, Desire and Loss in Western Culture* (Harmondsworth: Penguin, 1998)
DONNE, JOHN, *The Sermons of John Donne*, ed. by G. R. Potter and E. M. S. Simpson, 10 vols (Berkeley: University of California Press, 1953–62)
DRILLON, JACQUES, *Face à face* (Paris: Gallimard, 2003)
EDKINS, JENNY, *Trauma and the Memory of Politics* (Cambridge: Cambridge University Press, 2003)

Edwards, Tony, 'Gavin Bone and his Old English Translations', *Translation and Literature*, 30 (2021), 147–69
Eliot, George, 'The *Antigone* and its Moral', *Leader*, 7 (29 March 1856), 306
Elkins, James, 'Camera Dolorosa', *History of Photography*, 31 (2007), 22–30
—— *What Photography Is* (New York: Routledge, 2011)
Elsner, Anna Magdalena, *Mourning and Creativity in Proust* (New York: Palgrave Macmillan, 2017)
Fanning, David, *Shostakovich: String Quartet No. 8* (Burlington, VT: Ashgate, 2004)
Farin, Ingo, and Jeff Malpas, eds, *Reading Heidegger's 'Black Notebooks' 1931–1941* (Cambridge, MA: MIT Press, 2016)
Farrier, David, *Anthropocene Poetics: Deep Time, Sacrifice Zones, and Extinction* (Minneapolis: University of Minnesota Press, 2019)
Felman, Shoshana, 'To Open the Question', in *Literature and Psychoanalysis: The Question of Reading: Otherwise* (= *Yale French Studies*, 55/56 (1977)), 5–10 (repr. as *Literature and Psychoanalysis: The Question of Reading: Otherwise* (Baltimore, MD: Johns Hopkins University Press, 1982))
Felski, Rita, *Uses of Literature* (Oxford: Blackwell, 2008)
Ferrari, Stefano, *Scrittura come riparazione: saggio su letteratura e psicoanalisi* (Rome & Bari: Laterza, 2012)
Ferzoco, George, 'Dante and the Context of Medieval Preaching', in *Reviewing Dante's Theology*, ed. by Claire E. Honess and Matthew Treherne, 2 vols (Oxford: Lang, 2013), II, 187–210
Fisher, Philip, *The Vehement Passions* (Princeton, NJ: Princeton University Press, 2002)
Ford, David, *Self and Salvation: Being Transformed* (Cambridge: Cambridge University Press, 1999)
Fourcade, Dominique, *Deuil* (Paris: P.O.L., 2018)
Freud, Sigmund, *The Ego and the Id*, in *The Standard Edition of the Complete Psychological Works of Sigmund Freud*, ed. and trans. by James Strachey, 24 vols (London: Hogarth Press, 1953–74), XIX (1961), 12–66
—— *Letters of Sigmund Freud 1873–1939*, ed. by Ernst L. Freud and trans. by Tania Stern and James Stern (London: Hogarth Press, 1961)
—— 'Mourning and Melancholia' [1917], in *The Standard Edition to the Complete Psychological Works of Sigmund Freud*, ed. and trans. by James Strachey, 24 vols (London: Hogarth Press, 1953–74), XIV (1957), 243–58
Gallerani, Guido Mattia, 'Barthes et l'Italie: voyages, collaborations, traductions, réception, études', in *Barthes à l'étranger*, ed. by Claude Coste and Mathieu Messager, (= *Revue Roland Barthes*, 2 (October 2015)) <http://www.roland-barthes.org/article_gallerani.html>
Gardair, Jean-Michel, *Écrivains italiens* (Paris: Larousse, 1978)
Gardner, Callie, *Poetry and Barthes: Anglophone Responses 1970–2000* (Liverpool: Liverpool University Press, 2018)
——, ed., *Roland Barthes and Poetry* (= *Barthes Studies*, 2 (2016)) <http://sites.cardiff.ac.uk/barthes/category/volume-2/>
Gaunt, Simon, *Love and Death in Medieval French and Occitan Courtly Literature: Martyrs to Love* (Oxford: Oxford University Press, 2006)
Gefen, Alexandre, 'Philippe Forest et les injonctions paradoxales du *récit de deuil*', in *Philippe Forest: une vie à écrire: actes du colloque international*, ed. by Aurélie Foglia and others (Paris: Gallimard, 2018), pp. 26–38
Gilbert, Sandra M., *Death's Door: Modern Dying and the Ways We Grieve* (New York & London: Norton, 2006)

Giovanni da San Gimignano, *Opus aureum sermonum quadragesimalium* (Paris: Jean Petit, 1511)
Gneuss, Helmut, and Michael Lapidge, *Anglo-Saxon Manuscripts: A Bibliographical Handlist of Manuscripts and Manuscript Fragments Written or Owned in England up to 1100* (Toronto: University of Toronto Press, 2014)
Goldhill, Simon, 'Antigone and the Politics of Sisterhood', in *Laughing with Medusa: Classical Myth and Feminist Thought*, ed. by Vanda Zajko and Miriam Leonard (Oxford: Oxford University Press, 2016), pp. 141–62
Goodall, Jane, *Through a Window: My Thirty Years with the Chimpanzees of Gombe* (Boston, MA: Houghton-Mifflin, 1990)
Goodkin, Richard, *Around Proust* (Princeton, NJ: Princeton University Press, 1991)
Gorer, Geoffrey, *Death, Grief, and Mourning in Contemporary Britain* (London: Cresset Press, 1965)
Gragnolati, Manuele, *Amor che move: linguaggio del corpo e forma del desiderio in Dante, Pasolini e Morante* (Milan: Il Saggiatore, 2013)
——'(In-)Corporeality, Language, Performance in Dante's *Vita Nuova* and *Commedia*', in *Dante's Plurilingualism: Authority, Knowledge, Subjectivity*, ed. by Sara Fortuna, Manuele Gragnolati, and Jürgen Trabant (Oxford: Legenda, 2010), pp. 213–22
Gragnolati, Manuele, Fabio Camilletti, and Fabian Lampart, eds, *Metamorphosing Dante: Appropriations, Manipulations, and Rewritings in the Twentieth and Twenty-first Centuries* (Vienna: Turia & Kant, 2011)
Gregg, Melissa, and Gregory J. Seigworth, eds, *The Affect Theory Reader* (Durham, NC: Duke University Press, 2010)
Guibert, Hervé, *L'Image fantôme* (Paris: Minuit, 1981)
—— *Ghost Image*, trans. by Robert Bononno (Chicago: University of Chicago Press, 2014)
Guittone d'Arezzo, *Le rime*, ed. by Francesco Egidi (Bari: Laterza, 1940)
Gunn, Kirsty, '*Grief is the Thing with Feathers* by Max Porter Review — Words Take Flight', *Guardian*, 12 September 2015 <https://www.theguardian.com/books/2015/sep/18/grief-is-the-thing-with-feathers-by-max-porter-review-ted-hughes>
Hanson, Thor, *Buzz: The Nature and Necessity of Bees* (New York: Basic Books, 2018)
Haraway, Donna J., *Staying with the Trouble: Making Kin in the Chthulucene* (Durham, NC: Duke University Press, 2016)
Harrison, Robert Pogue, *The Body of Beatrice* (Baltimore, MD: Johns Hopkins University Press, 1988)
—— *The Dominion of the Dead* (Chicago: University of Chicago Press, 2003)
—— *Forests: The Shadow of Civilization* (Chicago: University of Chicago Press, 1992)
Harss, Marina, 'Running Like Shadows', *The Nation*, 16 July 2013 <http://www.thenation.com/article/running-shadows/>
Hartley, Julia, *Reading Dante and Proust by Analogy* (Oxford: Legenda, 2019)
Hawkins, Peter S., 'Dido, Beatrice, and the Signs of Ancient Love', in *The Poetry of Allusion: Virgil and Ovid in Dante's 'Commedia'*, ed. by Rachel Jacoff and Jeffrey T. Schnapp (Stanford, CA: Stanford University Press, 1991), pp. 113–30
Hawks, John, and others, 'New Fossil Remains of *Homo naledi* from the Lesedi Chamber, South Africa', *eLife*, 6 (2017) <https://elifesciences.org/articles/24232>
Hegel, G. W. F., *Phenomenology of Spirit*, trans. by A. V. Miller (Oxford: Clarendon, 1977)
Heidegger, Martin, *Poetry, Language, Thought*, trans. by Albert Hofstadter (New York: Harper Colophon Books, 1971)
—— *Vorträge und Aufsätze* (Pfullingen: Neske, 1954)
Heise, Ursula K., *Imagining Extinction: The Cultural Meaning of Endangered Species* (Chicago: University of Chicago Press, 2016)

HILL, MICHAEL, JOHN NEWMAN, and NIKOLAUS PEVSNER, *The Buildings of England: Dorset*, Pevsner Architectural Guides (New Haven, CT: Yale University Press, 2018)

HINES, JOHN, 'The Ruthwell Cross, the Brussels Cross, and *The Dream of the Rood*', in *Transitional States: Change, Tradition, and Memory in Medieval Literature and Culture*, ed. by Graham D. Caie and Michael D. C. Drout (Tempe: Arizona Center for Medieval and Renaissance Studies, 2018), pp. 175–92

HIRSCH, MARIANNE, *Family Frames: Photography, Narrative and Postmemory* (Cambridge, MA: Harvard University Press, 1997)

HOFFMANN, D. L., and OTHERS, 'U-Th Dating of Carbonate Crusts reveals Neandertal Origin of Iberian Cave Art', *Science*, 359 (2018), 912–15

HOLLOWAY, RALPH L., and OTHERS, 'Endocast Morphology of *Homo naledi* from the Dinaledi Chamber, South Africa', *Proceedings of the National Academy of Sciences of the USA*, 115 (2018) <https://www.pnas.org/content/115/22/5738>

HOLSINGER, BRUCE, *The Premodern Condition: Medievalism and the Making of Theory* (Chicago: University of Chicago Press, 2005)

HONIG, BONNIE, *Antigone, Interrupted* (Cambridge: Cambridge University Press, 2013)

HOROWITZ, M. J., B., and OTHERS, 'Diagnostic Criteria for Complicated Grief Disorder', *American Journal of Psychiatry*, 154 (1997), 904–10

HOWLETT, D. R., 'The Iconography of the Alfred Jewel', *Oxoniensia*, 39 (1974), 44–52

HUYGENS, CONSTANTIJN, *Korenbloemen*, ed. by Ton van Strien (Amsterdam: Querido, 1996)

—— *Mijn leven verteld aan mijn kinderen*, ed. by F. R. Blom, 2 vols (Amsterdam: Prometheus/ Bert Bakker, 2003)

IBBETT, KATHERINE, *Compassion's Edge: Fellow-feeling and Its Limits in Early Modern France* (Philadelphia: University of Pennsylvania Press, 2018)

JACOFF, RACHEL, 'Intertextualities in Arcadia: *Purgatorio* 30.49–51', in *The Poetry of Allusion: Virgil and Ovid in Dante's 'Commedia'*, ed. by Rachel Jacoff and Jeffrey T. Schnapp (Stanford, CA: Stanford University Press, 1991), pp. 131–44

JACOFF, RACHEL, and JEFFREY T. SCHNAPP, eds, *The Poetry of Allusion: Virgil and Ovid in Dante's 'Commedia'* (Stanford, CA: Stanford University Press, 1991)

JORDAN, SHIRLEY, 'Chronicles of Intimacy: Photography in Autobiographical Projects', in *Textual and Visual Selves: Photography, Film, and Comic Art in French Autobiography*, ed. by Natalie Edwards, Amy L. Hubbell, and Ann Miller (Lincoln: University of Nebraska Press, 2011), pp. 51–77

—— 'The Time of Our Lives: Repetition, Variation and Representation in French Women's Life Writing', in *What Forms Can Do: The Work of Form in 20th- and 21st-century French Literature and Thought*, ed. by Patrick Crowley and Shirley Jordan (Liverpool: Liverpool University Press, 2020), pp. 113–30

JUCHAU, MIREILLE, *The World Without Us* (London: Bloomsbury, 2015)

JUKES, HELEN, *A Honeybee Heart Has Five Openings: A Year of Keeping* Bees (New York: Pantheon Books, 2020)

KAFKA, FRANZ, *The Diaries of Franz Kafka, 1910–23*, ed. by Max Brod (London: Minerva, 1992)

KAPLAN, E. ANN, *Trauma Culture: The Politics of Terror and Loss in Media and Literature* (New Brunswick, NJ: Rutgers University Press, 2005)

KAY, DENNIS, *Melodious Tears: The English Funeral Elegy from Spenser to Milton* (Oxford: Clarendon Press, 1990)

KAY, TRISTAN, 'Dido, Aeneas, and the Evolution of Dante's Poetics', *Dante Studies*, 129 (2011), 135–60

KEESING, ELIZABETH, *Het volk met lange rokken: vrouwen rondom Constantijn Huygens* (Amsterdam: Querido, 1987)

Kennedy, David, *Elegy* (New York: Routledge, 2007)
Kennedy, William J., *The Site of Petrarchism* (Baltimore, MD: Johns Hopkins University Press, 2003)
Ker, N. R., *Catalogue of Manuscripts Containing Anglo-Saxon* (Oxford: Clarendon Press, 1957)
Kipling, Rudyard, *Just So Stories* (London: Collector's Library, 2002)
Knight, Diana, *Barthes and Utopia: Space, Travel, Writing* (Oxford: Clarendon Press, 1997)
——'Idle Thoughts: Barthes's *Vita Nova*', *Nottingham French Studies*, 36.1 (Spring 1997), 88–98
——'Roland Barthes, or The Woman without a Shadow', in *Writing the Image after Roland Barthes*, ed. by Jean-Michel Rabaté (Philadelphia: University of Pennsylvania Press, 1997), pp. 132–43
Kolbert, Elizabeth, *The Sixth Extinction: An Unnatural History* (New York: Henry Holt, 2014)
Kosek, Jake, 'Ecologies of Empire: On the Uses of the Honeybee', *Cultural Anthropology*, 25.4 (2010), 650–78
Küsters, P. M., 'Das Grab der Afrikaner', *Anthropos*, 14/15 (1919/20), 639–728, and 16/17 (1921), 183–229, 913–59
Lacan, Jacques, *The Ethics of Psychoanalysis 1959–1960: The Seminar of Jacques Lacan: Book VII*, ed. by Jacques-Alain Miller and trans. by Dennis Porter (London: Routledge, 1992)
Landy, Joshua, *Philosophy as Fiction: Self, Deception, and Knowledge in Proust* (Oxford: Oxford University Press, 2004)
Lansing, Carol, *Passion and Order: Restraint of Grief in the Medieval Italian Communes* (Ithaca, NY: Cornell University Press, 2008)
Laplanche, Jean, and J.-B. Pontalis, *The Language of Psycho-analysis*, trans. by Donald Nicholson-Smith (London: Hogarth Press, 1973)
Laqueur, Thomas W., *The Work of the Dead: A Cultural History of Mortal Remains* (Princeton, NJ: Princeton University Press, 2015)
Laurens, Camille, *L'Amour, roman* (Paris: P.O.L., 2003)
——*Cet absent-là: figures de Rémi Vinet* (Paris: Léo Scheer, 2004)
——*Philippe* (Paris: P.O.L., 1995)
Leonard, Miriam, 'Tragedy and the Seductions of Philosophy', *The Cambridge Classical Journal*, 58 (2012), 145–64
Levinas, Emmanuel, *Autrement qu'être ou au-delà de l'essence* (Dordrecht: Kluwer Academic, 1996)
Lewis, C. S., *A Grief Observed* [1961] (New York: Harper One, 1989)
Lieburg, Mart J. van, 'Constantijn Huygens en Suzanna van Baerle: een pathobiografische bijdrage', *De zeventiende eeuw*, 3 (1987), 171–78
Lievens, R., 'Huygens' Op de dood van Sterre', *Handelingen van de Koninklijke Zuidnederlandse Maatschappij*, 26 (1972), 325–33
Lindon, John, 'Notes on Nineteenth-century Dante Commentaries and Critical Editions', in *Interpreting Dante: Essays on the Traditions of Dante Commentary*, ed. by Paola Nasti and Claudia Rossignoli (Notre Dame, IN: University of Notre Dame Press, 2013), pp. 434–49
Lombardo, Patrizia, *The Three Paradoxes of Roland Barthes* (Athens: University of Georgia Press, 1989)
Loraux, Nicole, *The Invention of Athens: The Funeral Oration in the Classical City* (Cambridge, MA: Harvard University Press, 1986)
——*The Mourning Voice: An Essay on Greek Tragedy* (Ithaca, NY: Cornell University Press, 2002)
Lunde, Maja, *Bienes historie* (Olso: Aschehoug, 2015)

——*The History of Bees*, trans. by Diane Oatley (London: Simon & Schuster, 2015)
LUZZI, JOSEPH, *Dante's 'Divine Comedy': A Biography* (Princeton, NJ: Princeton University Press, forthcoming)
——*In a Dark Wood: A Memoir of Grief, Healing and the Mysteries of Love* (London: William Collins, 2015)
——*My Two Italies* (New York: Farrar, Straus & Giroux, 2014)
——*Romantic Europe and the Ghost of Italy* (New Haven, CT: Yale University Press, 2008)
MADISON, PAIGE, 'Who First Buried the Dead?', *Sapiens*, 16 February 2018 <https://www.sapiens.org/culture/hominin-burial/>
MALDINA, NICOLÒ, *In pro del mondo: Dante, la predicazione e i generi della letteratura religiosa medievale* (Rome: Salerno, 2017)
MALM, ANDREAS, *Corona, Climate, Chronic Emergency: War Communism in the Twenty-first Century* (London: Verso, 2020)
——*The Progress of the Storm: Nature and Society in a Warming World* (London: Verso, 2018)
MARRONE, ROBERT, 'Grieving and Mourning: Distinctions in Process', *Illness, Crisis & Loss*, 6 (1998), 320–32
MARTINEZ, RONALD L., 'Mourning Beatrice: The Rhetoric of Threnody in the *Vita nuova*', *Modern Language Notes*, 113 (1998), 1–29; repr. in *Dante: The Critical Complex*, ed. by Richard Lansing, 8 vols (New York: Routledge, 2003), I, 127–55
——'Mourning Laura in the *Canzoniere*: Lessons from Lamentations', *Modern Language Notes*, 118 (2003), 1–45
MATHEWS, FREYA, 'Planet Beehive', in *Unloved Others: Death of the Disregarded in the Time of Extinctions*, ed. by Deborah Bird Rose and Thomas van Doornen (= *Australian Humanities Review*, 50 (2011)) < http://australianhumanitiesreview.org/2011/05/01/issue-50-may-2011/>
MAZZOTTA, GIUSEPPE, 'The Language of Poetry in the *Vita nuova*', *Rivista di studi italiani*, 1.1 (1983), 3–14
MCCLURE, GEORGE W., *Sorrow and Consolation in Italian Humanism* (Princeton, NJ: Princeton University Press, 1991)
MCCUE, JIM, 'Laurence Whistler: An Oxford Artist', *Oxford Poetry*, 16.2 (2016), 36–39
MIDGLEY, MARY, *Beast and Man: The Roots of Human Nature*, rev. edn (London: Routledge Classics, 2002)
MITCHELL, ANDREW J., and PETER TRAWNY, eds, *Heidegger's 'Black Notebooks': Responses to Anti-semitism* (New York: Columbia University Press, 2017)
MITCHELL, W. J. T., *Picture Theory: Essays on Verbal and Visual Representation* (Chicago: University of Chicago Press, 1994)
MOEVS, CHRISTIAN, *The Metaphysics of Dante's 'Comedy'* (New York: Oxford University Press, 2005)
MOLLER, DAVID WENDELL, *Confronting Death: Values, Institutions, and Human Mortality* (Oxford: Oxford University Press, 1996)
MONTEMAGGI, VITTORIO, *Reading Dante's 'Commedia' as Theology: Divinity Realized in Human Encounter* (New York: Oxford University Press, 2016)
MOORE, JASON W., ed., *Anthropocene or Capitalocene? Nature, History and the Crisis of Capitalism* (Oakland, CA: PM Press, 2016)
MORIARTY, MICHAEL, *Roland Barthes* (Cambridge: Polity, 1991)
MORRIS, IAN, *Death-ritual and Social Structure in Classical Antiquity* (Cambridge: Cambridge University Press, 1992)
MORRISON, BLAKE, '*Levels of Life* by Julian Barnes — Review', *Guardian*, 10 April 2013 <https://www.theguardian.com/books/2013/apr/10/levels-life-julian-barnes-review>
MORTON, TIMOTHY, *Being Ecological* (Cambridge, MA: MIT Press, 2018)

——*Humankind: Solidarity with Nonhuman People* (London: Verso, 2017)
Mussgnug, Florian, 'Apocalyptic Narcissism and the Difficulty of Mourning', *Between*, 5.10 (2015) <doi:10.13125/2039–6597/2214>
Nagy, Piroska, *Le Don des larmes au Moyen Âge: un instrument spirituel en quête d'institution (Ve–XIIIe siècle)* (Paris: Michel, 2000)
Naiko, Natalia M., *Poznavshii tainu zvuka: stat'i o muzyke i muzykantakh* [Understanding the Secret of the Sound: Articles about Music and Musicians] (Krasnoyarsk: Krasnoyarsk Academy of Music and Theater, 2012)
Nancy, Jean-Luc, *After Fukushima: The Equivalence of Catastrophes*, trans. by Charlotte Mandell (New York: Fordham University Press, 2015)
Nasti, Paola, and Claudia Rossignoli, eds, *Interpreting Dante: Essays on the Traditions of Dante Commentary* (Notre Dame, IN: University of Notre Dame Press, 2013)
Neubauer, Simon, Jean-Jacques Hublin, and Philipp Gunz, 'The Evolution of Modern Human Brain Shape', *Science Advances*, 4.1 (2018) <https://advances.sciencemag.org/content/4/1/eaao5961.short>
Newby, Zahra, and Ruth E. Toulson, eds, *The Materiality of Mourning: Cross-disciplinary Perspectives* (Abingdon: Routledge, 2019)
Newell, Mike, dir., *Four Weddings and a Funeral* (Rank, 1994)
Niewoehner, Wesley A., 'Behavioral Inferences from the Skhul/Qafzeh Early Modern Human Hand Remains', *Proceedings of the National Academy of Sciences*, 98 (2001), 2979–84
O'Neill, Eugene, *Mourning Becomes Electra: A Trilogy* (New York: H. Liveright, 1931)
Osipenko, Olesya A., 'Mourning Themes in the Music of Dmitri Shostakovich', *Journal of Siberian Federal University. Humanities & Social Sciences*, 7.3 (2014), 404–15
Paolino, Laura, '"Ad acerbam rei memoriam": le carte del lutto nel codice Vaticano Latino 3196 di Francesco Petrarca', *Rivista di Letteratura Italiana*, 11 (1993), 73–102
Papadopoulou, Zoe, 'Grief — A Work in Progress' <www.griefaworkinprogress.net>
Paterson, Don, ed., *The Picador Book of Funeral Poems* (London: Picador, 2012)
Pearce, Eiluned, Chris Stringer, and R. I. M. Dunbar, 'New Insights into Differences in Brain Organization between Neanderthals and Anatomically Modern Humans', *Proceedings of the Royal Society B*, 280 (2013), 1–7
Pearson, Mike Parker, *The Archaeology of Death and Burial* (Stroud: Sutton, 1999)
Petrarca, Francesco, *Canzoniere*, ed. by Marco Santagata (Milan: Mondadori, 1996)
——*Canzoniere*, ed. by Marco Santagata, rev. edn (Milan: Arnoldo Mondadori, 2010)
——*The Complete Canzoniere*, trans. by A. S. Kline <https://www.poetryintranslation.com/PITBR/Italian/Petrarchhome.php>
——*Epistulae metricae: Briefe in Versen*, ed. by Otto and Eva Schönberger (Würzburg: Königshausen & Neumann 2004)
——*Letters of Old Age/Rerum senilium libri I–XVIII*, trans. by Aldo S. Bernardo, Saul Levin, and Reta A. Bernardo, 2 vols (Baltimore, MD: Johns Hopkins University Press, 1992)
——*Poëmata minora quae exstant omnia nunc primo ad trutinam revocata ac recensita*, ed. by Domenico de' Rossetti, 3 vols (Milan: Societas typographica classicorum Italiae scriptorum, 1829–34)
——*Les Remèdes aux deux fortunes/De remediis utriusque fortune (1354–1366)*, ed. and trans. by Christophe Carraud, 2 vols (Grenoble: Jérôme Millon, 2002)
——*Petrarch's Remedies for Fortune Fair and Foul*, ed. and trans. by Conrad H. Rawski, 5 vols (Bloomington: Indiana University Press, 1991)
——*Trionfi, rime estravaganti, codice degli abbozzi*, ed. by Vinicio Pacca and Laura Paolino (Milan: Arnoldo Mondadori, 2013)
Pettitt, Paul, 'The Neanderthal Dead: Exploring Mortuary Variability in Middle Palaeolithic Eurasia', *Before Farming*, 4.1 (2002), 1–26

PHILLIPS, ADAM, 'How to be your Father's Mother', *London Review of Books*, 13.17 (12 September 1991) <https://www.lrb.co.uk/the-paper/v13/n17/adam-phillips/how-to-be-your-father-s-mother> (repr. 'Philip Roth's Patrimony', in *On Flirtation* (London: Faber & Faber, 1994), pp. 167–74)
PICH, FEDERICA, 'L'immagine "donna de la mente" dalle *Rime* alla *Vita Nova*', in *Le Rime di Dante*, ed. by Claudia Berra and Paolo Borsa (Milan: Cisalpino, 2010), pp. 345–76
——'On the Threshold of Poems: A Paratextual Approach to the Narrative/Lyric Opposition in Italian Renaissance Poetry', in *Self-Commentary in Early Modern European Literature, 1400–1700*, ed. by Francesco Venturi (Leiden: Brill, 2019), pp. 99–134
PICONE, MICHELANGELO, 'Dante e Cino: una lunga amicizia. Prima parte: i tempi della *Vita nova*', *Dante*, 1 (2004), 39–53
——'La teoria dell'*auctoritas* nella *Vita Nova*', *Tenzone*, 6 (2005), 173–91
PIETERS, JÜRGEN, 'Fragments of a Consolatory Discourse: Literature and the Fiction of Comfort', *Barthes Studies*, 1 (2015), 123–47 <http://sites.cardiff.ac.uk/barthes/files/2015/11/PIETERS-Fragments-of-a-Consolatory-Discourse.pdf>
——*Literature and Consolation: Fictions of Comfort* (Edinburgh: Edinburgh University Press, 2021)
——*Op zoek naar Huygens: Italiaanse leesnotities* (Gent: KANTL/Poëziecentrum, 2014)
——, and CHRISTOPHE VAN DER VORST, '"Cui Dono Lepidum Novum Libellum?": Huygens' *Ooghen-troost* door een nieuwe bril', *Nederlandse letterkunde*, 14.1 (2009), 49–76
POISSON, CATHERINE, 'Frictions: mot et image chez Marie NDiaye et Camille Laurens', *Contemporary French and Francophone Studies*, 11.4 (2007), 489–96
POMEROY, EMMA, and OTHERS, 'New Neanderthal Remains associated with the "Flower Burial" at Shanidar Cave', *Antiquity*, 94 (2020), 11–26
PORTER, MAX, *Grief is the Thing with Feathers* (London: Faber & Faber, 2015)
PRESTON, CLAIRE, *Bee* (London: Reaktion Books, 2006)
PROUST, MARCEL, *In Search of Lost Time*, ed. by Christopher Prendergast, 6 vols (London: Penguin Classics, 2003)
RADDEN, JENNIFER, ed., *The Nature of Melancholy: From Aristotle to Kristeva* (Oxford: Oxford University Press, 2000)
RAMAZANI, JAHAN, *Poetry of Mourning: The Modern Elegy from Hardy to Heaney* (Chicago: University of Chicago Press, 1994)
RAVILIOUS, ROBIN, 'Whistler, Sir (Alan Charles) Laurence (1912–2000)' (23 September 2004; rev. 8 October 2009), in *Oxford Dictionary of National Biography* (Oxford: Oxford University Press, 2020) <http://doi.org/10.1093/ref:odnb/75009>
RENDU, WILLIAM, and OTHERS, 'Evidence Supporting an Intentional Neandertal Burial at La Chapelle-aux-Saints', *Proceedings of the National Academy of Sciences*, 111 (2014), 81–86
ROBERTS, JANE, 'Some Relationships between *The Dream of the Rood* and the Cross at Ruthwell', *Studies in Medieval English Language and Literature*, 15 (2000), 1–25
ROINE, HANNA RIIKKA, and HANNA SAMOLA, 'Johanna Sinisalo and the New Weird: Genres and Myths', in *Lingua Cosmica: Science Fiction from around the World*, ed. by Dale Knickerbocker (Champaign: University of Illinois Press, 2018), pp. 183–200
RONEN, AVRAHAM, 'The Oldest Burials and their Significance', in *African Genesis: Perspectives on Hominin Evolution*, ed. by Sally C. Reynolds and Andrew Gallagher (Cambridge: Cambridge University Press, 2012), pp. 554–70
ROSE, DEBORAH BIRD, *Wild Dog Dreaming: Love and Extinction* (Charlottesville: University of Virginia Press, 2011)
ROSE, GILLIAN, *Mourning Becomes the Law: Philosophy and Representation* (Cambridge: Cambridge University Press, 1996)
ROSE, H. J., 'Celestial and Terrestrial Orientation of the Dead', *The Journal of the Royal Anthropological Institute of Great Britain and Ireland*, 52 (1922), 127–40

Rossi, Vittorio, 'Il Petrarca a Pavia', *Bollettino della società pavese di storia patria*, 4 (1904), 367–437

Roth, Leon, ed., *Correspondence of Descartes and Constantyn Huygens: 1635–1647* (Oxford: Clarendon Press, 1926)

Roth, Philip, *Patrimony: A True Story* (London: Vintage, 1999)

Rousseau, Jean-Jacques, *The Discourses and Other Early Political Writings*, ed. by Victor Gourevitch, 2nd edn (Cambridge: Cambridge University Press, 2018)

Rushworth, Jennifer, 'Barthes as Reader of Dante: The Mediation of Sollers and the Role of Commentary', *Barthes Studies*, 4 (November 2018), 31–55 <http://sites.cardiff.ac.uk/barthes/article/barthes-as-reader-of-dante-the-mediation-of-sollers-and-the-role-of-commentary/>

——'Derrida, Proust, and the Promise of Writing', *French Studies*, 69.2 (April 2015), 205–19

——*Discourses of Mourning in Dante, Petrarch, and Proust* (Oxford: Oxford University Press, 2016)

——'Mourning and Intermittence between Proust and Barthes', *Paragraph*, 39.3 (2016), 269–86

——, and Francesca Southerden, eds, *Medieval Barthes* (= *Exemplaria*, 33.3 (2021))

Rutherford, Lucy, and Lindsay E. Murray, 'Personality and Behavioral Changes in Asian Elephants (*Elephas maximus*) Following the Death of Herd Members', *Integrative Zoology*, 16.2 (2021), 170–88

Rye, Gill, 'Family Tragedies in Recent French Literature', in *Affaires de famille: The Family in Contemporary French Culture and Theory*, ed. by Marie Claire Barnet and Edward Welch (Amsterdam: Rodopi, 2007), pp. 267–81

——*Narratives of Mothering: Women's Writing in Contemporary France* (Newark: University of Delaware Press, 2009)

Sacks, Peter, *The English Elegy: Studies in the Genre from Spenser to Yeats* (Baltimore, MD: Johns Hopkins University Press, 1985)

Samola, Hanna, 'From Gilead to Eusistocratia: The Dialogue between Margaret Atwood's Dystopian Novel *The Handmaid's Tale* and Johanna Sinisalo's *The Core of the Sun*', in *New Perspectives on Dystopian Fiction in Literature and Other Media*, ed. by Saija Isomaa, Jyrki Korpua, and Jouni Teittinen (Newcastle upon Tyne: Cambridge Scholars Publishing, 2020), pp. 45–64

Samoyault, Tiphaine, *Roland Barthes: biographie* (Paris: Seuil, 2015)

Sandel, Michael, *The Tyranny of Merit: What's Become of the Common Good?* (London: Allen Lane, 2020)

Santagata, Marco, *Amate e amanti: figure della lirica amorosa fra Dante e Petrarca* (Bologna: Il Mulino, 1999)

Schlauch, Margaret, '*The Dream of the Rood* as Prosopopoeia', in *Essays and Studies in Honour of Carleton Brown*, ed. by P. W. Long (New York: New York University Press, 1940), pp. 23–34

Schnapp, Jeffrey T., 'Dante's Sexual Solecisms: Gender and Genre in the *Commedia*', in *The New Medievalism*, ed. by Marina S. Brownlee, Kevin Brownlee, and Stephen G. Nichols (Baltimore, MD: Johns Hopkins University Press, 1991), pp. 201–25

Scott, John, ed., *A Dictionary of Sociology*, 4th edn (Oxford: Oxford University Press, 2014)

Scranton, Roy, *Learning to Die in the Anthropocene: Reflections on the End of a Civilization* (San Francisco: City Lights Books, 2015)

Screech, M. A., *Montaigne & Melancholy: The Wisdom of the Essays* (London: Duckworth, 2000)

Shostakovich, Dmitry, *Story of a Friendship: The Letters of Dmitry Shostakovich to Isaak Glikman, 1941–1975*, ed. by Isaak Glikman and trans. by Anthony Phillips (Ithaca, NY: Cornell University Press, 2001)

—— *Testimony: The Memoirs of Dmitri Shostakovich*, ed. by Solomon Volkov and trans. by Antonina W. Bouis (New York: Limelight Editions, 1995)

Singleton, Charles, *An Essay on the 'Vita nuova'* (Cambridge, MA: Harvard University Press, 1949)

Sinisalo, Johanna, *Enkelten verta* (Helsinki: Teos, 2011)

—— *The Blood of Angels*, trans. by Lola Rogers (London: Peter Owen, 2014)

Smit, Jacob, *De grootmeester van woord- en snarenspel* ('s Gravenhage: Nijhoff, 1980)

Sofaer, Joanna R., *The Body as Material Culture: A Theoretical Osteoarchaeology* (Cambridge: Cambridge University Press, 2006)

Solnit, Rebecca, 'The Way We Get Through This is Together', *Guardian*, 14 May 2020 <https://www.theguardian.com/world/2020/may/14/mutual-aid-coronavirus-pandemic-rebecca-solnit>

Sommer, Jeffrey D., 'The Shanidar IV "Flower Burial": A Re-evaluation of Neanderthal Burial Ritual', *Cambridge Archaeological Journal*, 9 (1999), 127–29

Sophocles, *Antigonick*, trans. by Anne Carson (New York: New Directions Books, 2015)

—— *The Three Theban Plays: Antigone, Oedipus the King, Oedipus at Colonus*, trans. by Robert Fagles (London: Penguin Classics, 1984)

Southerden, Francesca, 'Lost for Words: Recuperating Melancholy Subjectivity in Dante's Eden', in *Dante's Plurilingualism: Authority, Knowledge, Subjectivity*, ed. by Sara Fortuna, Manuele Gragnolati, and Jürgen Trabant (Oxford: Legenda, 2010), pp. 193–210

Sprengnether, Madelon, *Mourning Freud* (London: Bloomsbury Academic, 2018)

Steinberg, Justin, *Accounting for Dante: Urban Readers and Writers in Late Medieval Italy* (Notre Dame, IN: University of Notre Dame Press, 2007)

Steiner, George, *Antigones: The Antigone Myth in in Western Literature, Art, and Thought* (Oxford: Oxford University Press, 1986)

Stevens, Wallace, *The Collected Poems of Wallace Stevens*, ed. by John N. Serio and Chris Beyers (New York: Vintage Books, 2015)

Storey, H. Wayne, 'Following Instructions: Remaking Dante's *Vita Nova* in the Fourteenth Century', in *Medieval Constructions in Gender and Identity: Essays in Honor of Joan M. Ferrante*, ed. by Teodolinda Barolini (Tempe: Arizona Center for Medieval and Renaissance Studies, 2005), pp. 117–32

Stow, Simon, *American Mourning* (Cambridge: Cambridge University Press, 2017)

Strengholt, L., *Huygens Studies: Bijdragen tot het onderzoek van de poëzie van Constantijn Huygens* (Amsterdam: Buijten en Schipperheijn, 1976)

Stroia, Adina, 'Camille Laurens: l'écriture depuis soi', *Dalhousie French Studies*, 112 (2018), 27–35

Stroppa, Sabrina, *Petrarca e la morte: tra 'Familiari' e 'Canzoniere'* (Rome: Aracne, 2014)

Stroppa, Sabrina, and Nicole Volta, eds, *Forme della consolatoria tra Quattro e Cinquecento: poesia e prosa del lutto tra corte, accademie e 'solidalitas' amicale* (Lucca: Pacini Fazzi, 2019)

Stubbs, John, *Donne: The Reformed Soul* (London: Viking, 2006)

Svevo, Italo, *Further Confessions of Zeno*, trans. by Ben Johnson and P. N. Furbank (Berkeley & Los Angeles: University of California Press, 1969)

Swanton, Michael, ed., *The Dream of the Rood* (Manchester: Manchester University Press, 1970)

Takeshita, Rafaela S. C., and others, 'Changes in Social Behavior and Fecal Glucocorticoids in a Japanese Macaque (*Macaca fuscata*) Carrying her Dead Infant', *Primates*, 61 (2020), 5–40

Tambling, Jeremy, 'Thinking Melancholy: Allegory and the *Vita nuova*', *Romanic Review*, 96.1 (2005), 85–105

Taruskin, Richard, *Defining Russia Musically: Historical and Hermeneutical Essays* (Princeton, NJ: Princeton University Press, 1997)

Tattersall, Ian, 'The Minimalist Program and the Origin of Language: A View from Paleoanthropology', *Frontiers in Psychology*, 10 (2019) <https://www.frontiersin.org/articles/10.3389/fpsyg.2019.00677/full>

Taxidou, Olga, *Tragedy, Modernity and Mourning* (Edinburgh: Edinburgh University Press, 2004)

Todorović, Jelena, *Dante and the Dynamics of Textual Exchange* (New York: Fordham University Press, 2016)

Treherne, Matthew, 'Liturgical Personhood: Creation, Penitence, and Praise in the *Commedia*', in *Dante's 'Commedia': Theology as Poetry*, ed. by Vittorio Montemaggi and Matthew Treherne (Notre Dame, IN: University of Notre Dame Press, 2010), pp. 131–60

Tsing, Anna Lowenhaupt, *The Mushroom at the End of the World: On the Possibility of Life in Capitalist Ruins* (Princeton, NJ: Princeton University Press, 2015)

Tsintjilonis, Dimitri, 'Death and the Sacrifice of Signs: "Measuring" the Dead in Tana Toraja', *Oceania*, 71 (2000), 1–17

Tyler, John M., *The New Stone Age of Northern Europe* (New York: Charles Scribner's Sons, 1921)

Unger, J. H. W., ed., *Dagboek van Constantyn Huygens, voor de eerste maal naar het afschrift van diens kleinzoon uitgegeven* (Amsterdam: Gebr. Binger, 1885)

Valency, Maurice, *In Praise of Love: An Introduction to the Love-poetry of the Renaissance* (New York: Schocken Books, 1982)

Van Dooren, Thom, *Flight Ways: Life and Loss at the Edge of Extinction* (New York: Columbia University Press, 2014)

Van Dooren, Thom, and Deborah Bird Rose, 'Keeping Faith with the Dead: Mourning and De-extinction' (10 November 2013) <https://thomvandooren.org/2013/11/02/keeping-faith-with-death-mourning-and-de-extinction/>

Vandermeersch, Bernard, 'The Excavation of Qafzeh: Its Contribution to Knowledge of the Mousterian in the Levant', *Bulletin du Centre de recherche français à Jérusalem*, 10 (2002), 65–70

Vandermeersch, Bernard, and Ofer Bar-Yosef, 'The Paleolithic Burials at Qafzeh Cave, Israel', *PALEO*, 30–31 (2019), 256–75

Vecchio, Silvana, 'Giovanni da San Gimignano', in *Dizionario Biografico degli Italiani*, 100 vols (Rome: Istituto della Enciclopedia Italiana, 1960–), LVI (2001), 206–10

Vendler, Helen, *Last Looks, Last Books: Stevens, Plath, Lowell, Bishop* (Princeton, NJ: Princeton University Press, 2010)

Vernant, Jean-Pierre, and Pierre Vidal-Naquet, *Myth and Tragedy in Ancient Greece*, trans. by Janet Lloyd (New York: Zone Books, 1988)

Vickers, Nancy J., 'Widowed Words: Dante, Petrarch, and the Metaphors of Mourning', in *Discourses of Authority in Medieval and Renaissance Literature*, ed. by Kevin Brownlee and Walter Stephens (Hanover: University Press of New England for Dartmouth College, 1989), pp. 97–108

Vinchesi, Maria Assunta, 'L'inedita egloga "Parnasus" di G. De Bonis in morte del Petrarca', *Quaderni petrarcheschi*, 9–10 (1992–93), 315–31

Virgil, *Eclogues; Georgics; Aeneid: Books 1–6*, trans. by H. Rushton Fairclough, rev. by G.P. Goold, rev. edn (Cambridge, MA: Harvard University Press, 1999)

Vovelle, Michel, *La mort et l'Occident de 1300 à nos jours* (Paris: Gallimard, 1983)

Wallace-Wells, David, *The Uninhabitable Earth: A Story of the Future* (London: Penguin, 2019)

Warkentin, Germaine, 'The Form of Dante's "libello" and its Challenge to Petrarch', *Quaderni d'italianistica*, 11.2 (1981), 160–70

Watkin, William, *The Literary Agamben: Adventures in Logopoiesis* (London: Continuum, 2010)

Webb, Heather, *Dante's Persons: An Ethics of the Transhuman* (Oxford: Oxford University Press, 2016)
—— *The Medieval Heart* (New Haven, CT: Yale University Press, 2010)
Westenbroek, J. J. M., 'An Anatomy of Melancholy: Huygens' "Op de dood van sterre" en de afsluiting van "Dagh-werck"', *Spiegel der Letteren*, 13.3 (1970–71), 161–73
Whistler, Laurence, *Armed October* (London: Cobden-Sanderson, 1932)
—— *Four Walls* (London: Heinemann, 1934)
—— *The Image on the Glass* (London: John Murray, in association with the Cupid Press, 1975)
—— *The Laughter and the Urn: The Life of Rex Whistler* (London: Weidenfeld & Nicolson, 1985)
—— *Scenes and Signs on Glass* (Woodbridge: Cupid Press, 1985)
Wilkins, Ernest H., *Life of Petrarch* (Chicago: University of Chicago Press, 1961)
Wilson, E. O., *The Future of Life* (New York: Knopf, 2004)
—— *The Insect Societies* (Cambridge, MA: Belknap Press of Harvard University Press, 1971)
Wilson, E. O., and Bert Hölldobler, 'Eusociality: Origin and Consequences', *Proceedings of the National Academy of Sciences USA*, 120 (2005), 13367–71
Winston, Mark L., *Bee Time: Lessons from the Hive* (Cambridge, MA: Harvard University Press, 2014)
Witstein, Sonja, *Een Wett-steen vande Ieught* (Groningen: Wolters-Noordhoff, 1980)
Wolff, Tobias, *Old School* (London: Bloomsbury, 2004)
Woods, Angela, 'The Limits of Narrative: Provocations for the Medical Humanities', *Medical Humanities*, 37 (2011), 73–78
World Economic Forum, *Global Risks Report* <https://reports.weforum.org/global-risks-report-2020/survey-results/the-global-risks-interconnections-map-2020/>
Wright, Charles D., 'Why Sight Holds Flowers: An Apocryphal Source for the Iconography of the Alfred Jewel and Fuller Brooch', in *Text, Image, Interpretation: Studies in Anglo-Saxon Literature and its Insular Context in Honour of Éamonn Ó Carragáin*, ed. by Alastair Minnis and Jane Roberts (Turnhout: Brepols, 2007), pp. 169–86
Yusoff, Kathryn, *A Billion Black Anthropocenes or None* (Minneapolis: University of Minnesota Press, 2018)
Žižek, Slavoj, *The Plague of Fantasies* (London: Verso, 1997)
Zwaan, F. L., 'Repliek' [on the former contribution by R. Lievens], *Handelingen van de Koninklijke Zuidnederlandse Maatschappij*, 27 (1973), 152–56

INDEX

www.ingramcontent.com/pod-product-compliance
Lightning Source LLC
Chambersburg PA
CBHW080541090426
42734CB00016B/3175
9781839540356